The NIETZSCHE Question

Ever since Nietzsche first published his bold, revolutionary works, the storm of controversy has raged about his name. Was he the immoral preacher of the antichrist? Was he the theoretician of the Superman, and did he lay the groundwork for the advent of Hitler's barbaric Nazi philosophy in our own day? Does his anti-Christian philosophy *(the weak shall perish)* give moral support to totalitarian ideas now challenging the world order?

A great deal of the controversy is due to difficulty in understanding Nietzsche's almost lyrical, aphoristic style. Moreover, many of his posthumous works, now cited as evidence of his "evil intent," were never meant for publication or as a final representation of his ideas.

This edition is based primarily on those of Nietzsche's works that were published during his lifetime. It was prepared with new translations for all the works by the late Otto Manthey-Zorn, one of the outstanding scholars on the Nietzsche Question.

Professor Manthey-Zorn's other published works include: **DIONYSUS,** *The Tragedy of Nietzsche;* and **GERMANY IN TRAVA**~~~~ ~~~~ ~~~~ ~~~~ of ~~~~
Immanuel ~~~~

D0992969

NIETZSCHE:
An Anthology of His Works

Edited, newly translated,
and with critical Introductions
by Otto Manthey-Zorn

WASHINGTON SQUARE PRESS, INC. • NEW YORK

NIETZSCHE: AN ANTHOLOGY OF HIS WORKS

A *Washington Square Press* edition
1st printing..........................April, 1964

Parts of this book are taken from DIONYSUS: *The Tragedy of Nietzsche*, by O. Manthey-Zorn. Copyright, ©, 1956, Amherst College Press.

Published by
Washington Square Press, Inc., 630 Fifth Avenue, New York, N.Y.

WASHINGTON SQUARE PRESS editions are distributed in the U.S. by Affiliated Publishers, a division of Pocket Books, Inc., 630 Fifth Avenue, New York 20, N.Y.

Editor's Preface

This anthology of Friedrich Nietzsche's works is based in large part upon Professor Manthey-Zorn's earlier critical appraisal of Nietzsche's philosophy, DIONYSUS, THE TRAGEDY OF NIETZSCHE, which was published by the Amherst College Press in 1956. The detailed analysis of Nietzsche's Dionysian view of life in that work was the major inspiration for this present volume, which has employed whole segments of the DIONYSUS, both the criticism and the translations. Grateful acknowledgment is due the Amherst College Press for its kind permission to so employ the DIONYSUS in the framework of this anthology, intended to provide the general reader with a clearer perspective on the nature and meaning of Nietzsche's philosophy of sublimation. However, a great deal of the connective tissue, as it were, of the DIONYSUS had to be sacrificed in order to provide for the increased percentage of actual translations of Nietzsche's works now made available to the reader. It is earnestly recommended that a further study of Nietzsche begin with the DIONYSUS, which is rich in detail as it follows the whole tragic course of Nietzsche's growth and importance as an original thinker.

PHILIP C. FLAYDERMAN

A sincere expression of gratitude is due Professor Murray B. Peppard who assisted Professor Manthey-Zorn throughout with the preparation of this book, in matters both great and small, and who so generously gave of his time and talents to insure the successful completion of the book after the author's sudden passing only a few months before actual publication.

Author's Preface

This study pursues the writings of Friedrich Nietzsche in chronological order, whereby the inception and metamorphosis of the Dionysian view is presented with its expanding demand that it rule over the analysis and synthesis of all human culture. It is hoped that this will enable the reader of Nietzsche, who is attracted by the brilliance of his aphorisms, to understand more clearly the limits within which they apply, and help him to preserve his own intellectual sanity as he follows the spiritual battles and torment which this keen but increasingly dogmatic warrior for exclusive mundane culture waged with himself and society. When he knows with what he is confronted, it will increase the reader's enjoyment of this master of style; and as the artist's perspective becomes clear, his figures will be viewed in the proper light.

Discussed primarily are those publications which Nietzsche himself authorized and supervised. The voluminous posthumous material has served as background, but is not presented in detail, because it would not be fair to do so. The published works are a very carefully edited selection from this mass and thus constitute what Nietzsche wished to assume full responsibility for as products of his intellectual integrity. They are the thoughts by which he wanted to be judged, and he is, therefore, presented in them.

The references to the writings are identified by the numbering of the aphorisms or paragraphs of the separate books which is identical in all editions, both the original and the translations. The present translations are the author's own, but all italics are those found in the original, the sources for which are given in an appendix. Moreover, while the punctuation in the body of the critical remarks of this edition follow, more or less, the normal American practice, the punctuation of the translations has adhered as closely as possible to the standard of the original German.

OTTO MANTHEY-ZORN
Amherst College

Contents

xi

The Approach

Friedrich Nietzsche is one of the most stimulating, but also most disturbing, figures in modern German intellectual history. He found himself so much in violent opposition to the prevailing standards of the culture of his day that he undertook to examine them afresh and radically revise them. To do so he considered it necessary to define anew life itself. Thus he built for himself a new focus from which to revalue the institutions.

The results were brilliant and exciting. As they became increasingly popularly known, particularly after his death, they aroused angry opposition as well as blindly enthusiastic acceptance. But most interpretations of him, especially every popular one, were in some sense distorted. They were not based upon the painfully constructed focus from which he insisted life *must* be viewed. Each person or group judged or used him in support of the values he or it held essential or profitable. Hence the ever-changing myth about his meaning, and the opposition or support by groups of completely contradictory values.

It should seem possible, however, to follow him closely in order to determine his point of view. He was clear enough about it and so very insistent upon it that he rejected even the slightest compromise. He was a harsh disciplinarian, almost a martinet. But he was a great writer and teacher who will persist and so should be known for what he is.

Nietzsche liked to think of himself as the investigator of life by means of an intellectual integrity such as no philosopher before him had attained. He considered that by courage and discipline he had developed this into a dominant instinct

1

to serve as the reliable touchstone for the honesty and soundness of all human evaluations.

With all its exaggerations, this claim was nevertheless honestly held by Nietzsche, or at least his life was consistently
directed towards a justification of this claim. His prevailing
loneliness was the expression of the uniqueness which he believed he represented in this respect, as though no investigator
before him had possessed the insight or the courage to draw
the extreme conclusions or to seek the final fulfillment of the
spiritual and intellectual enlightenment of the Protestantism
which was his heritage.

In the *Antichrist* he says of Kant that, like Luther and
Leibniz, he is merely one more brake on German intellectual
integrity, meaning to accuse him, as he does repeatedly
throughout his writings, of impeding the development of intellectual enlightenment by setting limits to reason for the
"romantic" purpose of rescuing Christian religion and morality.
He would interpret Kant's famous definition in 1784 of enlightenment, if he knew of it, very literally: not merely as the
only dependable directive for the continuous development of
human culture, but equally as the proper touchstone for testing the genuineness of existing evaluations and institutions.

"Enlightenment," Kant says, "is the emergence of man from
his self-imposed dependency. Dependency is the inability of
man to make use of his reason without the guidance of anything else. The dependency is self-imposed if not caused by
lack of reason but the lack of the determination and courage
to make use of it without the guidance of anything else.
Sapere aude! (Have the courage to make use of your *own*
reason!) is consequently the motto of enlightenment."

Enlightenment in this definition is, of course, not meant in
an historical sense but in its fundamental meaning as a contrast to every authoritative dogmatism. Its motto might well
serve for the devotion to which Nietzsche strove to be true.
What he called integrity might well be understood as the
progressively clearer comprehension of the powers of autonomous human reason and the constant alertness to guard it
against compromises, irrespective of where it may lead. Kant,

he believed, had seriously compromised reason by postulating a metaphysical world of truth as the want of pure reason, and by attempting the desperate rescue of the autonomy of reason by establishing for that want what would seem to Nietzsche the self-contradictory "faith of reason" [*Vernunftglaube*]. To Kant the necessity for the faith of reason lies in his conviction that a truly moral person is in need of assurances beyond what can be known by any natural data of reason. These assurances are subjectively necessary, and so of sufficient reason to a moral person, even though objectively they are consciously insufficient. Though they can never satisfy all the demands of logic, they are still held to be not only valid, but unchanging and necessary truths, the postulates of practical reason. The need for these postulates is all-important to Kant, "because it is absolute and the existence of God must be postulated not only when we *want* to judge but because we *must judge*. For the pure practical use of reason lies in the prescripts of the moral law."

Two further quotations from Kant's essay, "What is Meant by Orienting Oneself by Reason," clearly illustrate what Nietzsche considered to be the brake which Kant applied to German intellectual integrity:

> If the right is denied to reason to speak *first* in things metaphysical, such as the existence of God and a future world, then the door is opened wide to all sorts of fanaticism, superstition, and even to every kind of atheism.

> The maxim of the independence of reason of its *own want* (dispensing with the faith of reason) is called *unbelief;* not an historical one, for that cannot be conceived as intentional and consequently not as responsible either; but an absence of the *faith of reason,* a sad condition of the human mind which denies to the moral law all its power over the heart and in time also all authority, and produces what is called *libertinism* (Freigeisterei), that is, the principle to acknowledge no duty whatever.

Nietzsche considered this an intellectually dishonest expansion of reason to include its opposite, engaged in out of fear of the consequences of an outright literal acceptance of the definition of enlightenment. If morality demanded this, then there must be something wrong with the concept of morality itself. He believed that every European philosopher had followed Kant to various degrees, and that none before himself had been willing to accept fully the consequences of the primacy of human reason free from further wants. To accomplish this he saw in reason not only the entirety of the intellectual powers of man, but also his all-inclusive force: the synthesis of his thinking and feeling; his informative senses and his creative imagination; his critical and his evaluating functions. The emergence of man's independence he equated with the fullness of reason as identical with the height of his power and his wholesomeness. To acknowledge wants beyond this conception of reason was to accept the defeat of reason and of man's autonomy. If this be taken as a dangerous undertaking or foolhardy, it is still to Nietzsche the only path by which to approach the full dignity of man and the highest worth of life. The more he struggled to solve this problem, the more he realized that it was indeed a tragic venture—but the more he was also convinced that the most courageous optimism of life was to face its tragedy joyously.

It was a matter of course to him that enlightenment must lead to the complete rejection of everything supernatural and, therefore, to a complete atheism, free from the compromises even of the deists and from the superficialities of popular freethinkers. He guarded and constantly tried to heighten this standard of intellectual integrity with a kind of desperation. If the autonomy of man means the rejection of all dependence upon God, it must then be made to mean the understanding, disciplinary training, and creative culture of man's power in its highest examples. If the autonomy of this life means the rejection of a life beyond, then this life must be accepted without reservation with all its changes and chances as eternal existence, to be humanized by man in an eternally recurring venture, each in proportion to his genuine ability to do so.

So the first requirement of intellectual honesty is to accept this life exactly as it is to the exclusion of any want beyond it, with all its physical drives and dark impulses, as well as the spiritual powers of man's intellect and creative force. The direction of all these forces is no other than the endless effort to find the opportunity to complete themselves; not in a straight line of progressive evolution, but in endlessly recurring cycles of effort with here and there the fortunate emergence of the philosopher who has gained wholesomeness beyond other men and who, through superior integrity, courage, and creative will, has surpassed in the power of sublimation. This is the surpassing man, the superman whom each cycle of life seeks as the hope toward its fulfillment.

For this conception of life, with its dark and beastly as well as its sublimating drives in eternal recurrence, Nietzsche held, as an inspiration, to the metaphor of the dismembered but recurrently reborn Dionysus. Like the will of Dionysus to rebirth, life is to him the will to power, to the fullness of its own potentialities. More and more Dionysus becomes the leading metaphor, both for life as the will to power, and for the creating philosopher driving with his disciplined instinct toward eternally recurring attempts to sublimate that power as the values and institutions of human culture. Almost like a religious symbol, this metaphor is meant to initiate into this specific meaning of life and of man's mission in life. Even a hierarchy is built into it, with the fully initiated as the lawgiver of sure instinct, sound health, and creative force; the disciples of sufficient courage and health to understand who, though they cannot create, act as executives; finally the great mass, with neither instinct nor health, that must be kept content so as not to interfere and impede, but which, nevertheless, is the basic supply of life and the foundation to hold the superstructure of culture.

Having in this metaphor set up the autonomy of this life and of man, the acts of man become autonomous also, beyond divine judgment or reward and outside of the moral law. This is in direct opposition not only to Kant's faith of reason, but equally to the rationalistic pietism of the conventional men of enlightenment or the cynicism of the nihilists. Never-

theless, judgments are continuous and severe with Nietzsche.
The standard, however, is the fullness of man's attained autonomy, consisting in the degree of his acceptance and comprehension of the Dionysian life by virtue of his instinct for the
breadth and depth of intellectual integrity.

Nietzsche makes unending attempts to clarify this instinct,
and the more he does so the more it becomes a unique, indeed, a mystic quality of his own. It gives him his sure sense
of reality out of complete devotion to the Dionysian view of
life. It defeats, so he believes, all threat of dualism, in that
matter and spirit are together expressions of reality; wherefore he insists that he is neither materialist nor metaphysician.
It provides for him the qualifications of a sound scholar and
keen observer of nature, and also the gift of a creative interpreter who understands and can fashion the metaphor
beyond other men to the future glimpse of truth. It is, he
would say, his unerring sense to discover the genuineness or
fullness, the health or degeneracy of every value and institution of society, because it tests the reality of each and is,
therefore, the basis of his claim to being a new and greater
psychologist. He would take this instinct to be his deepest self,
his personality, and so beyond the grasp of definition. But it
is also so much the object of constant vigilance against compromise, static satisfaction, or exhaustion, that, with its insistence upon uniqueness, it impels him to ever greater isolation; then to a loss of humor and even perspective; and in the
end to the frantic exaggeration of despair. He has a right to
his contention that of all modern philosophers he most consistently dared to make use of his "*own* reason"; that with
greatest determination he refused to admit the necessity of
the postulates of practical reason for the redemption of man;
and that he has struggled most to avoid the nihilism in which
attempts similar to his invariably ended. But his end was a
tragedy. Not merely the tragedy of his physical collapse, but
rather that of the final stage in the sublimation of the will to
power which his "instinct" finally forced him to accept.

The height of the fully optimistic acceptance of life he calls
the beginning of the tragedy. At long last it will be realized

that a true culture can begin only when there is recognition of the rarely but eternally recurring genius of true instinct for intellectual integrity. He will devote himself to the battle for the sublimation of the powers of life at the expense of himself, so that the future genius may be equally prepared for the sacrifice in an unending recurrence. Then the genius can emerge from his isolation to gather and take command of his followers whom an appreciation of his mission has made free; until the army of free spirits is mighty enough to join in the final, most terrible battle with the hallowed institutions and beliefs which are still based on a world-denying faith or on some philosophical compromise with the full autonomy of life and man. But even a victory in this battle would only mean that the tragedy can now fully begin in a joyous sacrifice for future and infinitely future culture—with the joyous acceptance of the cycles of eternal return and the voluntary discipline of the loyalty to reality, called *amor fati*.

It is a fantastic goal, if indeed it can be called a goal. Nietzsche dwells upon it mostly in moments of extreme excitement or even pathological euphoria. Nevertheless, it is there as an indication of his extreme loyalty to his Dionysian hypothesis. Or perhaps it is his peculiar brand of German efficiency, which in other respects he repeatedly excoriated. In his more sober moments conception of the tragedy of the genius is primarily an element of discipline, where the goal matters nothing and the process everything. He would first free himself from the prejudices within the philosophical, religious, and institutional values of the past, because each in varying degrees is built upon a pessimistic view of this life, the worth of which it either denies, or from which escape and redemption are sought. He would then be able to apply himself exclusively and "honestly" to the study of the powers of life's will to realize its highest potentialities by their sublimation in terms of culture.

Both efforts, however, are endless experiments of perspective to him, since the knowledge of the whole of life with its changes and chances can never be complete, and, therefore, a complete configuration of the final culture cannot be constructed either. The most accurate and inclusive critical observation of life provides the material for the experiment, gained with his instinct for reality. The great health of the genius acquired through this instinct provides the interpretation. Both are incomplete, especially the latter.

Since Nietzsche holds to the autonomy of life, he must conclude that it is eternal, without beginning or end, and that its will to power through sublimation is infinite, with the sublimating genius playing the agent of the endlessly recurring experiment. This genius is a sacrifice within the cycles of experiments of continuous trial and error, and thus tragic. But he gladly accepts this tragic role as a proof of his worth and dignity and as a guarantee, also, that the cycle of experiments must be eternally repeated. Thereby he believes he establishes his eternity as recurrent man—not personal, of course, for that to Nietzsche would be the height of vanity and the destruction of the dignity of tragedy. From this point of view the extreme goal, mentioned above, is a spur to continuous battle and a phantom cry pointing to the time when the battle will have found the support of many, whereas Nietzsche to the end found himself quite alone.

Because he was alone, his efforts were directed toward being the pathfinder of the Dionysian way and to clear away what seemed to be obstructions to it. It is in this latter respect that, together with the brilliance of his aphorisms, he is understood most and his influence has been widest—both for the better and the worst. It certainly cannot be said that he has succeeded in establishing his Dionysian view of life as the only honest view. He has won few adherents for his complete atheism out of intellectual integrity, or for his insistence that God is dead and His murderer the most courageous but most tragic man. With the uncompromising extremity of these views, he may be said to be as isolated as he was at the time of his collapse. He has not repudiated faith, but only substituted his own Dionysian faith as the principle of reality. The fiercely dogmatic adherence to this principle led him to some wholly arbitrary interpretations, of which his history of Christianity and his construction of the personality of Christ are the most glaring.

But when he does not indulge in such wide dogmatic sweeps, and, instead, examines social and individual evaluations to discover what elements of escape they contain, though they claim to express reality, he is very interesting and at times inescapable in the many analyses which have given him a significant place as forerunner of modern depth psychology. However, it must be kept in mind that his yardstick is always the same: the complete and exclusive loyalty to this life. Therefore, wherever a cultural value in philosophy, religion, the State, or any other political and social institution claims a realistic basis in his sense, he is sharp in examining the genuineness of it and exposing the lack of it in pithy aphorisms. He is so confident of his instinct for this, that he delights in the widest use of it, and thereby has provided comfort and authority to a great variety of critics as well as to dogmatists of society who have preached and still preach in his name, though they have no conception of the exclusiveness of his Dionysian premise or of the severity of his standard of intellectual integrity. Thus Hitler succeeded, for a time, in elevating him as a patron of his leadership principle, until closer study turned him into an opponent. The socialists built upon his attack on the State, though to do so they had to neglect his exposure of the false power with which they were usurping the State. Even the Church has made attempts to point to him as a reformer who attacked Christianity to restore it to its original purity, and morals to original honesty.

These are extreme examples of the suggestiveness of Nietzsche's aphoristic writings which, when taken piecemeal, extend into many fields. They easily lend themselves because of his dithyrambic style and avoidance of system. Therefore it is not unfair to Nietzsche to hold him responsible for the great mass of contradictory interpretations which he has suffered, or for the changing myth that has grown out of his writings when dismembered. However, they all still belong to followers for whom he would have shown some sympathy, but then rejected for their lack of sufficient training and understanding.

He was extremely severe with himself and expected the same of others. He would allow himself or those who would follow him no deviation from the reality which his Dionysian faith represented to him. From it arose the responsibility of ever more complete knowledge of the powers of life and the unending task for the man of clear understanding to approach the synthesis of those powers by the values of human culture. It may be said that the aim of enlightenment has always been to find in mundane culture a substitute for Christian piety and otherworldliness, but never with the exclusiveness and severity of Nietzsche. Generally, the full development of man and the height of culture was taken to evidence itself in human happiness, the disregard of which was considered a curse, to be lifted only by a new idealism based on a superrational reality which promised grace and redemption. To Nietzsche this search for happiness is escape and weakness. He insisted that the sublimation of life's powers in culture is a ceaseless battle of the free spirit. The more severe and the more sacrificing he is, the more hope he will produce. For this battle all idealism and every superrational absolute must be avoided and the comprehensive human reason alone be depended upon to know and fashion life, if only a sure instinct of intellectual integrity has been won.

This intellectual severity was his substitute for every shade of asceticism, moral and religious, all of which he found to be escapist and a pessimistic denial of life. Indeed, his genius is taken to have surpassed the conflict between pessimism and optimism of former men of enlightenment. He would be a new type of saint and prophet of man's dignity, whose optimism in spite of all severity still sees some worth in every grade of man, however weakened or diseased he may have been made by false physicians. In every man, even the slave, he finds some sense of dignity, some sense of awe of his worth —he calls it *Scham*—to violate which is the meanest crime. Its growth distinguishes man's rank, its vitality is the will to power, and its flower the sublimation of power in culture. In that sense the severity of the genius is still kind and saintly in spite of the insistence upon rank, and even in spite of his disgust with the broad mass of the diseased, the *Chandala*. But this kindness has none of the sentimentality of the ideal of human bliss of German enlightenment, for that threatens to make men static. He discards all praise of sympathy for its softness and demands intellectual fairness instead.

In his attack upon the Church, however, he is closely related to the general spirit of enlightenment which has always made the Church its most direct target, even when the object was to reform it and the result an authority of similar power. The purpose has always been to deny to the Church and its priesthood the right to decide human fate, but it was not followed through to the complete autonomy of life and man as Nietzsche would have it. To him the priest is the complete antithesis of his new philosopher and teacher, as he must be from the Dionysian premise: he is himself exhausted and diseased, but clever enough to know it, whereas the masses do not. With cunning deception he gains power over the masses by the prescription of such narcotics and stimulants as will keep them pliant and useful. His will to power is in every particular composed of drives diametrically opposite to the sublimation sought for by Nietzsche's prophet. This priesthood is the enemy which Nietzsche all too obviously constructed into the antithesis of his Dionysian faith. He builds upon it the history of the Jewish priesthood, with its continuance in the Christian Church, and claims that thereby he has proved himself the first to have interpreted this history accurately. It is the most striking example of how exclusively his intellectual integrity is limited by his Dionysian view of life as the only reality. In that restricted sense he remains honest with himself, but dogmatic, and consequently so exacting in his judgments of all evaluations in any way related to his view. Insofar as social and, to varying degrees, religious evaluations lay claim to being realistic—that is, expressive of the worth of this life—they become proper objects of Nietzsche's examination by which he has significantly sharpened the sense for the detection of escapes and hidden unrealities. His contributions in that respect are not to be denied.

However, to Nietzsche himself that achievement was merely

preparatory and the exercise of his proud instinct for truth-fulness and falsity, which his exclusive acceptance of the Dionysian view of life gave him. When interpreted without regard to that view, much that is interesting and stimulating may still be garnered from him, but it would not be what he would want. Besides, it may lead, as it has done variously and repeatedly, to serious abuses of him. On the other hand, if this view is taken with all the severity that he exercised upon it, he then emerges as a truly tragic figure who frantically seeks, with the discipline of an ever renewed intellectual integrity, to complete the autonomy of man in a completely autonomous world. In the end he arrives at no further conclusion than that his hypothesis must be true and, therefore, must lead to a more truthful and sound configuration of society. But the realization of it is a mere beckoning phantom to entice even the most robust and wisest wayfarer to the further determination of self-sacrifice. He is neither the intellectual libertine, cynic, nor nihilist that Kant warned would result from such an attitude as his. His challenge, however, arrives only at further defiance, showing stages of the road to many in brilliant expositions, but promising only the happiness of the will to tragedy.

He is the figure of the tragic thinker and artist who would extend his limits beyond the power of man. He might have thought of himself as a more courageous Faust who refuses to acknowledge all need of redemption and wards off every desire for it. Eternal striving is itself eternally enough for him, provided it is directed by the sharply disciplined instinct for reality and a superb power of creative insight. To accept the tragedy of its endless dissatisfaction is his proof of man's dignity and evidence of the joyousness of his faith. He would need no Mephistopheles as a companion to keep him going. He would agree with the Lord in the prologue to Goethe's *Faust* that the activity of man can all too easily become exhausted. But he would undertake to diagnose and eliminate that exhaustion quite by himself; eradicate all that is human, all-too-human, and build this "intransient" world into a culture that is the sublimation of the truly human here on earth.

He tries to face the certainty that his individual efforts will destroy him. But that destruction will profit some greater warrior in the endless series of self-sacrificing leaders, until perhaps the cause will rally an army of "free spirits" to produce, not victory, but the cataclysm that will destroy all that impedes the way to the possible realization of what a victory might be.

So stark is this "joyous tragedy," Nietzsche broke under the tension of it, physically and spiritually, as would every man who took himself as seriously as he did. It finally destroyed his sense of humor and his balance. Nevertheless, there are many moments in his writings when this same tension produced marvellous aphorisms on human all-too-human weaknesses and playful exposure free of cynicism. They are often very helpful and more often of high poetic quality. They justify his place among the very best of modern German writers and psychologists. But they are of little value and some danger, unless the drive of the Dionysian view that directs them be understood and clearly kept in mind.

1.

Boy and Student

Friedrich Nietzsche was of an ancestry proud and cultured, but not extraordinarily distinguished either by blood or achievement. His ancestors were all people of the better middle class in modest but comfortable circumstances, among them a few artisans, some civil servants, and many pastors. They were satisfied to know themselves respectable in position, manners and taste, based on a long tradition of humanistic interests and a piety out of reverence for their spiritual and intellectual roots. Nietzsche's immediate ancestors may be said to have been refined to the point of sensitiveness, if not preciousness. There seems to have been no trace of a daring adventurer in any field, but rather a progressive development of the spirit of the contemplative and mildly inquiring study and the refined drawing room that has played its significant part in German intellecual history.

Nietzsche's father had been tutor at the ducal court at Altenburg where he acquired the courtly manners his son later affected. In 1842, at special command of King Friedrich of Prussia, he was given the parish of the village of Roecken near Leipzig, to which he brought his bride the following year, and where Friedrich was born on October 15, 1844. At his baptism he was given the name of the admired king.

The father was a rather unctuous parish pastor of a nervous temperament. He enjoyed the dignity of his office but also the opportunity for leisure that his small charge afforded and which he used to pursue his studies and his music. The mother was eleven years younger than her husband, of similar social background, but more robust and enterprising. With the family also lived the grandmother and two maiden aunts and so the young Friedrich received an abundance of feminine attention, though he was allowed to invade the sacred precincts of the study at will.

There was a strong mutual attachment between father and son. But before Friedrich's fourth birthday his father became seriously ill and, in July 1849, died of softening of the brain. It was a severe shock to the young boy quite apart from the change of fortune that it signified. The wound of it persisted with him. In July 1846, his sister Elisabeth was born, to whom Nietzsche was always strongly attached and who became his literary executor and the rather autocratic guardian and interpreter of his writings.

At the death of the father, the family moved to the larger city of Naumburg, where they had relatives and friends and could live in the refined circles of their inclinations. There Friedrich was sent to the public primary school, but he remained less than a year because even then, barely six years old, he kept himself apart and was avoided by his schoolmates who were estranged by his precocious and polite manners. He then attended a small, select private school for four years, and spent another four years at the classical Gymnasium where he received the traditional preparation of the better social circles of his day. He was a very serious and shy lad, induced probably by the pampering which he received at home as the only masculine heir to the proud family tradition. Nor was he particularly robust. Eyestrain, due to extreme nearsightedness, brought on persistent headaches, and his family pride encouraged a precocity by which he avoided the ordinary boyish games and sought his recreation in the intellectual sport of music, the writing of poems, and discussions and walks with a very few intimate friends of similar tastes. Even then he was spoken of as "the little pastor."

In October 1858, at the age of fourteen, he entered on a scholarship the famous school of Pforta near Naumburg, one of the oldest and most highly reputed preparatory schools of Germany. The curriculum was centered wholly around the study of the classics and the humanities. While it was what

Nietzsche later described as a "hard school" of high standards and close discipline, it was still liberal in the sense that its teachers were more intent upon arousing the latent scholarly talents and intellectual curiosity of the students, than upon mere drill. Nietzsche fully appreciated its excellent qualities and he applied himself seriously and loyally. However, he still complained that his teachers did not allow him time enough for his own reading and contemplating.

There is little doubt that his lasting interest in the world of Hellas and Rome received its foundation at this school, as well as his preoccupation with the aristocratic values of the earlier Greeks, probably even beyond the interpretation given them by his teachers. It is quite characteristic of him that during the fall months of 1864, at home on vacation before entering the university, he prepared a critical study of the elegies of Theognis of Megara in which he hoped to prove that the poems were all on an aristocratic note, expressions of his love, irony, and anger, and meant to be sung in select aristocratic circles which suffered from the same difficulties of fate and love as he did. Thus early, by a sharp differentiation between moral and aristocratic, he declares:

> But the old aristocracy did not survive after the Persian Wars; wealth was transferred to the people and the popularizing of education and art destroyed the nobility of blood. With this the necessary basis for the understanding of the elegies of Theognis was lost. The burghers approached them with other views. Now moral principles were discovered in them while formerly only aristocratic ones prevailed.[1]

Besides the ancient classics, he also took an interest in German literature, with emphasis on Goethe and Schiller and the older sagas, though that interest was largely dictated by the opportunity to develop his own style in the writing of essays for the school and for the literary club, Germania, which he had formed with a few friends. In the autobiographical sketch which he prepared for the school at graduation, he pays tribute to the influence of his father, his courses, and the games, his two friends in the Germania, music, the writing of poems, thorough specialization, but mentions no modern foreign literature. Nevertheless, there are numerous evidences that Emerson's "Conduct of Life" impressed him strongly, a translation of which had appeared in Leipzig in 1862.

The reading of Emerson had a far more personal interest for him, as though he had discovered a mature guide to help him in formulating the anti-conventional ideas that his classical studies had begun in him and that he must not expose to his teachers. He seems to have read the book zealously and to have absorbed the ideas of Emerson quite carefully, but primarily in order to use them as support for his own reflections on Christianity and the still vague and mystic eternal recurrence of the cycles of becoming.

On September 7, 1864, Nietzsche graduated from Pforta, and on the first of October took a leisurely trip to Bonn where he matriculated at the university, intent more upon this first opportunity fully to enjoy his freedom from all restraint than upon serious study. Within a week he had been admitted into the *Burschenschaft Frankonia,* a fraternity with many of the romantic traditions and customs of German student life, but professing more serious intellectual and national purposes than others of its kind and which was, therefore, preferred by Pforta graduates. It is Nietzsche's first attempt to identify himself with a larger group and to accommodate his ways and thinking to it. He made a determined effort and at first even participated in the drinking and duelling more than was required of him. But it was not in him to treat it as more than an experiment. In a few months he discovered that the fraternity had little to offer him and that he could not honestly pay to it the expected loyalties. Within a year, he sent his resignation to the fraternity in curt and awkwardly pedantic terms:

To the Corporation of the *Burschenschaft Frankonia.*

Oct. 20th, 1865

I am herewith notifying the Corporation of "Frankonia" that I am returning my colors and am declaring my resignation. I shall continue to treasure the idea of the *Burschenschaft.* But I admit frankly that the present form of its ex-

> pression pleases me little. Partly this may be my fault. It has
> been difficult for me to endure a year in the Frankonia. But
> I considered it my duty to learn to know it. I no longer have
> closer bonds with it. Therefore I say farewell. May the Fran-
> konia soon outlive its present stage of development. May it
> always restrict itself to members of high mind and good
> behavior.
>
> FRIEDRICH NIETZSCHE.

Later, in his first public lectures at Basel, he examined the
experience more soberly; for the time, however, it seemed a
serious waste of time and energy except for the acquisition of
a very few friends.

Indeed, the year at Bonn offered him very little and produced nothing of value, due probably to the confusion of his
fraternity experience. To please his mother he had registered
as a student of theology and philology, but he paid no attention to the theological lectures and was very casual also with
the philological studies, even those with his admired Professor Ritschl. There exist also insufficiently authenticated
stories of adolescent excesses during this year from the effects
of which he is said to have suffered throughout his life.
Whether this is true or not, the year at Bonn, though a costly
experiment, made clearer to him the limits of his personality
and kept him aware of the need of discipline and responsibility in the pursuit of freedom.

He arrived at Leipzig on October 17, 1865, to embark upon
the last of his student days. The next day he was matriculated
at the university by a special and, he thought, auspicious
ceremony, the day marking the hundredth anniversary of
Goethe's matriculation. He now devoted himself wholly to
the opportunities offered by the university and its scholars,
whether teachers or fellow students, to develop his intellectual
powers.

His favorite teacher of philology, Professor Ritschl, had accepted a chair at Leipzig and took very special interest in his
former student when he discovered his new seriousness. A
friendship developed between the two which proved to be of
significant help to Nietzsche. Inspired by Ritschl, he formed a

philological club together with a few friends at which the young scholars tested their talent for philological research and literary interpretation. The first paper prepared by Nietzsche for it found such good acclaim that he emendated and revised it and then presented it to Professor Ritschl for criticism. The latter was so astounded by its thoroughness of understanding and originality in interpretation that he encouraged him to elaborate it further into a book. This undoubtedly heightened Nietzsche's ambition, but it made him in no sense a grind; rather, it encouraged him to seek his own way increasingly. He attended lectures with only fair regularity and quite neglected the factual information in them since he could glean that for himself. His whole attention, he claims in a review of his first two years at Leipzig, was upon the "form in which the academic teacher imparted his wisdom," [1] always sharply critical of all pedantry even when discovered in his favored Ritschl. He made up his mind quite early to adopt the teaching of philology as his profession, but also that he would be no philologist in the narrow professional sense; that he must rather develop and perfect as far as possible a philosophical point of view. "I am setting as my goal," he says, "to be a truly practical teacher and above all to arouse in my students the necessary concentration and reflection that will enable them to keep in mind the Why, What, and How of their investigations."

If he was critical of his teachers, he was equally so of himself, guarding against false originality and endeavoring to find a genuine style of his own. The problem of intellectual integrity seems to have been his dominant drive as a student and remained his most absorbing concern throughout his activity. Queries, which he made the subject of his first public lectures as professor at the University of Basel, appear early in the student: how much integrity is there in German thoroughness, with its painstaking labor, but inability to penetrate to the idea interrelating the mass of accumulated material; can there be an honest literary historian without the philosophical power of penetration; especially, what constitutes an honest philosopher?

His chance discovery in a bookshop, in the early days at Leipzig, of Schopenhauer's *World as Will and Idea* helped to formulate and intensify this problem. At once Schopenhauer became his unofficial but consecrated teacher, critic, and philosopher. He nourished what remained of the gloom of Bonn and the desire to submit himself to a philosopher. Nietzsche so reveled in the pessimism of Schopenhauer that he characteristically applied it to himself, even to being perverse about it, and became "bitter, unjust, and unrestrained" in hatred of himself.[1] For a time he was not only an enthusiastic admirer, but a fanatical disciple of Schopenhauer. He made much of his vocabulary his own and felt for a while that he could communicate intimately only with those who were initiated into these new relations.

This extreme experience is an early but striking illustration of the way in which Nietzsche approached what seemed to him a significant intellectual attainment. Much later, when in his *Zarathustra* he attempts to construct the picture of the ideal philosopher, he lists the "three metamorphoses" which the spirit must undergo to have a proper claim to intellectual integrity and productivity. First, like a camel, he must bear his burden gladly and even with reverence. It is as though he would say that there can be no honest claim to a thorough knowledge of a significant intellectual experience, unless it be approached first with reverence and without skepticism. Then only is it thoroughly one's own to test, as one must, with clear analysis, honest doubt, and even the antagonism demanded by one's intellectual powers.

Before Nietzsche finished his student days at Leipzig, he tried himself in the second metamorphosis of the destructive lion in the desert and erased from Schopenhauer what did not agree with his own intellectual direction. He had come to see Schopenhauer's *pure will* as an experiment to explain the world with the help of a leading metaphor which, however, had failed. Moreover, this leading metaphor had become a serious error because its author would not admit of its experimental nature and shaped it into an absolute.[2] He little realized that he would soon persist in doing the very same thing with Dionysus. Even though Nietzsche took the point of view that Schopenhauer's basic premise was an error, he considered the by-products of the experiment of great value and the method essential. "The errors of great men," he says even now, "are more worthy of respect than the truths of lesser men because they are more fruitful." [1] What of Schopenhauer finally could be incorporated into his own thinking and what must be laid aside as foreign to himself did not appear until the publication of "Schopenhauer as Educator" in 1878. By that time it had so fused with other strong influences that Nietzsche had reason for saying the figure in the essay reflects less of Schopenhauer than of himself.

At the end of his second year at Leipzig, Nietzsche decided to serve his year as "volunteer" in the army, as required of every able-bodied student. He had no particular liking for military service or for the interruption of his studies and even hoped that he would be rejected. When accepted, he joined a unit of mounted artillery in his home town, on October 9, 1867. After four months he was rated as the best rider among the recruits of his class. At about that time he crushed his chest severely on mounting his horse. He was completely incapacitated for five months, most of which he was allowed to spend at home, and then was honorably discharged.

He was unable to return to Leipzig until October 1868. The many months of convalescence he employed to carry on his studies and more particularly to prepare himself for the career of a professor of classical philology upon which he was determined. The enforced isolation he utilized, as he strove to do in later life, as a discipline to be the more exacting with himself, not only in the interpretation of his studies, but equally in the evaluation of the opportunities and duties of a teacher. Consequently he returned to Leipzig not as a mere student, but as a serious scholar with so clearly defined a purpose that he strongly impressed his friends, his fellow students, and also his professors.

A little over two months after his return, a professorship in classical philology became vacant at the University of Basel. Professor Ritschl, upon being consulted for possible candi-

dates, proposed Nietzsche's name, even though he was still
without a degree.

He received the appointment as Associate Professor in
spite of his youth and incomplete degree and though the
position had been sought by men of experience and reputation. It was a most unusual distinction for so young a man,
increased by the awarding of the doctorate by the University
of Leipzig without the requirement of a dissertation or examination, merely on the basis of a few previously published
articles. The honor brought about in Nietzsche more serious
reflection than exuberance. He applied himself to the preparation for his new duties not so much by increasing his scholarship as by a conscientious examination of his responsibilities
to his future students.

In the early part of the last semester at Leipzig he had met
Richard Wagner, with whose music he had early become
acquainted and over which he had enthused. Wagner was
completely charmed by the young man; Nietzsche, in turn,
was carried away by the attention shown him by the much
older and famous hero of the day, upon whom he looked as
the best possible illustration of what he had learned to know
as genius from the study of Schopenhauer. This friendship
was to grow after Nietzsche's migration to Basel, but, like all
his deeper emotional and intellectual devotions, was also to be
the occasion for serious conflict.

2.

Works:
The Greek Musicdrama
The Birth of Tragedy
Socrates and the Tragedy

On April 7, 1869, Nietzsche arrived at Basel with an intensely sober reflection upon the responsibilities which the unusual honor and opportunities of his appointment afforded. His duties, as was the convention at Basel, consisted not only in the lectures at the University: he had also to teach certain courses in Greek at the Gymnasium and besides was expected to give occasional public lectures for the benefit of the citizens upon whose support the University depended. He began with the rank of Associate Professor of Greek, but had been promised a promotion to a full professorship after a single year.

This confidence imposed upon him a responsibility as interpreter of Greek which his innate passion for integrity impelled him to take very seriously, and not simply in the conventional sense of attendance to duty. Besides, he must have believed that his selection meant that more than mere scholarship was expected of him and that the opportunity was afforded for originality in interpretation and for free experiment with his students. Originality did not mean to him a new philological twist or a brilliant exhibition of learning: he wanted above all to draw out the personalities of his students and to present Greek to them so that the study of its culture would develop a sense of wonder in them for what had given rise to the great individuals of the past.

At this time the University of Basel was not very flourishing and attendance at the lectures in Greek was small. Also, Nietzsche's health was uneven and consequently his lectures were sometimes, brilliant, sometimes depressed. Not much is known about his work at the Gymnasium. Fully known and of principal importance for the understanding of his mind and influence are his writings and his public lectures, to which he gave himself with careful reflection and full frankness.

His first public address before the University on May 28, 1869, he called "Homer and Classical Philology." In this he outlined as the purpose of his teaching the hope to draw attention away from and beyond all the bickerings of professional philologists, so that, with the development of an aesthetic and philosophical insight, he might bridge the gap between the familiar idealistic ancient world, "which perhaps is only the most beautiful fond Germanic longing for the South," and the real world of the ancients. "For," he says, "all and every philological activity must be fenced in with a philosophical attitude by which everything that is separate and separated evaporates and only the whole and unified remains."

Once engaged upon his duties, however, he set to work on what his earlier studies of pre-Socratic Greek literature had begun in him, in order to clarify and make a first formulation of the Dionysian element in the Greek interpretation of life. This was to be the basic idea of his *The Birth of Tragedy*, and with increasing clarity and simplification it was to remain dominant throughout his development.

In the spring of 1871, he completed his original version of *The Birth of Tragedy*, in which there was as yet no elaborate mention of Wagner or any direct interpretation of his ideas upon the Wagner operas. According to the editor it was offered for publication. The publisher, however, hesitated to accept it, whereupon Nietzsche had a few copies of the latter half of it printed and distributed to a few friends under the title "Socrates and the Greek Tragedy." This seems to have been intended as the ultimate title as well, until service to the cause of Wagner brought with it significant changes and necessary additions.

In "The Greek Musicdrama," a public address delivered in 1870, a year before the completion of *The Birth of Tragedy,* the tragedy of the Dionysian festivals is described as in its most primitive, but also unspoiled state. "The soul of the Athenian who came to view the tragedy in the great Dionysian festival still retained something of that element out of which the tragedy was born. This is the immense outburst of the impulse of spring; a storm and raving of mingled emotions such as all naïve peoples and the whole of nature knows at the approach of spring."[1] In the ecstasy of this condition the servants of Dionysus, the Bacchi, from whom, as chorus, the poet viewed the actors and with whom it in turn viewed the audience, represented man as beside himself and so transfigured by the spell that he does not again return to himself. This transfiguration produces that intense pathos which demands, by its very intensity, the complete but natural unity of the arts where the author must be productive simultaneously as a poet and musician, as director of the orchestra on the stage, and finally as actor. Thus the original tragedy is the most genuine and difficult simplicity, free from all modern studied procedure and intrigue, but still "takes place in the deepest night like all evolving and growth in the realm of art."[2] It is a fond hope for the future at most, he says, that the modern musicdrama will ever be able to recapture such genuine unity.

In his second address, in 1870, entitled "Socrates and the Tragedy," Nietzsche spells out how the critical intellectualism of Socrates destroyed the true nature of the naïve Dionysian power. Socrates, he says, was well acquainted with it but distrusted it; and when it spoke to him he took it as the voice of what he called his daemon that was warning him away. So it lost its productive power. By such behavior, Nietzsche explains, "is revealed how Socrates belongs to a topsy-turvy world. With all productive natures it is the unconscious that acts in a creative and affirmative way, while consciousness behaves critically and as a warning. In Socrates instinct becomes the critic and consciousness the creator." [1] As an end result the original pathos and music of the Dionysian is finally wholly crowded out by the dialectic and intrigue; the tragedy turns increasingly optimistic and ends in comedy. "To speak quite plainly, the flower and zenith of the Greek musicdrama is Aeschylus in his first great period before he was influenced by Sophocles. With Sophocles the very radical decay begins, until Euripides with his conscious reaction to the tragedy of Aeschylus brings about the end with the speed of lightning." [2]

However, in this discussion of the Dionysian as the naïve and creative power of nature and of the danger of consciousness to the productivity of the artist, Nietzsche still labors heavily under the influence of Schopenhauer's aesthetics which he later modified considerably.

The essay entitled "The Dionysian View of Life" seems to be a first attempt to formulate the central idea of *The Birth of Tragedy:* the union of the Dionysian and the Apollonian in the Greek tragedy. It was not meant for publication, but merely as an attempt to clarify the idea for himself. Apart from the terminology, which is still wholly in the language of Schopenhauer, the essay presents the problem of Dionysus and Apollo and their union in the tragedy almost exactly as finally formulated in *The Birth of Tragedy*.

Apollo is *"der Scheinende,"* god of the image or the metaphor, containing the "true insight in contrast to the imperfectly understood actualities of the day." [3] The metaphor, while an illusion, never deludes but results rather from "the restraint, freedom from all wilder emotions, the wisdom and repose of the artist-god." [4] This is the original Hellenic god of art. His power is able to restrain the Dionysus as he storms in from Asia where his cult of nature still signified the crudest release of base instincts and a "panhetaeric animal life which for a time loosens all bonds." [5] This restraint enabled the Greek to sublimate the power of Dionysus and turn the wild orgies into a festival of world salvation and a day of transfiguration. "The myth relates that Apollo restored the torn Dionysus and rescued him from his Asiatic dismemberment." [6] Now the most intimate bond could arise between them and find its consummation in the tragedy. The terror and absurdity of life, disgust with which might have made life intolerable, the sensitive Greek was now able to transmute into attitudes he could bear. "These are the *Erhabene*, the *sublime*, as the artistic control of the terror, and the *ridiculous* as the artistic release from the disgust with the absurd." [1] In the resultant tragicomic art, the Apollonian illusion is no longer enjoyed as illusion, but made into a symbol of truth through the power of music which Nietzsche calls the symbolism of the tone.

The Birth of Tragedy itself, as the challenging result of these preparations, was ready for the publisher in November 1871 and appeared the following January. It was to be the first book of the young professor to establish his position among the classicists, not only with a new and wholly unconventional interpretation of the Greek spirit, but also with a cavalier fluency and emotional style which was certain to arouse professional opposition—as it universally did. This, however, only increased his pride in his originality and heightened his conviction of the philosophical blindness of academic philologians. It made him the more certain of his own penetration and the prouder that he could not be confused with them. He did not think of himself as a scholar in their sense, but as a bold experimenter with ideas, and sought his equals among the geniuses and not the plodders.

At this time Wagner and his wife, Frau Cosima, were living at their villa in Tribschen not far from Basel. Nietzsche had called upon them during his very first holiday and had found himself enthusiastically received and flattered. He then visited them frequently and read and discussed with them all the essays preparatory to his book. For the time being it was a highly emotional intimacy by which Wagner, prodded by Frau Cosima, saw in the young genius a most understanding disciple of his theories of art, and Nietzsche, in Wagner's art, saw an illustration of his new theory of the tragedy. The height of the mutual excitement was reached during the Christmas holidays of 1870 when Nietzsche presented Frau Cosima with a copy of *The Dionysian View of Life*, and when the completed book was accepted by Wagner's publisher, Fritzsch, in

Leipzig, to appear in a format similar to the works of Wagner. While the manuscript was being printed, Nietzsche added a final chapter devoted primarily to Wagner's art in a spirit of grateful tribute to the master. As such it was welcomed at Tribschen with an enthusiasm which even now, at the height of friendship, gave Nietzsche some slight pause for fear that he had surrendered some of his originality and, consequently, some integrity. It evidences itself in the strained superlatives by which he explains the tribute to his friend Rhode in a letter of December 12, 1871, and more directly in a later letter to this same friend when the latter sent him a review of the book as an answer to the many unfavorable discussions by conventional reviewers. In it he says: "No one has an idea of the manner by which such a book comes into being; of the care and trouble taken to keep oneself free to this extent of all the *other* ideas that crowd upon one; of the courage of the conception and the honesty of its execution; probably least of all of my enormous task in relation to Wagner which truly caused me much severe distress—the task to maintain my originality even when assuming a position foreign to myself, so to speak." It became increasingly foreign to him and the emotional excess of it he soon regretted and then attacked.

In the criticism which Nietzsche wrote of his *The Birth of Tragedy* in 1886, he realized quite accurately that at the time of its composition the strong influence of Schopenhauer's aesthetics and his devotion to Wagner had given his ideas too mystic and vague formulations. Above all, he insists that his formulation of the Dionysian is still far too hazy, but still of basic importance to all his further thinking.

The Greeks are again represented as highly sensitive in their feelings, impetuous in their desires, and capable of suffering as no other peoples. They could not have borne the titanic terror and horror of this world had they not created the clear and cheerful gods—and Apollo as the symbol of all the gods—as mediators and thereby won the cheer of life for themselves. But this artistic act in no way implied for them a denial of the original suffering and ambiguity of life, as the Dionysian is called, but rather a protection against the

sensitiveness to suffering and a struggle for the wisdom which
it promotes.

Without Dionysus, Apollo has no existence. Out of life itself, with all its changes, contradictions, crudities, and its
eternal becoming, he can, in moments of extreme ecstasy,
reveal himself as the god; the comforting redeeming illusion;
the basic myth; as that which is indestructible in life beyond
all its changes and antagonisms. This comfort appears in clear
actuality in the chorus which, by its enchantment, lives, as it
were, "beyond all civilization, beyond destruction, and will always be the same in spite of all the changes of generations
and the history of peoples." [1] In this enchantment the Dionysian enthusiast sees a new vision outside of himself in the
heroes of the stage as the Apollonian perfection of his condition, the redeeming illusion of the illusion. "Could we imagine the Dionysian dissonance taking on the form of man
(and man is just that) then this dissonance, to be able to
exist, would require that a splendid illusion should spread the
veil of beauty over itself. This is the real intention of Apollo
in whose name we concentrate all those many illusions of
beautiful phenomena which make life worth living at every
moment of existence and urge on to the experience of the
next." [2]

The basic idea in this first book is thus the Dionysian metaphor for the permanence of life with all its inherent changes
and dissonances and the eternal becoming and suffering. This
is the inescapable myth without which no faith in life or courage for life is possible. It is this that the Greeks teach us first
of all. That life, then, as with the Greeks, needs Apollo to
spread the veil of beauty over it, is a second lesson to which
Nietzsche did not adhere to the extent emphasized in this
book, nor did he keep to the extreme interpretation here
given it. Later, indeed, Apollo is wholly merged with Dionysus
as a single principle. However, the idea of what Nietzsche
called "tragic culture," and later "distinguished culture," persisted with him. It is an attitude of heroic affirmation which
with Dionysian wisdom steadily affirms the picture of life as a
whole and makes the suffering of life its own. Later he will

examine anew whether art alone by means of "the healing balsam of illusion" can supply this courage, or whether German music will again restore the Dionysian character to culture as, he says, it did from Bach to Beethoven.

In this book the accent on art is exclusive and the understanding of the myth the basis of the creative instinct of the Dionysian artist. In him consciousness and rationalism act only as critic and admonisher. From this point of view Socrates becomes a destroyer who reverses the process by making consciousness the creator and instinct merely the critic. "A truly perfect monstrosity!" The Alexandrian culture resulting from this inversion, he says, degenerated to the cheap optimism of modern civilization with its need of a class of slaves to maintain it. "There is nothing more terrible than the barbaric class of slaves which has learned to look upon existence as an injustice and is preparing to take revenge not only for itself, but for all generations. In face of such a threatening storm who would dare appeal to the religions which themselves have degenerated in their fundamentals to learned theology, whereby the myth, as the necessary basis of all religions, is laid lame everywhere, so that there prevailed the spirit of easy optimism which [is] the germ of the destruction of our society." [1]

Thus Dionysus and the myth constitute the important accent of the book, and the union of Dionysus and Apollo, with its resultant heroic culture, is perhaps only the present perspective which, like every perspective, his integrity must test with bold antagonism.

from:

The Greek Musicdrama

It is neither an arbitrary matter nor playful exuberance when, in the first beginnings of the drama, wildly excited mobs roam through fields and woods costumed as satyrs and sileni, their faces smeared with soot and plant juices, and wearing wreaths. The overpowering, suddenly manifested effect of spring here also increases the vital forces to such excess that ecstatic conditions, visions and the belief in one's own enchantment appear everywhere, and others of similar mood roam through the land in swarms. Here is the cradle of the drama. For it does not begin in that somebody disguises himself and tries to arouse illusions in others; rather in that man is beside himself and believes himself transformed and enchanted. In the condition of this "being beside oneself," the ecstasy, there is only one more step needed: we do not return to ourselves but pass over into another being so that we behave as though enchanted. From that in the last analysis comes the deep wonder at viewing the drama: one step becomes uncertain and with it the belief in the permanence and fixity of the individual. And just as the Dionysian ecstatic believes in his transformation, so the dramatic poet believes in the reality of his characters. Without this belief one may, to be sure, belong to the dilettanti but not to the real servants of Dionysus, the Bacchi.

[THE GREEK MUSICDRAMA, *p. 11 ff.*]

from:

The Birth of Tragedy

From the two deities of art, Apollo and Dionysus, we derive our realization that there exists in the Greek world, in respect to its origin and goals, an immense contrast between the plastic art of the image, that of Apollo, and the imageless art of music, that of Dionysus. These two very different tendencies usually go side by side, mostly in open discord with each other and inciting each other to ever new and more powerful creations by means of which they perpetuate the conflict of this contrast; until finally by an act of a metaphysical miracle of the Hellenic "will" they appear paired and in this

union finally produce the Attic tragedy, an art equally Dionysian and Apollonian.

[SECTION 1]

In order to bring these two impulses nearer, they should be
thought of as distinct worlds of art, that of the dream and
that of the intoxication. Between these two physiological
phenomena a corresponding contrast can be seen like that
between the Apollonian and the Dionysian.

[SECTION 1]

But that delicate line which the dream-picture must not
overstep—lest it have a physiological effect and the illusion
deceive us as crude reality—must be observed in the picture
of Apollo: that measured restraint, that absence of all the
wilder emotions, that wise serenity of the god of the image.

[SECTION 1]

Either by the influence of narcotic potions of which the
paeans of all primitive men and peoples speak, or at the
powerful approach of the spring as it joyously penetrates all
of nature, there awaken those Dionysian emotions at the increase of which all that is subjective disappears into complete
self-forgetfulness.

[SECTION 1]

Under the magic of the Dionysian not only is the bond
between man and man established again—even the estranged,
inimical or subjected nature again celebrates its festival of
reconciliation with man, its prodigal son—Now the slave is a
free man; now all those rigid, hostile divisions which distress,
wilfulness, or "insolent fashion" have established between
men disappear.

[SECTION 1]

In the presence of these art conditions of nature, every artist is an "imitator," namely, either an artist of the Apollonian dream or an artist of the Dionysian intoxication, or finally, as for example in the Greek tragedy, both at once. As such we must consider him, when in the Dionysian intoxication and mystic self-abnegation, alone and apart from the ecstatic chorus, he is overcome, and now, because of the effect of the Apollonian dream, his own state reveals itself to him in a metaphorical dream of his oneness with the innermost basis of the world.

[SECTION 2]

It is an indisputable tradition that in its oldest form the Greek tragedy had as its exclusive subject only the sufferings of Dionysus and that for a long time Dionysus was the only hero on the stage. But it can be maintained with the same assurance that up to the time of Euripides Dionysus never ceased to be the tragic hero, but that all the famous figures of the Greek stage—Prometheus, Oedipus, and so on—were merely masks of the original hero, Dionysus.

[SECTION 10]

This striving of the spirit of music for metaphorical and mystic manifestation which had been increasing from the beginnings of the lyric up to the Attic tragedy suddenly, after having just attained its most luxurious development, breaks off and disappears, as it were, from the surface of Hellenic art. Meanwhile the Dionysian view of life born of this striving lives on in the mysteries and, even in the strangest metamorphoses and distortions, does not cease to attract more serious natures. Will it perhaps once again rise as art out of its mystic depths?

[SECTION 17]

from:

Socrates and the Tragedy

The tragedy foundered on optimistic ethics and dialectics; the musicdrama foundered because of a lack of music. By invading the tragedy Socratism prevented the music from fusing with the dialogue and monologue, even though in the drama of Aeschylus a most successful beginning had been made in this respect. Another result was that music, more and more limited and forced into more and more narrow bounds, no longer felt at home in the tragedy but developed more freely and boldly outside of it as a sovereign art. It is ridiculous to have a ghost appear at a noonday meal; it is ridiculous to demand of so mysterious and seriously enthused a muse as that of tragic music that it should sing in the halls of the courts in the intervals between dialectic contests. Conscious of this absurdity music became silent, frightened as it were by this unheard-of desecration. It dares less and less to raise its voice; finally gets confused and sings things that are inappropriate; then becomes shy and flees from the theater altogether.

3.

Works:

On the Future of Our Academic Institutions

Philosophy in the Tragic Age of the Greeks

Truth and Lie in an Extra-moral Sense

From January to March 1872, Nietzsche delivered five public addresses at the request of *Akademische Gesellschaft* of Basel "On the Future of Our Academic Institutions," the purpose of which, as stated in a preface published posthumously, was to arouse a "feeling for the specific elements of our present barbarism or that which distinguishes us as barbarians of the nineteenth century from other *barbarians.*" He is referring, of course, to German institutions generally.

The language of these lectures is still very decidedly that of Schopenhauer. In spite of that, however, his own specific ideas evolve very clearly. He is concerned with the student and the necessary first step he must take if he is to progress toward being the future herald of culture. If he avoids that first step he is violating his nature and so becomes unnatural, confused, and what Nietzsche calls degenerate. "*Natura non fecit saltus.*" This first and only proper, because natural, attitude of the student is that of reverence, the reverent and tolerant camel, by which alone that overabundance of riches can be gained which will enable him to give to others.

35

The lectures are cast in the form of a chance meeting of two students who have retired from the distractions of collegiate life to examine their progress with a philosopher and his friend who have come to expound on the nature of culture. Thus the students can illustrate what directions they have received at the preparatory schools and the university, and the philosopher can help to evaluate them from his mature position. The question then is: what does current, here specifically modern Prussian, education offer in preparation for genuine culture? Current education is taken to pursue two principal objects, both of which are barbarous if judged by the nature of genuine culture. It either promotes a general extension of education, called popular education, with its goal that of a successful businessman, or a utilitarian and narrow specialization to train servants for the state at the expense of the self-sufficiency of culture. Out of this there arises at best the modern pseudogenius, the clever journalistic talent living by the maxim: knowledge is power and power is money. Out of antagonism to this, the philosopher bids the students take a courageous look at the modern trends in education and insists that the preparatory schools be examined first, since university education is based upon them.

The significance of these lectures, it must be emphasized, lies not in the propounding of general views, but in the repeated insistence that there is no road to culture unless the path through reverence for the leaders in philosophy, art, and literature be taken first. Otherwise there can be no integrity in its pursuit; nature can not really be known; the result can be only unreal, unnatural, and degenerate, or, at best, merely superficially clever journalism. The premise for an understanding of the lectures, however, is the comprehension of nature in the Dionysian sense, which is so central to Nietzsche that he assumes its acceptance by his audience.

His university lectures on Greek Philosophy he seems to have used to promote the above attitudes. He planned to use the material of these lectures for a publication to be called "Philosophy in the Tragic Age of the Greeks," a fragment of which is now to be found in his posthumous works and deals with Greek philosophy from Thales to Anaxagoras. In the two forewords, the one presumably of 1874 and the other of 1879, he explains that he is only slightly interested in presenting systems, not at all in imparting learned information, but wholly in the great personalities. They are always true whatever may be true about their philosophies.

The interpretations are bold and used to show what constitutes a philosopher, what his relation to nature is, and how he proceeds. He chooses the Greeks before Socrates because he believes that their philosophies are products of greatest maturity and integrity. Also, they are the seers and, therefore, genuinely artists, as he insists great philosophers must be.

He dwells most fondly on Heraclitus to whom he consistently owed most. Heraclitus is to him the "real seer," the "divine sage of the highest power of intuitive expression." Many of the ideas and directions that Nietzsche developed later, by what he considered highly original formulations, he here emphasized in Heraclitus. He finds in him a great dislike of abstractions and a delight in the senses. Nietzsche rejects the idea of essence as a vain abstraction and clings to what he describes as actualities. "I see nothing but becoming. Do not be fooled." "Becoming" receives a Dionysian connotation as the striving of one quality to produce its opposite and then to unite, and to continue this process *ad infinitum*.

At about this time, in an attempt to formulate his own more distinctive approach, Nietzsche was working at an essay he never finished. It is an attempt to clarify for himself the fundamental question whether absolute truth is possible or even desirable for man. He speaks of "Truth and Lie in an Extra-moral Sense." "Extra-moral" here, it is important to note, means unconventional, specifically in the sense of a psychological and social investigation. The implication is that investigations by conventional moral attitudes have all been far too superficial.

This essay is a mere fragment but it is still interesting to see Nietzsche groping to establish the relative nature of truth as man's interpretation of his weapon for the fullest life for him-

self and society. The claim, however, that the artist wields the
weapon most beneficially, he will modify later as Dionysus
increases in importance and Apollo assumes a lesser part.

The next few years, from 1873 to 1875, Nietzsche progressively retired within himself. In outside philological circles
he had become suspect as a brilliant but superficial radical,
and his hope that he be accepted as a philosopher met with
no success. In the University and the civic circles of Basel he
found respectful but in no sense warm support. His classes at
the Gymnasium afforded him some satisfaction, but he was a
moody and uneven teacher and the attitude of his students
varied between enthusiasm and non-comprehension. At the
University his students became fewer and then shrank to a
very small number of enthused disciples. He offered them
great stimuli for a radical revaluation of ideas, but, so it
seemed to them, little help toward orderly professional training. Also, his health became increasingly precarious.

The effect of all this was to make him the more exacting
with himself and others. In his lectures on the future of the
academic institutions he had already set up very high standards of intellectual integrity in all educational pursuits and
demanded that culture be as organic as a great work of art.
The more he retired within himself, the more severely he
examined the demands of integrity within himself, as well
as in the so-called cultured society.

from:

On the Future of Our Academic Institutions

The culture of the masses cannot be our goal but solely
the culture of select individuals who are equipped for great
and lasting works. We know well enough that an enlightened
posterity will judge the configuration of the culture of a
people solely by the great, isolated heroes of the age and
will give its approval in accordance with the manner in which

these heroes were recognized, furthered and honored or, on the other hand, neglected, abused or destroyed. What we generally call popular culture can be attained directly, for example by universal, compulsory elementary education, only very superficially and crudely. The real, deeper levels where the great mass has any contact with culture—there where the mass cherishes its religious instincts, where it keeps evolving its mystic images, where it remains loyal to its customs, its law, its native home and its language—all these can scarcely be reached directly or, if so, only by disturbing acts. Truly to promote the culture of the masses in these serious matters means to ward off such destructive acts and to foster that wholesome unconsciousness, that restorative sleep of the people, without which countering action as a remedy no culture can persist because of the exhausting tension and irritation of its effects.

[THIRD LECTURE]

Free! Take a look at this free student, this herald of autonomous education, discover him from his instincts, find out what he is from his needs! How would you rate his culture if you undertook to measure it by three standards: first by his need of philosophy, then by his instinct for art, and finally by Greek and Roman antiquity as the embodied categorical imperative of all culture.

Man is so surrounded by the most serious and difficult problems that, if led to them in the proper way, he will find an early approach to that persistent philosophical wonder from which, as the only useful foundation, a deeper and nobler culture can arise.

[FIFTH LECTURE]

For, if you take away the Greeks together with their philosophy and their art, what ladder will there be by which to climb the rungs of culture? For at the attempt to climb this ladder without such help your learning will be an awkward

burden on your back rather than supply you with wings or
elevate you.

[FIFTH LECTURE]

I repeat, my friends! All culture begins with the opposite
of the presently vaunted academic freedom: with obedience,
subordination, with discipline and willingness to serve.

[FIFTH LECTURE]

from:

Philosophy in the Tragic Age of the Greeks

Other peoples have saints, the Greeks have sages.
The philosopher [he says in treating of Thales] tries to let
the harmony of the world penetrate him and then to project
it in concepts. While he is contemplative like a plastic artist;
has the sympathy of a religious person; hunts for causes and
purposes like a scholar; even feels himself expanding to a
macrocosm, he still maintains the calm clarity to view himself
as the reflection of the world. This clarity is identical with that
of the dramatic artist as he transforms himself into other
bodies, speaks out of them and yet knows how to project the
transfiguration in verses. Dialectical thinking is to the philosopher what the verse is to the poet. It is this that he seizes
upon in order to hold to his transfiguration and to project
it. . . . [So he claims to find in Anaximander the style most
suited to the artio-philosopher] Lapidary writing in grand
style, sentence for sentence witness of a new enlightenment
and the expression of dwelling in lofty contemplation.

[SECTIONS 3 AND 4]

All becoming arises from the war of opposites. The definite
qualities that seem so persistent to us merely express the
momentary superiority of the one contestant. But that is not

the end of the war; the conflict persists eternally. Everything takes place in accordance with this conflict and it is this very struggle that reveals eternal justice. It is a marvellous idea taken from the purest source of the Hellenic that conflict is considered as the persistent reign of an undivided, strict justice bound to eternal laws. Only a Greek had the ability to find in this idea the basis of a "cosmodicy." Just as each Greek carries on his fight as though he alone were in the right and an infinitely assured judgment were determining at each moment the direction of victory, so the qualities contend with each other in accordance with laws that are immutable and immanent to the contest. The things themselves, which only the limited brains of men and animals believe fixed and stationary, have no real existence at all. They are the flashing and sparks of drawn swords, the glow of victory in the conflict of opposing qualities.

[SECTION 5]

from:

Truth and Lie in an Extra-moral Sense

The various languages, placed side by side, show that with words it is never a matter of the truth or of adequate expression. Otherwise there would not be so many different languages. The "thing per se"—that of course would be the pure, dead-end truth—is wholly incomprehensible even to the creator of language and in no sense worth striving for. He merely describes the relations of things to man and resorts for their expression to the boldest metaphors. A nerve stimulus first translated into an image! First metaphor. The image then again transformed into a sound! Second metaphor. And each time a complete leap from one sphere into another and new one.

[We] possess nothing but the metaphors of things.

What then is truth? A mobile army of metaphors, metonyms, anthropomorphisms, in short the sum of human relationships which, on poetic and rhetorical heights, were transformed and adorned and, after long usage, are considered by the people to be established, canonical and authoritative. Truths are illusions forgotten as such: metaphors that have become stale and have lost their sensual power, or coins that have lost their image and now are thought of merely as metal and no longer as coins.

We still do not know the origin of the urge to truth. For up to now we have heard only of the obligation which society sets up in order to exist, namely to be truthful; which means that it uses ordinary metaphors; or, expressed in moral terms, that it lies in accordance with a firm convention: that is, lies collectively in a style binding upon all. Man, to be sure, forgets this fact. Then in the manner described above he lies unconsciously according to century-old habits—*through this very unconsciousness*, through this forgetting, he arrives at the feeling of truth.

For the liberated intellect that immense structure of concepts, by clinging to which man in his need has saved himself throughout his life, is merely a scaffolding and plaything for his most daring feats. When he breaks it, throws it into a heap, and ironically puts it together again, pairing the least related and separating the most so, he thereby shows that he is in no need of such makeshifts born of his distress and that now he is directed not by concepts but by intuitions. No regular path leads from these intuitions into the land of the spectral patterns, the abstractions. The word has not been made for them; man has no voice when he sees them or he speaks only in forbidden metaphors or unheard-of conceptual combinations in order, by breaking down and mocking the old conceptual barriers, at least to approach creatively the impressions of the present mighty intuitions.

4.

Works:
Human, All-Too-Human,
Parts I and II

Part I

As early as 1876, and as a result of a decline in the state of his health, after seven short years of service, he considered the necessity of resigning his position, but remained another three years at the urging of the university authorities and his friends. He saved most of his strength, however, to apply himself to the writing of a book that seemed of greater importance to him than his present teaching.

The theme has now changed considerably. He is no longer addressing himself primarily to the education of youth, but assumes the responsibility of talking to wider audiences, as though to educate them to an integrity similar to the kind he wished to instill in youth. When he now had students in mind, moreover, he was thinking of those who were to be active at the building of a future culture and leaders of it. Consequently, they could be treated as potential co-workers with himself and share his concern for his own genuineness, justice, and wisdom. Also, he could present to them, and perhaps felt that he must in order to be wholly honest with them, the process by which he himself had fought through to independent, free, and intellectually responsible thinking: his experience with pre-Socratic Greek culture; the inspiration

43

which his reverence for and his interpretation of Schopenhauer had given him; and the excitement of his first devotion to Wagner and his intimacy with him. In a word, thus far the path to integrity, to a thorough affirmation of life, a wholeness of self, and a genuine creative activity was under the guidance of the genius, the philosopher, and of art.

Now, however, he necessarily had to reexamine the comparatively facile answers which he had given thus far. He had to test every step of his own as to its integrity and also, of course, every social institution, value, and conviction of the Europe which he was preparing to address. It looked like a serious undertaking, weighty and dangerously ambitious, and for that reason alone a threat to a full integrity. Besides, he was depressed and of precarious health; yet clarity of mind and health were synonymous to him with freedom and integrity. So he had at least to pretend that he was making this reexamination a sort of game, a highly entertaining experiment out of curiosity as to where it will lead.

To a degree the book, under the title *Human, All-Too-Human*, which he published in May 1878, just a year before his resignation from the University, is just that: a mixture of very serious and sometimes trivial examinations of institutions, customs, and values. Some of these concerned him deeply and he had thought long and thoroughly on them, especially those of moral sentiments; about others he is merely audacious and imperfectly informed, as for example, practical politics and, especially, women.

Ten years after the publication of *Human, All-Too-Human*, he wrote the preface which now introduces the book. There he describes it as an important transitional step in his development, as though the period of youthful reverence and obedience, the stage of the camel, had been completed and he were starting out with this book on his wanderings in the desert, as a lion, to learn what of his prized possessions must be destroyed, and to find the attitude by which to win the right, power, freedom, and wisdom for a new creation.

The principles dominating this book are these: Values are created by man for the preservation of life in society and for service to it; the view of life must maintain its Dionysian character by embracing every element of it to the extent of man's ability; life must be penetrated by the sharpest possible power of observation and analysis. This last is, perhaps, the leading influence of the book, whereby the accent on the creative artist is strongly modified in favor of the experimenter. The method of experimentation and of analysis strives to be as exact as that of the natural scientist. Nietzsche strives to be the psychologist, the exact observer and analyst, or, as he likes to say, the tester and mystery-solver of man's mind and emotions. Thereby he does indeed discover his own most individual genius. He is here the psychologist, not to say psychoanalyst in the making.

In the opening section, which he calls "On the First and Last Things," he undertakes to clear the way for his perspective thinking and understanding by freeing himself from all philosophical approaches that assume more than a strictly scientific procedure. This means to him freedom from all metaphysical beliefs, which, since they hope for and rely on things that cannot be known, must mislead.

However, in all this Nietzsche was merely shaking off from himself the authority that Schopenhauer, for example, once exercised over him or that Kant exerted over his times, so that he might devote himself to the experiment with its scientific method, as he called his psychological procedure. He was deliberately restricting himself to test his own integrity. Even this new method was taken up in a somewhat playful spirit, as though he were afraid that it might dominate him and close his mind to an entirely different approach, if the new discoveries which resulted from it should so demand.

The history of morals which he is demanding is not a history in the ordinary sense, but rather sharp psychological analyses of moral behavior in general, in order to discover, if possible, what is basic and consequently antecedent in such behavior. He tries to peel off the emotional elements, since they interfere with scientific accuracy, and then to arrive at whatever prejudices and wishful illusions are active in moral judgments. For the only cure for prejudices, he believes, is

a keen knowledge of them, and the only purpose in dissecting
emotions and acts is to find the degree of integrity in them.

He defines moral sentiments as those upon which responsibility is based. But in examining this responsibility he finds
whole series of inversions and distortions of logic. Originally
acts were called good or evil because they produced beneficial
or harmful effects. This is then forgotten, effects are translated
into sources, and the acts themselves given the attribute good
or evil. Next, the attributes of the acts are put further back
into the motives and then, finally, into the nature of man himself, as, for example, Schopenhauer's "intelligible freedom"
is moral in so far as man attains his relation to the "will." [1]

The scientific observer, however, sees man's nature as the
product of innumerable elements and influences of past and
present things, wherefore he can be intelligent and fair, but
in no way responsible by virtue of an "intelligible freedom,"
or out of a sense of duty based on his obedience to a "universal
law." The latter he cannot possibly know, and so cannot, with
integrity, claim to follow it. So the "freedom of the will," in
this moral sense of obedience to a universal law or of responsibility to his essence as related to a divine will, must be an
error. It may indeed be a beneficial illusion, a deception of
necessity (*Notlüge*) to defend man against the beast within
himself, but it nevertheless is intellectually false. The problem
imposed upon man is therefore to aim at being a wise man
rather than what is conventionally called moral. Nietzsche
realizes that it is bitter and disagreeable to be asked to lay
aside as untenable the belief in moral responsibility and in
the freedom of the will which upholds it. But, on the other
hand, to him such an attitude adds to the dignity of man
rather than detracting from it, in that it increases the courage
of intellectual integrity, sharpens the understanding of his
nature, and may lead to wisdom. The welfare of society can
be promoted more lastingly when keen and cold integrity,
rather than moral judgments, determine it, and fairness,
rather than judgments, is sought for.

By his dissection of what has been thought of as morality
up to the present, he believed he had found three stages of

development. The earliest evidence of the rule of reason in man was when he treasured an act as of enduring, rather than just monetary usefulness to himself. In the second and higher application of his reason, he realized his community with others and sought the enduring usefulness of the community together with his own. He wanted to be respected by others and acted according to the principle of respectability *(Ehre)*. The last and highest stage that has been sought hitherto by the increasing application of the intellect, Nietzsche calls that of the lawgiver, who determines what is useful and honorable for himself and the community in accordance with an increasingly higher standard of enduring usefulness and honor. He has learned to prefer the common, enduring usefulness to the personal, and to value the honor of the enduring repute more highly than any monetary recognition. "He lives and acts as a collective individual."

Moral behavior then, like every progress in nature, is experimental. Every good is an evil or trial error, sublimated by reason to a new, more enlightened experiment, and then called good. However, even the most enlightened good may still be an evil in the light of the degree of reason that man may at some future time reach. At this juncture morality is primarily piety in respect to the community and its manners and customs, and is used in this sense as the touchstone for its genuineness in the analysis of current behavior. But even in that Nietzsche is not strictly consistent and often he engages in playful intellectual exercises. His scientific keenness is like a new toy to him, the more when, like a child with a knife, he thinks it dangerous.

In the next section, in which he undertakes to deal "scientifically" with what he calls the religious life, he is very strained and often awkward, as if his integrity demanded that he treat it, but were also warning him against deceiving himself with a show of assurance. He asserts that the application of the intellect to an analysis of faith is a very painful process, "But without pain one cannot get to be a leader and teacher of mankind, and woe to him who would try it and thereby lose a clean conscience." [1] The reconciliation of science and religion is patently impossible for him. Much in religion he can comprehend as wishful misunderstanding by men deeply concerned for the welfare of humanity, but it must nevertheless be attacked as romantic and unenlightened. Purely religious sentiments are very appealing and, therefore, even many philosophers resort to mystic presentiments as wishful hypotheses. But that is bad thinking and a lack of integrity. Where such wishful metaphors not only go beyond the reach of reason, but also represent an escape from life—as in the idea of grace and an eternal justice that compensates in the beyond for the misery here and makes the weaker the masters of the stronger—he attacks them because all such beliefs humiliate man and are in the deepest sense "barbaric, Asiatic, non-distinguished, and non-Greek." [1] Evidently his own faith in man, as the creator of all things and himself the perfection of nature, is quite scientific to him. Man can be known if only by virtue of "scientific," sharp, psychological methods we proceed boldly on the road to such knowledge and avoid the wishful presentiments of religious romantics. It is this sort of thing that he tries in this particular investigation, but hardly with the clarity that he demands of a clear intellectual conscience.

In the section on "The Souls of Artists and Writers," the experiment of science as the necessary approach to integrity goes further still. To be sure, it primarily contains an attack upon the revolutionary behavior of naturalistic writers who misunderstand both art and nature. Nevertheless, the demand upon authors for scientific procedure is often strained to the point where the definition of science itself becomes vague.

When Nietzsche examines the evidences of higher and lower culture in individuals and society, the importance of art appears again and, though there is still emphasis on the natural sciences and history, science essentially has the meaning of "severe thinking, careful judgment, and consequential conclusions." He is now seeking to get a clearer grasp on what constitutes the "free spirit," free from the tyranny of the emotionalism of religion and art, as well as from the tyranny of the orthodoxy of science; for integrity is taken as impossible under either. In describing what he calls the phases of the intellectual development of modern man, he seems to describe the changes which he had observed within himself.

from:

Human, All Too-Human, I

THE POSSIBILITY OF PROGRESS

A scholar of the old culture is quite right when he decides that he will have nothing more to do with people who believe in progress. For the greatness and the values of the old culture have been left behind and our historical training forces us to admit that they can never again be restored. It takes an insufferable stupidity and an equally intolerable sentimentality to deny this. But people can *consciously* decide to develop themselves toward a new culture, whereas in earlier times they developed unconsciously and by chance. They can now create better conditions for human living, its nourishment, training and education; administer the world as a whole economically; in general balance the powers of men against each other and put them to work. This new conscious culture erases the old which, taken as a whole, has carried on the unconscious life of animals and plants. It also erases the distrust about progress—it is *possible*. I mean to say: it is premature and almost nonsense to believe that progress must *necessarily* follow, but how can it be denied that it is possible?

[SECTION 24]

PRIVATE AND WORLD MORALITY

Ever since the belief has been abandoned that a God directs the fate of the world as a whole and, in spite of all the windings on the path of mankind, splendidly directs all things for the best, man must himself set goals which embrace the whole world. The older morality, specifically that of Kant, demands acts from the individual which are desirable for all men. That was a beautiful, naïve thing; as though each individual automatically knows what manner of acting is best for the whole of mankind, in other words, what actions are generally desirable. . . . Perhaps a future survey of the needs of mankind may show that it is not at all desirable that all men act in the same way. It may be possible that special, perhaps under certain circumstances even evil tasks must be set for whole sections of mankind. . . . At all events, if man is not to bring about his downfall by such a conscious totalitarian rule, there first must be found a *knowledge of the conditions of culture* as a scientific standard for ecumenical goals far beyond all that is presently known. In this lies the immense task of the great spirits of the next century.

[SECTION 25]

SUBSTITUTE FOR RELIGION

One believes he is praising philosophy when it is presented to the people as a substitute for religion. In intellectual economy there is indeed an occasional need for *transitional* ways of thinking. Thus the transition from religion to scientific observation is indeed a violent, dangerous leap, something to be cautioned against. Insofar the above recommendation is right. But it is about time to learn that the needs themselves which religion has satisfied and philosophy now is to satisfy are not beyond change. They can be *weakened* and *eradicated*. For example, consider the Christian spiritual agony, the sighs over inner corruption, the worries about salvation. . . . All these are ideas originating from errors of reason which in no way deserve satisfaction but rather eradication. Philosophy can be of use either by satisfying such needs or by removing them, for they are merely acquired ideas, are limited in time and rest upon hypotheses which contradict those of science. To make a transition here it is much better to resort to art in order to relieve the mind overburdened with sentiments. For by means of art such sentiments are entertained much less than by means of a metaphysical philosophy. From art it is much easier to make the transition to a truly liberating philosophical science.

[SECTION 27]

Aside from all theology and the attacks upon it, it is evident that the world is not good and not evil, and certainly not the best or the worst, and that these concepts "good" and "evil" have meaning only in relation to man. Perhaps they are not even justified in the way they are usually used. At all events we must get rid of the fault-finding and glorifying view of the world.

[SECTION 28]

THE GRIEF OF KNOWLEDGE

Those false assertions of the priests that there is a God who sees and guards every act of ours, every moment, every thought; who loves us and in all misfortune desires our best— how pleasant it would be to exchange these errors with truths which are equally wholesome, quieting and comforting! But such truths do not exist. At best philosophy can set up against them comparable metaphysical illusions. But the tragedy is this: one can not *believe* these dogmas of religion and metaphysics if one is devoted head and heart to the severe methods of science; and yet the development of mankind has made us so tender, sensitive and suffering that we are in need of the highest kind of remedies and comfort. Consequently there arises the danger that man will bleed to death from his acquired truth. Byron expresses this in the immortal verses:

Sorrow is knowledge; they who know the most
Must mourn the deepest o'er the fatal truth;
The Tree of Knowledge is not that of Life.

[I, 109]

There is no doubt that in the Age of Enlightenment one had been unfair to the significance of religion. But it is equally certain that the ensuing reaction to enlightenment had gone considerably beyond what is just by treating religion with intense affection and attributing to it a deeper, even the deepest understanding of the world, which science need only strip of its dogmatic garment in order then to possess "truth."

[I, 110]

Indeed, between religion and real science there is no relationship, nor friendship, nor even enmity; they live on different planets. Every philosophy which trails a comet's tail of religion into the darkness of its ultimate views makes every thing suspect that parades as science. All of it is presumably religion even though it wears the garment of science.

[I, 110]

OF THE CHRISTIAN NEED OF REDEMPTION

Careful consideration should be able to uncover an explanation for the Christian's need of redemption which is free of mythology, in other words purely psychological. . . . Man is conscious of certain acts which are customarily ranked very low. Indeed he discovers in himself a tendency toward such acts which seems as unchangeable as his whole nature. How gladly he would engage in the other order of acts which are universally rated as the most lofty; how gladly he would like to have his fill of that good conscience which is said to follow upon an unselfish way of thinking, but he gets no further than the wish for it. The dissatisfaction at not being able to satisfy it is added to all the other types of dissatisfaction which are generally the lot of his life or which the results of his so-called evil acts have aroused in him. Consequently a deep discontent arises in him and with it a search for the physician who might cure it and all its causes. This condition would not be felt so bitterly if he would only compare himself frankly with other men. Then he would have no reason to be especially dissatisfied with himself; he merely would bear his part of the general human dissatisfaction and imperfection. But he compares himself with the one being who alone is capable of those acts which are called unselfish, and lives in a constant awareness of unselfish attitudes, namely with God. By looking into this bright mirror his own nature seems to him to be so very clouded and uncommonly distorted. Consequently the thought of that divine being frightens him, since it hovers before his imagination as an avenging justice; in every kind of great or small experience he believes he sees this being's anger and threat and even anticipates the scourge of the judge and executioner. Who will help him in this danger which transcends all other fears of his imagination as he considers the horror and eternity of this punishment?

[I, 132]

They [modern men] begin their entry into culture as children with religious emotions and reach the highest vivacity of this phase about the tenth year. By approaching science they then change over to weaker emotional forms, such as pantheism, and free themselves wholly from God, immortality, and the like but succumb to the magic of metaphysical philosophy. However, this finally appears to be untenable, and art seems to offer more, so that for a time metaphysics barely lives on, transformed into art or an artistically transfigured mood. Then the scientific sense becomes more demanding and leads the mature man to the natural sciences and history and, above all, to the severest method of thinking, while art attains an increasingly milder and less demanding significance.

Today all this usually takes place within the first thirty years of a man's life. However, it is the recapitulation of an assignment for which man has expended his powers for perhaps thirty thousand years.

[I, END OF 272]

[Like the balance between illusion and severe reason, Nietzsche sees culture depending upon the union of the ancient and the modern world. The Italian Renaissance promised well, in its beginnings, to lead to such a union, but was degenerated by the scholastic and regressive German Reformation which the Counter Reformation then used for its own purpose.]

[I, 237]

[The Renaissance] was the golden age of this millennium in spite of all its blemishes and vices. Then there arose against it the German Reformation as the energetic protest of retarded spirits who had not yet tired of the views of the Middle Ages and who were deeply distressed by the symptoms of its dissolution, the extraordinary loss of vigor and the superficiality of the religious life, instead of rejoicing over it as they should. With their Nordic vigor and stubbornness they reversed the progress of mankind and, with the violence of a state of siege, forced upon it the Counter Reformation, this Catholic Christianity of self-defense. Thus they delayed by two or three centuries not only the complete awakening and reign of science, but also made impossible perhaps forever the complete union of the ancient and modern spirit of life. The great task of the Renaissance could not be brought to fruition; the protest of the still retarded German character (which in the Middle Ages again and again had sense enough to seek its salvation beyond the Alps) prevented it. It was because of the accident of an extraordinary configuration of politics that Luther was spared at that time and that the protest prevailed. The emperor protected him in order to use his reforms to exert pressure upon the Pope, just as the Pope secretly favored him in order to use the Protestant princes against the Emperor. Without this strange interplay of intentions Luther would have been burned at the stake like Huss—and the dawn of enlightenment would perhaps have risen earlier and with a more beautiful glow than we can imagine.

[I, 273]

THE FUTURE OF SCIENCE

. . . Science affords a great deal of joy for him
works and searches in it, but very little to him who merely
studies its results. Since gradually all the important truths of
science must become commonplace, this remnant of satisfaction also ceases, just as we have long since ceased rejoicing in
the marvellous multiplication table. But if science affords less
and less joy because of itself and finds more and more of it in
throwing suspicion upon comforting metaphysics, religion, and
art, then the greatest source of joy to which mankind owes
almost the whole of its humanity disappears. Therefore a
higher culture must supply man with a double brain, two
brain chambers, so to speak, one for the appreciation of
science, the other for non-science, lying side by side without
confusion and separable. This is a requirement of health. In
the one lies the source of energy, in the other the regulator.
Illusions, onesidedness, passions must supply the heat, discerning science must prevent the malicious and dangerous
results of overheating. . . . If this requirement of higher culture
is not satisfied, the whole future course of human development
can be foretold with certainty: the interest in truth will cease
as it affords less satisfaction; illusions, error, and phantasies
step by step will regain the ground they once maintained because they are associated with pleasure. The next result will
be the ruin of science and the return to barbarism. Mankind
must begin anew to weave its web after, like Penelope, it un-
did it in the night. But who will guarantee that it will always
find the strength for this?

[I, 251]

[When examining the State, as he does in a separate section, he is particularly awkward. Modern democracy, and
especially the socialism that seems to expend so much of human energy which might be applied to cultural development,
is clearly in his way, though he gains comfort from his analysis
of it as merely an intermediate and transitory stage. The

mand for justice without any intellectual
ice, he finds impelled only by envy and
their demand for equality and self-
their own class only, they are forced to
p, cruelty, and deceit, just as all special
have done. But they are doomed to a short
existe... f this unreality. He foresees that when such
a dictatorship reaches its height, the state, with its bulky
bureaucracy, will increase its control also over the masses, and
the cry, "as much state as possible," will more and more,
though gradually and by necessity rather than by agitation,
produce the opposite demand, "as little state as possible."
This may even bring into disrepute every traditional concept
of the state and begin the search for an entirely new form,
the configuration of which cannot now be imagined. To in-
stigate this new development by means of revolutionary agitation is to him a presumption of knowledge that must lack
genuineness and so can have only a disturbing and vainly destructive effect.]

A QUESTION OF MIGHT, NOT OF RIGHT

For people who in every instance are intent upon the
highest advantage, socialism, if it *really* is the revolt of those
who have been suppressed and kept down for thousands of
years against their oppressors, is not a problem of *right* (with
the ridiculous question: "how far ought one to yield to its
demands"), but a problem of *might*: "how far can one make
use of its demands." It is similar to a natural force, for example
steam, which men either force into their service, as god of the
machine, or which in case of human miscalculation in its construction destroys itself and men. In order to solve this question one must know how strong socialism is, with what modification it can be of use as a powerful lever for the present
political power game. Under certain conditions one might
even have to do everything to strengthen it. In case of every
great force, even the most dangerous, one must always keep
in mind how to make of it an instrument of his intentions.

Socialism wins a right only when war seems to threaten between the two powers, the representatives of the old and the new, but at the same time wise calculation of the highest possible preservation and adjustment of the two parties produces a desire for a treaty. Without contract no right. But until now there is neither war nor treaties in this field, consequently no rights, no "Thou shalt."

[I, 446]

Socialism in Respect to Its Means

Socialism is the fantastic younger brother of the almost outlived despotism whose heir it desires to be. Consequently its efforts are reactionary in the fullest sense of the word. For it desires a degree of political power as high as despotism ever has had. Indeed, it outrivals all the past in that it aims at the complete annihilation of the individual which appears to be an unjustified luxury of nature and which it intends to change over into a *purposeful organ of the community*. Because of its relationship it always appears very close to every excessive development of power, as the typical socialist of old Plato appeared at the court of the Sicilian tyrants. It desires (and under certain circumstances promotes) the Caesarian despotism because it wishes to be its heir. But even this heritage would not be sufficient for its purposes. It has need of obedience and subjugation of all its citizens beyond anything that ever existed. Because it dares not even count upon the old religious piety toward the state but must involuntarily keep working at its elimination—just because it is working at the abolition of all *states*—therefore it can hope to exist only here and there and only for a short time by means of extreme terrorism. Therefor it quietly prepares itself for a reign of terror of the most extreme sort and, like a nail, drives the word "justice" into the head of the half-cultured masses in order to rob them wholly of their reason and to build up in them a good conscience for the evil game which they are to play. Socialism can serve to teach in the most brutal and convincing way the danger of every accumulation of political power and thus make the state itself suspect. When its harsh voice resounds in the battle cry "as much state as possible," it grows noisier and noisier, but soon the opposing cry emerges with even greater force: "as little state as possible."

[I, 473]

Onward

. . . One must have loved religion and art like a mother or nurse . . . otherwise one cannot attain wisdom. But one must be able to look beyond them, to outgrow them. If one stays under their spell one will not understand them. Just so you must be familiar with history and with the careful game of "on the one hand, on the other." Retrace the way, following in the footsteps by which mankind once made its painful, long journey through the desert of the past. Then you are most certain to know whither all later mankind cannot and must not go again. And as you use all your powers to explore how the knot of the future will be tied, your own life will acquire the value of a tool and means to understanding. You have it within your grasp to succeed in making all that you have experienced, your trials, errors, bypaths, passions, your love and hopes, serve your goal exclusively. This goal is: to become yourself a necessary link in the chain of culture, and from this necessity to draw a conclusion as to the necessity within the progress of general culture.

[I, 292]

[In the final section of this book on intellectual experimentation, Nietzsche makes the attempt to clarify for himself the nature of the scientific investigator of human behavior and the human evaluator. He is not the ordinary, proud scientist who, having made a discovery after careful and exacting investigation, now proclaims that he has made the final advance in truth which must henceforth be an accepted authority.

Such a person is the enemy, rather than furtherer of truth.
Nor can he be the man who seeks change merely for change's
sake, for then he would possess neither character nor that
drive for assurance out of which wisdom may grow. Long
practice must have made him keen to discover and suspect all
"deviousness of thinking," but even in that he must be restrained and meticulously fair. The genius of science is, here,
that of fairness and quite on a par with the genius of the
philosopher or artist. Fairness means to be just to all things
and men; to have examined them with complete devotion and
to have given them their just due; to be willing to accept what
is found to be of worth, but then, and only then, to attack or,
as Nietzsche calls it, "turn traitor" to that which can and
therefore must be betrayed in the service of a higher culture.

This formula is still quite vague, and far in the offing there
is a longing for certainty and a hope for the wisdom that will
permit action. But it is the formula for the kind of psychologist he now is: the diviner of men's behavior and evaluations,
disciplined against personal convictions and emotions. He
thinks himself, or longs to be, a "free, completely alive spirit"
who is able to guard himself against anything that may para-
lyze his thinking. Especially against convictions of any kind
whatever, for they threaten an end to questioning and experimenting.]

ENEMIES OF TRUTH

Convictions are greater enemies of truth than lies.

[I, 483]

Conviction is the belief at some point of understanding
that one is in possession of the absolute truth. Consequently
this belief presupposes that there are absolute truths; also that
perfect methods have been found by which to arrive at them;
finally that every man of convictions makes use of these perfect methods. All three assertions clearly prove that the man
of convictions does no scientific thinking; that he is innocent

of theories like a child, however mature he may otherwise be.
Whole millenniums have lived with these childish presupposi-
tions and they have been the source of the mightiest human
energies. Those innumerable men who sacrificed themselves
for their convictions believed that they were doing so for the
absolute truth. All of them were wrong in this. Perhaps no
man has ever sacrificed himself for the truth; at least the dogmatic expression of his belief will have been unscientific or
semi-scientific. Actually one insisted on being right because
one believed it *necessary* to be right. To permit one's being deprived of one's faith perhaps meant to jeopardize one's eternal
salvation. In a matter of such extreme importance the "will"
all too clearly prompted the intellect. The presupposition of
every man of faith of any shade was that he *could not* be refuted. If the arguments against it prove to be too strong he
could still take resource in belittling reason itself and perhaps
even raise the banner of the most extreme fanaticism, the
"*credo quia absurdum est.*" It is not the conflict of opinions
which has produced such a history of violence but the conflict
of the belief in opinions, that is to say the convictions. If only
all those who put such great store by their convictions brought
sacrifices of every kind and spared neither honor nor life in
their service, had devoted even half that energy to investigat-
ing with what right they were clinging to this or that conviction, by what paths they had arrived at it, how peaceful the
history of mankind would appear!

[I, 630]

CONVICTIONS AND JUSTICE

Are we under obligation to be true to our errors even
when we realize that by doing so we do harm to our higher
selves? . . . No, there is no law, no obligation of this kind;
we *must* be traitors, must be disloyal, again and again must
abandon our ideals. We do not progess from one period of life
to the other without causing the pains of treason and, in turn,
suffering from them. In order to avoid these pains is it perhaps

necessary to avoid outbursts of emotion? Would not then the world be too barren, too colorless? Rather let us ask whether the pains that accompany a change in convictions are *necessary*, or whether they depend upon some *mistaken* opinion or judgment. . . . Why is the man admired who remains true to his convictions and he who changes them despised? I fear the answer must be: because everybody presupposes that only motives of baser advantage or personal fear cause such changes. That is to say: basically we believe that nobody changes his opinions as long as they are to his advantage or at least do him no harm. If true, that is a very poor testimony for the *intellectual* significance of all convictions. If we examine how convictions arise and ask ourselves whether they are not greatly overrated, then we will realize that also the *change* of convictions is always measured by a false standard and that we have been in the habit of suffering too much because of this change.

[I, 629]

[The book ends with the following lyric description of what he calls the "Wanderer and Philosopher of the Forenoon."]

He who has at all approached freedom of the intellect cannot help but feel himself a wanderer on earth—even though not as traveling toward a final goal, for such does not exist. To be sure, he will want to watch and keep his eyes open for everything that really is happening in the world. That is why he must not cling fast to any one thing; there must be something wandering about him that delights in change and transition. Such a man will surely have bad nights when he is tired and finds closed the gates of the city that was to offer him rest. Perhaps, as in the Orient, the desert will extend to the very gates, and wild beasts will howl, now nearer, now farther; a violent storm will arise or robbers take from him his pack animals. It may be that a terrible night will descend upon him like a second desert and his heart will tire of wandering. When then the morning sun arises, glowing like a goddess of anger, and the city opens, he may see on the faces of the dwellers

more desert, dirt, deceit, and insecurity than he saw before
the gates—and the day is almost worse than the night. Thus
the wanderer may at times fare. But then, as recompense,
come the delightful mornings of other regions and days, where
in the earliest dawn he sees the muses swarm and dance
closely by him, and later, when the day is quiet in the harmony of the forenoon, he will amble among the trees from
whose tops and leafy shadows all sorts of good and clear things
are sent as gifts from all those free spirits who are at home in
hills, woods, and solitude, and who, like himself, in their now
joyful, now thoughtful manner are wanderers and philosophers. Born of the spirit of the dawn, they contemplate how
the day between the tenth and the twelfth hour can have such
a clear, translucid, cheerfully transfigured appearance—they
are seeking *the philosophy of the forenoon.*

Part II

In the spring of 1879, at the early age of thirty-five, Nietzsche retired from his professorship at Basel, forced to do so
largely by his health, but also driven to it by the restless worry
that his professional duties were cutting across his higher
responsibilities to culture. If he was to be the kind of teacher
that he envisioned for himself, he would have to find disciples
as honestly searching as himself. This meant that he would
have to go aside by himself and, under the stress of solitude,
further test and develop his own honesty. For some time his
health had interfered seriously with a proper attendance to
duty and had forced him to take a leave of absence for the
academic year 1876-77. He continued for another two years
under increasing physical, social, and particularly spiritual
difficulties, and then retired to live a life of wandering in
search for relief from his physical discomforts, and more for
the clarity and assurance as to how to point the way to higher
culture and become the worthy teacher of worthy pathfinders.
He now meant to assume responsibility to humanity, but to a
humanity cleansed of the all-too-human errors and sublimated
to a preserver, renewer, and creator of its highest values. He

was embarking upon a lonely journey and burdening himself with tasks that could not possibly promise final or even clearly satisfying solutions. For every station on the way could be only a new perspective which, however clarifying, he would still have to seek to change, for fear that there may have been a spot of prejudice in the eye of the observer or too narrow a field observed. He may have believed that he was setting himself the task of reasonable, scientific experimentation as a process of trial and error in which he could sublimate each regulatory trial and each error to a substantial good. But he had none of the clear controls of the natural scientist. Instead, he had to rely on severe intellectual integrity, on sharp and deep penetration, or on his gifted divining of human behavior and values. These, however, are neither ready nor precise controls, but are themselves objects of experimentation and perspective search. At best, they serve as valuable but endlessly changing stimuli for future experimenters. But in a pathfinder they permit of no relaxation and repose, and threaten to exhaust him physically and mentally, unless he has more humor than Nietzsche was able to muster and can smile at his own deficiencies.

The section of opinions and sayings in *Human, All-Too-Human*, II, is an attempt to discover a control for his search of spiritual values which promised to be more definite than the still vague intellectual integrity, but well adapted to his kind of psychological search and penetration. Instead of laborious scholarly procedure, he demands of himself and the philosopher, above all, an overabundance of knowledge and the power to command it. But that power is a very individual gift: clarity of insight and thinking, together with a clear instinct for that which is robust and distinctive. This instinct is to him the very nature of wisdom. He calls it "good taste," and in one of his rather brash etymologies[1] maintains that the Greek word for wisdom ($\sigma o \phi \iota a$) can properly be interpreted only as good taste. This instinct must act as the directive in the procession of experiments toward truth. Together with clarity of insight and the unflagging courage to experiment, instinct seems to be his present meaning of integrity.

The second section of this second volume is more direct and personal, or at least a kind of pause in the struggle, as though to see how far he had progressed. He calls it "The Wanderer and His Shadow," suggesting that the wayfaring experimenter is watching his own shadow to test the sharpness of his interpretations and, beyond that, what interpretations those capable of observing him were putting upon his sayings. Again, it is a collection of epigrams and aphorisms, short experimental comments with occasional proud pronouncements of what might be a final insight.

The wanderer is the courageous experimenter who has finally freed himself from those prejudices which, even though most revered, have primarily impeded his search. The first is that of the various forms of the religious and philosophical faith in absolute truth which Nietzsche had discarded for himself long since and assumed to have disposed of forever. The second is that of the freedom of the moral will, which he had also repeatedly contested earlier, but which he attacks anew here as though he had not finished with it sufficiently, either for himself or for his followers. Besides, he seems to have found it a much more stubborn problem than that of absolute truth, and much more difficult to find a substitute.

He calls the belief in the freedom of the will one of man's significant self-deceptions. It is a natural habit in man, he says, to consider himself free in that which gives him the strongest feeling of vitality, whether it be his passions, his sense of duty, his intellectual drives, or even his arbitrariness. In order to secure the satisfaction of such freedom man is quite willing to close his eyes to obvious experiences, to distort his logic, and to take recourse in metaphysical and religious faiths that are quite beyond the reach of his cognition, until he finally asserts that to believe is better than to know. "We must," Nietzsche answers to this, "again be *good neighbors of the things nearest* to us and not look beyond them so superciliously toward clouds and goblins of the night." This is again the antimetaphysician who would avoid with the strictest integrity all leaps into absolutes, who would keep his eye upon the Dionysian world in its flow of necessities, and continue his knowledge of it by means of ever more enlightened experiments. Since the experiment is concerned with the evaluation of ever truer culture, the process by which it must progress cannot be that of moral world denial, but one of seeking to improve upon error—that is to say, a steady process of sublimation of values through the clearer humanizing of them. Thus the whole of his argument about the freedom of the will is far less a philosophical speculation, in which he is very high-handed, than an effort to replace morality in the accepted sense with his theory of the sublimation of values. He finds that even the accepted morality with its teaching of responsibility, its good and evil, its punishment and reward, is, if not sublimation, still an attempt to lighten the burden of those virtues that are valued most by means of a leap into distant faith.

To the present psychologist, which he eminently is in this "scientific" period which he now calls "being good neighbors to what is nearest in us," virtues are powers or potentialities and nothing besides. The conventional moral interpretation of such powers, with its responsibility to the moral law, may have been a necessary and beneficial attitude during the naïve and unenlightened periods of man's culture, but with the growth of insight they must be sublimated to a more genuine power. The freedom of the will is to him merely one of the better illusionary values which later insight must set aside in favor of the wisdom which can face the Dionysian world and also force it into the service of culture by sublimation.

Being superior power, virtues have always been aristocratic and have arisen among individuals rather than in society. They have been taught to society for its preservation. When society relies upon them merely as a cherished inheritance and enjoys them as unearned increment, it is certain to become a "waster of morality" and an "attractive, weak good-for-nothing." [1] For it is then without the power of sublimation with its requirement of highly discerning reason, the ability of subtlest selection, and a *strong inclination toward restraint.* Consequently, if every virtue is basically potentiality and aristocratic, sublimation, with its demand of wisdom and restraint, is superlatively so; and the values of sublimation are quite naturally the morality of the rulers of culture, a *Herrschermoral*. Also, sublimation can be genuine only out of a super-abundance of powers, since that alone gives meaning to selectivity, restraint, and insight.

Even here Nietzsche envisions the highest degree of sublimation as the culmination of insight and wisdom into what he calls joy, where head and heart join. This would indicate that, even in this severe period, he is going beyond a strictly scientific procedure. But that is true of him anyway. The scientific method is merely a necessary experiment, however seriously taken. As it promotes the psychologist in him more and more, his search for integrity demands increasing attention to the affects rather than to mere reasoning. It is as if joy at the end of these aphorisms were indeed a new word for full integrity; a rich, perfectly clear insight to the point of complete rhythm, what he will later call a dance.

While working at this book, Nietzsche reviewed, as he must in the light of its requirements of constant experimentation, integrity, and the search for sublimation, those past influences which he had felt most strongly, especially that of Wagner. This review is a mere series of notes from the year 1878 collected posthumously and certainly not meant for publication.

He finds Wagner to have been a very stimulating figure which he had been inspired to draw as an "ideal monstrosity," but against which he now had to turn out of clearer insight. He is grateful to Wagner for that experience, however, for "insight must rise above craft," since by that process "man gets to be a series of Alpine valleys which constantly rise to greater heights." He now calls the actual Wagner merely a "very last print on very poor paper of the etching" which he had originally made of him; a "misplaced histrionic genius" who lacked the figure, voice, and modesty of a good actor and had resorted to the agitation of a strange music drama instead. Above all, he finds in him a dislike of the "just, restrained, those who delight in this world; of the mild, considering, scientific man;" in a word, of all those seriously concerned with the persistent cultural sublimation of powers. Thus Wagner becomes to him, very much like Schopenhauer, an important experience of a glorious wrong, the insight into which has helped him to reach a higher level.

from:
Human, All-Too-Human, II

IMMORALISTS

Today moralists cannot avoid being decried as immoralists merely because they dissect morality. However, in order to dissect one must kill, but only to improve our knowledge, our judgment and our living, and not to teach everybody to dissect. Unfortunately, people still think that every moralist in all his actions must be a model for all others to imitate. They confuse him with the preacher of morals. The older moralists did not dissect enough and preached too much. That is the reason for the confusion and for the disagreeable consequences for the present-day moralist.

[THE WANDERER AND HIS SHADOW, 19]

STAGES OF MORALITY

First of all morality is a means merely to keep the community going and to ward off its extinction. Then it is the means to maintain the community at a certain level and a certain worth. Its motives are *fear* and *hope,* and they are the more sturdy, powerful and crude as long as the inclination to be mistaken, one-sided and personal is strong. The most terrible incitements to fear must be called upon as long as milder ones have no effect and preservation cannot be attained otherwise. (Among the strongest is the invention of a world beyond with an eternal hell.) Further stages of morality or means to preservation are the commandments of a God (like the Mosaic Law); further and higher ones still the categorical imperatives

of duty with the "Thou Shalt". . . . All these are quite roughly-
hewn but *broad* steps because man has not yet learned to set
his foot on finer and narrower steps. Then comes the morality
of *inclination*, of *good taste*, finally that of *insight*—which,
though it is far beyond all illusionary motives, still has seen
clearly that for long stretches mankind could not do without
them.

[THE WANDERER AND HIS SHADOW, 44]

THE MOST DISTINGUISHED VIRTUE

In the first era of higher humanity bravery was considered the most distinguished virtue, in the second justice, in
the third moderation, in the fourth wisdom. In which era are
we living? In which do *you* live?

[THE WANDERER AND HIS SHADOW, 64]

THE THREE GOOD THINGS

Greatness, serenity, sunlight—these three embrace
everything that a thinker desires or demands of himself: his
hopes and duties, his intellectual and moral pretensions, even
his daily mode of living including the surroundings of his
home. Corresponding to them are, first, *elevating* thoughts,
then *quieting* ones, in the third place those that *enlighten*. In
the fourth place, however, thoughts that share in all three
qualities and by which all the things of this world are transfigured. This is the realm where the great *trinity of joy* rules.

[THE WANDERER AND HIS SHADOW, 332]

[In the last aphorism of these psychological investigations
of the human, all-too-human, Nietzsche gives an enthusiastic
view of what he now hopes to have attained. He entitles it
"The Golden Password" and explains the process of sublimation thus:]

Many chains have been laid upon man so that he might

learn no longer to behave like a beast. And really, he has grown milder, more spiritual, more joyous and reflective than any beast. However, he still suffers from having borne his chains so long and having been deprived of free air and movement. These chains are—I repeat it again and again—those grave and significant errors of moral, religious and metaphysical conceptions.

Not until he has recovered from this *chain-disease* has his first goal been reached: the separation of man from the beast.

Now we are in the midst of our effort to take off the chains and must exercise the greatest care. The *freedom of spirit* must be given to the ennobled man only; for him alone it will mean *easement of life* and will salve his wounds; he alone has a right to say that he is living only for the *joy* of life and nothing else. Used by any other there would be danger in this watchword; *Peace about me and good will toward all the nearest things.*

As this watchword for the few he recalls an old, great and moving saying which was meant for *all* and still stands above all mankind as watchword and symbol, fatal to everyone who sets it on his banner too soon—which sealed the fate of Christianity. It seems that *the time has still not come* when *all* may fare like those shepherds who saw the heavens lightened above them and heard that word: "Peace on earth, good will among all men." Still it is the *time of the separate man.*"

5.

Works:
The Dawn of Day
The Eternal Return
The Gay Science

After his retirement Nietzsche spent a decade of rest-less wandering in search of a climate that might promise re-lief from the persistently recurring physical ills so that he might have the energy to produce the writings that were crowding in upon him. But even more, he was trying to attain, but never quite reaching, the calm which would give him the assurance that he was finding greater clarity for his perspec-tives and, therefore, a greater confidence in his intellectual and spiritual integrity. Though his physical as well as his intellectual and spiritual difficulties continued to be severe, he nevertheless fought a steady battle with them and made good use of the shorter or longer periods of relief for an astound-ing productivity under most difficult circumstances.

He completed his first book in the autumn of 1880 and called it *The Dawn of Day*, suggesting that his ideas were now beginning to clear and that his mission was taking on a definite configuration. But that is true only in the sense that he knew himself more clearly than ever to be the pathfinder of a higher culture and that he must therefore continue to clear the path toward it. This meant, as before, that he must not merely examine the integrity of the past or, better, the conventional human behavior and morality, but also, and more important, he must scrutinize with greatest care the integrity of himself as one who would set up new values of behavior, as well as of those who would follow him. For, he says, "Has never the fear tormented you that you are not good enough to recognize that which is true? The fear that your senses are dull and the sensitiveness of your sight still far too crude? . . . Is this not perhaps some gruesome comedy in which you thoughtlessly desire to play a part?" [1]

In the preface to this book, written in the form of a review in 1886, he calls it an attack on morality out of morality. He means, of course, that his integrity, the scientific spirit as the attention to the "nearest things," must make him challenge conventional moral values and behavior as based upon prejudices that are outlived, especially the metaphysical ideas which he calls the "bridges of lies" (*Lügenbrücken*) that led to German idealism.

He has made these attacks before, though they may here be more direct. His dawn of day, as he calls it, is at most a more determined groping toward the attitude that will give him the right to claim he is not deceiving himself, as he points to a new direction along which the idea of morality might be found. Indeed, he considers his insistence on intellectual integrity as perhaps his most important discovery thus far. "If you look back you will see that among the Socratic and Christian virtues there is no mention of integrity. This is one of the latest virtues, still little mature, still often misunderstood, hardly conscious of itself—something in being that we can further or obstruct according to our inclinations." [2]

To his psychological acumen—his interpretation of the "nearest things"—morality arises from a behavior which proves to be useful for the preservation of a society, then becomes a norm, and still later a law. In time this origin is forgotten and the laws of behavior and their ceremonials are dignified to the point of being hallowed as original causes. Whoever must regularly obey such laws is considered to be the most moral, together with him who sacrifices most for the dignity of their authority. But he who acts out of individual

integrity, out of self-discipline and restraint, is considered an
enemy of proper behavior and so also of society. He is not
only persecuted as such, but feels the evil of it himself. Consequently individualism is considered to be evil and is accompanied by bad conscience.

Since such values have been arrived at by confusing the
effect for the cause, the very reverse must be taken as true.
The individual who attempts to change the laws of behavior,
whatever danger it may entail—even to the point of self-
castigation or madness, is still the agent of the history of the
world, the free spirit with a most important though dangerous
mission. He calls the concern about authoritative customs engaged in by the free spirit, the "playing field of the intellect."

This is for him the day of the exercise of the dangerously
experimenting free spirit, free to attempt an intellectual
study of morality; willfully choosing intellectual integrity as
his point of departure to see where it may lead. It may even
be a restricted point of view, but all thinking in each age has
had some such restriction. Especially must that be true of
this age of science—science, to be sure, in Nietzsche's particular sense of psychology which can see and interpret the
depths of human behavior. "To observe a law of nature for
the first time and wholly, that is to *prove* it (e.g. gravitation,
light or sound reflection) is something quite other and the
affair of others than to *interpret* such a law. Thus the moralists
who observe and expose human laws and behavior—the
moralists with fine ears, noses, and eyes—are very different
from those who interpret what has been observed. The latter
must above all be *inventive* and must have an imagination *set
free* by acute discernment and knowledge." [1] But they will always remember that they are experimenters and seekers and
will not, like former moralists, try to set up imperatives of
authoritative morality. For restraint is essential to their integrity, as is the realization that *as yet* mankind has no goal.
He insists that there is far too much that we do not know; our
discernment is still far from keen; there is far too little
watchful integrity in our use of words. Nietzsche devoted a
large number of aphorisms to the illustration of this, and

tests a great variety of conventional attitudes, approaches, and beliefs for that purpose.

In place of the conventional code of morals he calls for the progressive sublimation of genuine human powers or virtues. Life, he insists, cannot be put to the service of higher culture by its denial as demanded by the older Christian morality. Instead, his integrity demands that life be affirmed in the Dionysian sense, even to acceptance of chance, and then be sublimated to the highest possible degree in an endless, experimental effort, since no one can be wise enough to foresee the final goal.

As an experimenter, however, Nietzsche cannot honestly be interested in giving a definite answer as to the final stage of man's development. His integrity rather demands that he be without the presumption of the need for such an answer. "We are experiments. Let us be willing to be just that." [1] "What matter I! is written over the door of the future thinker." [2]

Meanwhile, the experimenting itself with sublimation must be guarded against the failure of integrity occasioned primarily by pride, fear, and, especially, exhaustion. Fear and pride may obstruct the search for integrity, or exhaustion may evidence itself by the impatient desire for disciples or for too early a change of institutions. There is, he says, a "viciousness of the intellect" in the passionate enthusiasm for an idea that may include hatred of criticism, science, and thinking. All changes, if they are to be thorough, must be gradual and in small doses, until a new evaluation has created a new nature in us. Sudden changes he calls quackery and misleading.

Passions, unless sublimated, are dangerous to thinking and never a substitute for it, however attractive they may seem, and though they are more readily appreciated by others than is severe thinking. When naked, to be sure, passions show merely the "wild, disgusting, unbearable beast" in some men; another they may elevate to lofty, grand, and splendid gesture; a third, thoroughly ennobled person, may appear in his lofty Storm and Stress like wild, beautiful nature and cause awe and ecstasy, but for that very reason men may fail to see the greatness and serenity of the nature that he really is.[1]

Sublimation, then, is not only hard to attain, but not easily recognized and appreciated, though Nietzsche seems to believe that advances have been made in modern times even beyond those of his beloved Greeks. "Loyalty, magnanimity, the sanctity (Scham) of a good name: these three united in one sentiment is what we call *noble, distinguished, precious,* and in that we outrank the Greeks." [2] He thinks that we are less physical in our drives than they were; that "men born and disciplined to be noble" no longer hesitate to look up to that "ideal of *victorious wisdom* which no age was permitted to erect for itself with so good a conscience as the age which is just about to begin." [3]

Above all, sublimation is the stamp of the aristocrat, the harmony of "bearing, spirit, and mission" for which the higher man continuously searches. He recognizes, however, that it was also sought for by the better among those who did not have the courage or rectitude of Dionysian acceptance, but enthusiastically and with subtlety embraced the escape of Christian humility. The courage and the sincerity of their conviction fashioned some of the "finest figures that human society has hitherto produced," like some of the outstanding princes of the Catholic Church who, he thinks, were more than ought else taken by the people as proof of the truth of the Church. If that is so, he argues, then why should not a higher culture be attainable with the new sentiment of greater integrity and courage?

The aristocrat—with his harmony of bearing, spirit and mission, and his courage—is necessarily a man of power, but of sublimated power. Power in itself he calls perhaps the strongest natural drive and most difficult honestly to sublimate. In its natural state it is the daemon. "Take away from them [men] everything and satisfy this and they are almost happy —as happy as men and daemons can be." [4] He sees the love of power playing curious tricks with men. Those who pursue it most passionately are periodically overcome with exhaustion and, because of that, a desire for the "happiness of the opposite" and the delight of being overpowered by "wars, the arts, religions, or genius." He calls this the modern festival mood. After that they are again "freer, relaxed, colder, more disciplined, and tirelessly continue again to strive for an opposite: for power." [1]

The sublimation of power is something quite different from such a passion. The integrity of it is out of fullness and, like the joy of the abundance of knowledge, is mildness in the full possession of power. "To be able to be lowly so as to be approachable to many and humiliating to none! To bear much injustice and to have wormed your way through all sorts of errors so as to be able to approach many hidden souls on their secretive paths! Always with a sort of love and always with a kind of self-seeking and enjoyment of self! To be in possession of sovereignty and yet obscure and resigning. To lie constantly in the sun of mildness and charm and yet to know that the ascent to the lofty is near by! That would be a life! That would be a reason to live long!" [2] All this is a hoped-for sublimation of a power acquired only by strictest integrity. Its truest manifestation is courtesy to all and understanding of all who possess any relation whatever to the free spirit. The "four cardinal virtues" of the free spirit he lists as being *"honest* toward yourself and all *else* that is friendly to you; *courageous* in the face of the enemy; *magnanimous* to all who have been conquered; *courteous*—always: thus the four cardinal virtues would have us be." [3]

The dawn of the day, then, is the first sight of the way by which man can lift himself by his own bootstraps to a realization of his truest self; awareness that he can win his own salvation by virtue of his own integrity of thought and insight and seek his own redemption by the sublimation of the powers that are most truly his. It is hazardous and even frightful to venture out upon such a path of self-dependence. To be thus free, the adventurer must not only be able to dispense with all vicarious help and the refuge of the escapes and comforts offered by conventional creeds, metaphysics, and idealistic art. He must also be able to guard himself against the fear of his own adventure or its exhaustion, which might lead him to a premature goal, and then to claim authority for it with less reason and honesty than had those whom he discarded. However, this dawn of day is merely an outlook as upon a promise of great beauty in the far distance, the intense glare of which does not yet threaten him seriously. The idea of self-reliance, the courage of the acceptance of the Dionysian fate, the prospect of sublimation make for the moment almost automatic the refusal of all outside help; the denial of a helping God; rejection of all metaphysics, and every intermediary. It is, however, a mere theory still, and so still calls for little responsibility.

If the experiment with the idea of sublimation was but the first glimpse of a new day to Nietzsche, it also meant a new courage to venture into bolder experiments to try to clear the way to it. In the Engadines and in Genoa his health improved, and in Peter Gast he had found a companion upon whose understanding he believed he could rely. For the next two years, 1881 and 1882, he felt that he was going on merrily; that his integrity was becoming surer; and that the psychologist in him, the diviner of men and their drives, had penetrated to the first sight of an enlightening answer. It was only necessary, somehow, to dispel the last gloom of old prejudices, even in himself or particularly in himself, to be able to impart his joy in his latest discovery and thereby to give it the stamp of fullness and clarity.

At the end of June 1882 the new manuscript was about finished and plans were made to publish it under the title *The Gay Science*, or *"la gaya scienza,"* but he still thought of it, at least at first, as the continuation to *The Dawn of Day*. He now calls his science or understanding and penetration "gay," and in the preface, written in 1886, translates that to mean sportive, exuberant, as though he had come upon so liberating and clarifying an idea that with its help he could dance over all obstructions and make sport of them. But in the same preface he also warns that the idea is but a new transformation: at best, the "u" has been transformed into the "x," the very next to the last immediately preceding the very last; no further.

This new discovery is the idea of the "Eternal Return." In essence, however, it is a reformulation and adaptation to his mission of the acceptance of the Dionysian basis of life; the acceptance of life in its entirety; life constantly transfiguring itself in eternally recurring cycles, each of immeasurable duration, and yet as a whole eternally remaining itself.

The book is introduced by a separate treatise, not originally printed with it, on the theory of the Eternal Return in which he attempts to make of it a scientific postulate, even a sort of cosmology. But it does not prove to be very convincing as such, and it is important to note that this treatise is taken from the posthumous notes and was not included in the book as published originally. Moreover, in the second half of the treatise the idea reveals itself frankly as a regulative principle which he needs for the basis of his teaching, if, as he insisted that it must, his teaching is to function independently of an arbitrarily creating and directing God; if life is to explain itself or man is to accept it as he must, and thereby have the opportunity to make it the more truly itself by sublimating that which he is. The idea also, so he believes, protects him against a mechanistic interpretation of life in which nature itself merely substitutes for God.

The conservation of energy and of matter, he argues, are scientific postulates, as is infinite time. Consequently, there can have been no beginning but only an infinite activity of equal energy upon equal matter, and therefore infinite cycles of a practically immeasurable but definite number of combinations, changes, and positions. If a balance had ever been achieved in the course of this activity, the balance could not have been disturbed and would have lasted infinitely. Therefore no balance did or ever will come about, and conversely no complete chaos. So the cycle and its eternal recurrence must be and is the entelechy of nature. "This movement in cycles is not something that has developed; it is the original law, just as the supply of energy is a basic law, without exception or infringement." [1] He also calls it an irrational necessity and it is indeed a necessary presupposition to his approach. Even in the first, supposedly wholly scientific part of this treatise, the theory is summed up into an exhortation: "Man, like an hourglass your life will be turned about infinite times and run out again and again. One long moment of time in between until all the conditions which produced you will come together again in the cyclic motion of the world." [1]

The second part of this treatise is wholly devoted to the effect of the theory upon mankind and clearly discloses that Nietzsche's interests lay wholly here. He could have taken the theory itself from Pythagoras. But because of his own particular application of it, he considered it originally his own as an indispensable part of his teaching. He interprets it directly upon his theory of sublimation.

The main body of *The Gay Science* displays many instances of Nietzsche as psychologist or, as he pleases to call it, the "trier of men's reins" *(Nierenprüfer)*, in which he examines the known passions and drives to see what is real or assumed in them, its main topic is still the further investigation of intellectual integrity. He is now dissatisfied with describing it as the scientific approach, because he finds that that designation has been taken over by the mechanists whom he considers shallow and too easily satisfied and ready to make claims far beyond the reach of their experiments. Instead, he demands an intellectual good conscience, as he calls it, which he goes to great pains to define. It is really a combination of the careful but passionate scholar and the gifted psychologist: to tremble with the desire for and the joy of questioning, but with a passion for certainty as to the intellectual integrity of beliefs and feelings. While a skeptic like himself is always conscious of the great uncertainty and fantasy of his judgments and of the constant change in all human laws and concepts, he can still delight in the realization that scholarship is able to ascertain certain firm things from which to start— "similar," he says, "to the happiness of one wrecked at sea who finds a footing on the old, firm earth—astonished that it does not give way under him." [2]

Experiment is still the only proper procedure for him, but experiment in the service of a progressively better understood life. Hereticism for its own sake he calls a "modern evil witchcraft," rather than evidence of intellectual integrity or courage. The latter he describes again as a late development, after the realization that though two contradictory hypotheses both be basic errors, nevertheless both serve life and develop human power.

To Nietzsche life itself is the *"means toward knowledge"* [1] and because of that a succession of battles, dangers, and victories; but also of gayety and laughter, and quite different from the calm pursuit of the pure thinker. The "good conscience," which he seeks as the experimental psychologist of integrity in the pursuit of knowledge, focused his attention upon the drives that are active in the process. He sees their sublimation as a progressive compromise between them, "a sort of peace treaty, a justice" rather than their elimination, and he calls this knowledge. [2] It is a never-ending process rather than a final attainment. He compares such thinking to a breaker that pours into the crevices of rocks as though in search of something, then retreats and another breaker tries the same thing even more violently. [3]

The interpretation of life as a means toward knowledge with a good intellectual conscience makes him wary of the conventional words used to express attitudes and values and leads him to give them what he considers to be a better conscience by finding more honest connotations for them. Some he discards altogether because he finds them so laden with fond prejudices that it is best to replace them by a diametrically contradictory term. The most important of those that he retains but interprets anew is "power." It is a basic word to him for every kind of increase and a more honest name for many a human attitude. Thus he calls love the desire to possess a person; pity too often the desire to get the better of another's weakness, or in almost all cases an intrusion upon suffering that cannot possibly be known sufficiently and is therefore dishonest.

The concept of God and Nietzsche's compulsion to deny its supreme religious value, not only caused him much concern, but haunted him. His integrity, as he saw it, demanded that man's only honest concern can be with the "nearest things";

they alone can be understood and evaluated, and by those values alone can the significance of life be determined. All beyond that is unknown and cannot be known by any means except by a conjecture into a distance which a good conscience cannot reach. To deify the unknowable not only depreciates life as a means toward knowledge, but moreover denies its entire significance in comparison with the unknown. This amounts to a nihilism which would make Nietzsche's every hypothesis worthless, as well as his whole process of experimentation meaningless. This at least he thinks and drives himself to assume—however much Christian theism has done for society, or whatever great skeptics and philosophers there were who clung to their deism. Since man's concern for life is limited by his reach, God, being out of reach, must be dead for him. On the other hand, if man's reach must involve him in endless experiments dictated by an endless chain of hypotheses, contradictions, and new hypotheses, then this process may also approach a nihilism as faulty as the denial of life contained in theism or life's depreciation in deism.

It was a haunting problem to Nietzsche, however necessary it seemed to his integrity. Also, it must be remembered that reverence was an essential element to him in the pursuit of knowledge and a skepticism devoid of reverence he considered merely superficial libertinism. In his early years he had experienced full reverence for God. To deny Him now, even out of "good conscience," was to be a murderer of the most gruesome sort, a "madman," as he describes him painfully.

From this attitude Nietzsche called the denial of God an unavoidable hypothesis which in the long run—perhaps a hundred thousand years—must become more powerful, he believed, than the best-held faith in something not "true." He even insists that it is not very apt to call him an atheist, or unbelieving, or immoralist in any older sense, though he also says that he is all three but at too late a date to be understood by modern men.[1] Modern man, whether conservative believer or fashionable scoffer, is still sorely lacking in the kind of integrity which he demands inasmuch as he yields to false prejudices or overweening pride. But the same integrity causes him some uneasiness about the degree of overbearance, and more about the nihilism his skepticism may contain. He may also have fallen a victim to pessimism because of his distrust of what he can know of life. "Has it not perhaps made us suspect of a contrast, a contrast between the world in which we have hitherto been at home with our reverence —and because of which we are willing to *endure* this life— and another world *that we ourselves are;* a relentless, thorough, deepest skepticism about ourselves which is getting a worse and worse hold on us Europeans and may confront future generations with the terrible either-or: Either get rid of your reverences or yourselves! The latter would be nihilism; but is not the former perhaps—nihilism? That is *our* question mark." This may read like an astounding presentiment of modern existentialism, but it is more significant as an expression of his concern over his fearsome murder of God.

The fourth, and originally the final, book of *The Gay Science* is entitled "Sanctus Januarius," to suggest that in spite and in the midst of the severe chill of his skepticism, he will hold fast to his optimism and to the joy of affirmation. He will be of those who make things beautiful by seeing beauty in what is necessary in things. "Amor fati, let that be my love henceforth!—All in all and in the large; sometime or other I will be a yea-sayer and nothing besides." [1] This love of fate, this yea-saying to necessity in turn is the substance of his teaching of the Eternal Return.

In 1886, when Nietzsche was preparing a new edition of his *The Gay Science,* he appended a fifth book which he entitled "We Fearless," as though he wished by means of a resumé of the preceding books to define the experimenter with a good intellectual conscience of man's values and behavior. But the definition succeeds only to a degree. It is only the course upon which the man of integrity must embark but which will lead him out into unforeseen distances and futures. The more courageously he travels, the more dangerously he will have to protect himself against the errors of false certainties and "truths"; but when he has finally gained the superfluity of knowledge which might entitle him to create or propose an answer, the danger multiplies and the "tragedy begins."

The "fearless," the free spirit, no longer fears to deny old prejudgments however sacred they may be or whatever service they once may have performed for society, if they are in any sense world-denying or an escape from the Dionysian realities of life. With the courage of his *amor fati* he will accept life as it is in all its aspects; the Dionysian view of life is to him the only genuinely honest and full acceptance. "The richest in fullness of life, the Dionysian god and man, can afford not only the sight of what is terrible and questionable, but even the terrible deed and every luxury of destruction, disintegration and denial; to him evil, nonsense, and the ugly seems permissible, so to speak, because of the superfluity of generating, fructifying powers which are capable of creating luscious gardens out of every desert." [1] This is an extravagant description and yet in the last metaphor it contains what seemed to require his highest courage. It not only points to an endless struggle into an infinite future, but also eludes a clear definition of the sublimation that must result from the destruction, change, and becoming of the Dionysian *amor fati* and Eternal Return, and its creativeness. It is clear enough that by sublimation is meant to create the wholesome out of error, to find the affirmation in every denial, and to substitute the good intellectual conscience for the timid "bad conscience" of conventional morality. But Nietzsche lets us see clearly enough that to a man of his aspiring integrity all this is still very vague, and that the further the process develops, the greater the difficulties grow, even to the point of threatening despair. Consequently, this last book is also almost wholly preparatory, in spite of its call upon the joy of clarity. It is more the laughing daring of the acrobat who delights in "walking a thin rope even over abysses."

At the end of the book Nietzsche tries to defend himself against its impression of vagueness. He explains that he is writing only for those who are of his own kind and have ears to take it in; that his terse paragraphs are merely quick dives towards the ideal and a quick emerging; but that it must not for that reason be assumed that he had discovered nothing. He still had proved himself a lithe dancer and a subtle investigator and philosopher. The subtle dancer, he explains, has need of "the great health" to assure the integrity and courage of the experimenting free spirit, a health which constantly must be guarded anew. "Who wishes to know by the adventures of his own experience how it feels to be a discoverer and conqueror of the ideal; likewise an artist, a saint, a lawgiver, a sage, a scholar, a man of piety, a sooth-sayer, or a divine recluse of the old style, he first needs one thing above all else: *the great health*." [1] He calls it a new health, "stranger, subtler, more daring and joyous than any health has ever been." It will play, perhaps wantonly, with all that present convention treats as serious and important; will engage even in playful parodies of it; but nevertheless it must lead to the *great seriousness* when "the real question is posed, the soul's fate turns,—the tragedy begins." Thus all definite answers, all real affirmations are still far in the future, and *The Gay Science* is primarily a further assurance to him only of the integrity of the approach.

from:

The Dawn of Day

Not only are religions spun and fashioned here; here developed the poet, the thinker, physician, lawgiver. The fear of the incomprehensible which in ambiguous manner demanded ceremonies from us, gradually changed into the charm of that which is difficult of understanding; and where it was hard to fathom one learned to create.

[DAWN OF DAY, 40]

To observe a law of nature for the first time and wholly, that is to *prove* it (e.g. gravitation, light or sound reflection)

is something quite other and the affair of others than to
interpret such a law. Thus the moralists who observe and
expose human laws and behavior—the moralists with fine
ears, noses, and eyes—are very different from those who
interpret what has been observed. The latter must above all
be *inventive* and must have an imagination *set free by* acute
discernment and knowledge.

[DAWN OF DAY, 423]

SEARCHERS AND RESEARCHERS OR ATTEMPTERS AND TEMPTERS

No method of scientific research has a monopoly! We
must be cruel and then kind to things, we must treat them in
turn with justice, passion and indifference. One will approach
things like a policeman, another like a father confessor, a
third like a wanderer and out of curiosity. A sympathetic approach may induce them to reveal something, or a violent one.
Reverence for their mysteries may be of help to the one and
lead to an insight, and then again an indiscreet and frivolous
approach may lead to an explanation of the mysteries. We researchers are all of us conquerors, discoverers, navigators, adventurers of an audacious morality and must not be sur-
prised when people generally call us evil.

[DAWN OF DAY, 432]

AGAINST THE TYRANNY OF THE TRUTH

Even if we were mad enough to take all of our
opinions to be true, we still would not want them to be the
only truths. I would not know what to find desirable in the
autonomy and omnipotence of truth; it is quite enough if it
has *great power*. But it must be able to *fight* and have opposition, and it must have a chance by errors to *recover* from
the conflict—otherwise it will become tedious, powerless and
insipid, and make us so also.

[DAWN OF DAY, 507]

THE CLARIFYING EYE

One could most properly speak of "genius" in the case of such people whose spirit, as with Plato, Spinoza and Goethe, seems only loosely bound to the character and temperament, as though winged and able to soar high above character and temperament. On the other hand, those people have spoken most enthusiastically of their "genius" who never detached themselves from their temperament and were able to give it the most spiritual, greatest, universal, under certain circumstances even cosmic expression (as e.g. Schopenhauer). These geniuses could not soar above themselves but believed that they discovered and rediscovered *themselves* wherever they flew. . . . That *is their greatness*, and *may* indeed be greatness. The others, who really deserve the name of genius, have the *clear, clarifying* eye which does not seem to have developed out of their temperament and character, but independent of them and mostly in mild contradiction to them, looks upon the world as upon a god and loves this god. To them, too, the eye is not a sudden gift; there is a training and preparatory schooling for seeing and the lucky person at the proper time will find a teacher of clear seeing.

[DAWN OF DAY, 497]

[However, in place of the conventional code of morals he here calls for the progressive sublimation of genuine human powers or virtues. Life, he insists, cannot be put to the service of higher culture by its denial as demanded by the older Christian morality. Instead, his integrity demands that life be affirmed in the Dionysian sense, even to acceptance of chance, and then be sublimated to the highest possible degree in an endless, experimental effort, since no one can be wise enough to foresee the final goal.]

Those iron hands of necessity which shake the dice of chance play their game infinitely; there *must* among them be throws that have the appearance of purposefulness and rea-

sonableness of every degree. *Perhaps* the acts of our will,
our purposes, are merely such throws—and we are too limited and too vain to realize our severe limitation, namely,
that we ourselves with iron hands are shaking the dice and
that in our most intentional acts we are doing nothing but
playing the game of necessity. Perhaps! To get beyond this
perhaps we must already have been guests in the underworld
and at home beyond all surface things and have shaken dice
and gambled with Persephone herself.

[DAWN OF DAY, 130]

[Thus far his sublimation does not demand a new goal but
that a new sentiment be developed, or better, a new drive—
namely, that of intellectual integrity and veracity.]

THERE ARE TWO TYPES OF DENIERS OF MORALITY

"To deny morality"—this may mean *on the one hand:*
to deny that the moral motives claimed by people have really
impelled them to their actions. Consequently it claims that
morality consists of words and belongs to crude or subtle
human deceptions (especially self-deception), and perhaps
especially in the case of those who are most reputed for their
virtue. *Also* it may mean: to deny that moral judgments rest
upon truths. This admits that there are real motives of action,
but that *errors,* as the basis of all moral judgment, impel the
moral acts of men. This is *my* point of view. But I would be
the last not to realize that in a *great many cases* the fine suspicion in the manner of the first point of view, as in the
spirit of La Rochefoucauld, also has some justification and
surely is of the highest general usefulness. . . . I therefor deny
morality as I deny alchemy, that is I deny its assumptions.
But I do not deny that there have been alchemists who believed in these assumptions and acted upon them. I also
deny immorality; *not* that countless people feel that they are
immoral but that they have reason in *truth* to feel thus. I
of course do not deny—provided I am no fool—that many

acts are called immoral that should be avoided and battled against; also that many that are called moral should be performed and encouraged. But, I say, the one as well as the other for *different reasons than before*. We must learn anew —in order later, perhaps very late, to achieve even more: to develop a new discernment.

[DAWN OF DAY, 103]

THE NEW PASSION

Why do we fear a possible return to barbarism? Because it would make men unhappier than they are? Not at all. Don't let us deceive ourselves: the barbarians of all ages had *more* happiness. However, our drive for knowledge is too strong for us to place any value on a stout, firm delusion; it pains us even to imagine such conditions. The restlessness of our discovering and divining has become as attractive and indispensable as the forlorn love of the lover which on no account he would exchange for indifference. Perhaps we also are forlorn lovers. Knowledge has become a passion in us which shrinks from no sacrifice and really fears nothing but its extinction. We honestly believe that under the drive and pain of *this* passion all mankind must believe itself loftier and more content than at the time when it had not yet overcome the envy and the cruder contentment that accompanies barbarism. It may even be that mankind will perish because of this passion for knowledge! This thought also affects us not at all. Has Christianity ever hesitated at such a thought? Are not love and death like brother and sister? Yes, we hate barbarism—we prefer the extinction of mankind to the retrogression of knowledge. And finally: if mankind does not perish through some *passion* it will perish because of some *weakness*. Which is to be preferred? That is the main question. Do we prefer an end in fire and light or in the sands?

[DAWN OF DAY, 429]

NOTHING TOO MUCH!

How often is a person advised to set a goal which he cannot attain and which exceeds his powers in order at least to arrive at what his powers at their *highest exertion* can perform! Is this really desirable? Do not the best men who live by this doctrine as well as their best acts acquire something exaggerated and distorted just because they are too tense? And does not a gray haze of *failure* spread over the world because everywhere one sees struggling athletes and immense gestures, and nowhere a crowned and proud victor?

[DAWN OF DAY, 559]

THE FUTURE OF THE NOBILITY

The incontestable happiness of distinguished culture which rests upon the feeling of superiority is now beginning to rise to a higher level, in that now, owing to all free spirits, it is no longer a disgrace for people of noble birth and training to enter the ranks of scholars and there to win more intellectual distinction and to perform higher chivalrous services than before, and to look up to the ideal of victorious wisdom to which no age with such good conscience could aspire as the age just about to begin.

[DAWN OF DAY, 201]

WHERE ARE THE POOR IN SPIRIT?

How I dislike to *impose* my thoughts upon others! How I rejoice at every mood and change of mind when the thoughts of others prevail against my own! But now and then there is an even greater joy, when the opportunity is offered to *give away* my spiritual possessions, much like a father-confessor who sits in his nook anxiously waiting for *someone in need* to come and tell him of his distress of mind so that he again can make him feel confident and *lighten* his distressed soul. He is not looking for credit; he would even avoid all gratitude, for gratitude is obtrusive and insensitive in the presence of solitude and silence. But he lives nameless and slightly laughed at, too lowly to awaken envy or enmity, his head free of fever, supplied with a handful of knowledge and a bag of experiences; much like a country doctor helping this person and that person whose head is *confused because of his opinions* without his really noticing that he is being helped. Not trying to impress him or scoring a victory over him, but speaking to him so that at a slight, insignificant pointer or contradiction he will say the right thing himself and go away proud of it! Like a modest inn that refuses no one in need but then is forgotten or laughed at. To claim no advantage, neither better food nor purer air nor even a more joyous spirit, but to give, share, to give back and become poorer! To know how to be humble so as to be approachable for many and humiliating to none! To bear much injustice and to have wormed your way through all kinds of errors so as to be able to reach many a hidden soul on his hidden path. Always with a kind of affection, yet always with a kind of self-seeking and enjoyment of self! In possession of command, yet at the same time to be obscure and resigned! Always to lie in the sun and mildness of charm and still know that the ascent to the distinguished is nearby! . . . That would be a life! That would be a reason to live long!

[DAWN OF DAY, 449]

THE FOUR CARDINAL VIRTUES

Honest with ourselves and all else friendly to us; *brave* in face of the enemy; *magnanimous* with the vanquished; *courteous*—always; thus the four cardinal virtues want us to be.

[DAWN OF DAY, 556]

from:

The Eternal Return

The world of energy suffers no diminution, otherwise in eternal time it would have weakened and disappeared. The world of energy suffers no point of rest, otherwise that point would have been reached and the clock of life would be standing still. The world of energy never comes into balance, it never has a moment of rest, its force and movement are the same for every period of time. Whatever condition this world can attain, it must have attained, and not once, but an infinite number of times. Just so this moment: it was already there once, and will return exactly many times. All forces will be divided exactly as they are now. It is the same way with the moment which gave birth to it, and with the one which is the child of the present moment. Your whole life will always be turned over like an hourglass and will run out again and again—with one great moment in between, until all conditions from which you arose, will come together again in the cyclic motion of the world. And then you will find again every pain, every joy, every friend and enemy, and every hope and error, and every blade of grass and ray of light, the whole interrelationship of all things. This ring, of which you are a particle, will shine forth again and again. And in every cycle of human life there is always an hour when first to one, then to many, then to all the mightiest idea appears: —that of the eternal recurrence. Each time this is the hour of *noon* for mankind.

[THE ETERNAL RETURN, 25]

The political delusion, at which I smile just as my contemporaries do at the religious delusions of earlier times, is above all that of *worldliness,* the belief in the *world,* and of ridding yourself of the "beyond" and the "other world." Its aim is the well-being of the fleeting individual and therefor produces socialism in that the *fleeting separate individuals* seek their happiness by means of socialization. They see no reason to *wait* like the men with eternal souls and eternal growth and future changes for the better. I teach: the task is to live so that you must *wish* to live again—you will have to, anyway! Whoever finds his highest emotion is striving, let him strive; to him whom repose affords the highest emotion, let him rest; if conforming, following and obedience produce the highest feeling, let him obey. However, it *must be clear* to him what affords the highest emotion, and he must shun *no means* toward it. It is a question of *eternity!*

[THE ETERNAL RETURN, 27]

"But if everything is determined, what power have I over my actions?" This idea and faith is a dead weight which rests upon me in addition to all other weights and more than they. You say that nourishment, location, atmosphere and society change and determine you? Well, your opinions do so even more, for they determine your choice of nourishment, location, atmosphere and society. . . . If you accept totally this idea of ideas, it will transform you. At everything you are about to do, the query: "Is it of the kind that I am willing to do an infinite number of times?" is the *greatest* dead weight.

[THE ETERNAL RETURN, 28]

from:

The Gay Science

The acquisition of knowledge and the striving for truth finally took its place as a need among the other needs of life. From this point on not only faith and conviction but examination, denial, suspicion, contradiction became a *power*. —Finally cognition and those old basic errors clashed, both as life, both as power, both in the same person. The thinker now means the person in whom the drive for truth and those life-preserving errors fought their first battle after the drive for truth had also *proven* itself to be a life-preserving power. Everything else is insignificant in comparison with the importance of this battle. Here the final question is posed about the condition of life; here the first attempt is made to answer this question by means of the experiment. How far can truth be incorporated into life?—that is the question, that the experiment.

[THE GAY SCIENCE, 110]

OUR ASTONISHMENT

There is a deep and thorough satisfaction in knowing that science ascertains things that are firm and again and again provide the basis for new discoveries. It could be quite different. We are so convinced of the uncertainty and fantasy of all our judgments and of the eternal change of all human laws and concepts that we are astonished when we realize how very reliable are the results of science. In earlier days nothing was known of this inconstancy of all human things; habitual morality upheld the belief that the whole inner life of man was held fast by the unyielding jaws of necessity. At that time there was probably a similar voluptuous astonishment when people listened to fairy tales. The miraculous was so pleasing to those people who may at times have tired of law and eternity. For once to be able to lose your footing, to soar, to wander aimlessly, to enjoy madness: that was considered paradise and revelry in earlier days. Our happiness, however, is like that of a person wrecked at sea, who has reached the shore and has both feet planted on familiar, firm ground, and is astonished that it does not give way under him.

[THE GAY SCIENCE, 46]

[The entire process of continuous experimentation is the endless courage for the battle with "truths," which Nietzsche expresses ecstatically in his description of the pathfinders:]

I welcome every indication that a more manly and warlike age is about to begin, which will again bring bravery into esteem! For it is to prepare the way for a still higher age and gather the strength which that age at one time will require,—that age which transfers heroism to the acquisition of knowledge and *carries on wars* for its ideas and their consequences. That will require many brave pathfinders who cannot arise out of nothing—and just as little from the sand and sticky mud of the present civilization of metropolitan culture; men who in reticence, loneliness, and determination know how to be satisfied and constant with invisible activity; men who with an inner inclination seek in all things that which can be overcome; men who possess cheerfulness, simplicity, and dislike of great vanities as they possess magnanimity in victory and tolerance for the small vanities of all conquered; men who are keen and frank judges of all victors and of the part that chance plays in every victory and fame; men with festivals and days of work and mourning of their own; accustomed and assured in commanding and equally prepared to obey when necessary, as proud of the one as of the other, in both serving their own cause equally. Men who are more endangered, more productive, and happier! For, believe me!— the secret to harvest the greatest productivity and the greatest enjoyment from life is: *to live dangerously!* Build your cities at the Vesuvius! Send your ships into unexplored oceans! Live at war with yourselves and your equals! Be robbers and conquerors as long as you cannot be rulers and possessors, you seekers after knowledge! The time will soon be over when you might be satisfied to live in the woods like timid deer! Finally your knowledge will stretch out its hand for that which is its due:—it will want to *rule* and *possess,* and you also!

[THE GAY SCIENCE, 283]

[The entire passage is produced here so that it may be clear that in talking of war and robbery and the dangerous life, Nietzsche is describing solely the militant experimenter in search of "truth," and that the ecstasy is mainly the passionate urge that the battle be carried on with the sharpest intellectual integrity, free of trickery and overbearance. But the "finally" at the very end shows how much the search for integrity is still in the making, and how far in the distant future still lies the attainment of "rule" and "possession." It well describes what Nietzsche repeatedly calls the higher man. It already gives a good clue to the *Uebermensch*, the no-longer human, all-too-human, the overman. The superman (if this now almost meaningless word must be used) is a wish-picture, a metaphor which, like all good metaphors, sends out an experimental picture toward the expression of the perception of that which will ever elude finality.]

Have you heard of that madman who lit his lantern in bright daylight, ran into the marketplace and cried continuously: "I am looking for God! I am looking for God!" Since many happened to be gathered about who did not believe in God there arose a great laughter. "Has He gone astray?," one asked. "Has He lost his way like a child?," said another. "Or is He hiding? Is He afraid of us?" "Has He boarded some boat, perhaps emigrated?" Thus the cries and laughter went. The madman leaped into their midst and pierced them with his eyes. "What has become of God?" he cried, "I will tell you! *We have murdered Him*, you and I. All of us are murderers. But how did we do it? How were we able to drink up the ocean? Who gave us the sponge to wipe out the horizon? What did we do when we unchained this earth from its sun? Whereto is it moving now? Whither are we moving? Away from every sun? Are we not continuously falling? And backwards, sidewards, forward to all sides? Is there still an up and down? Are we not wandering aimlessly through an infinite void? Does not an empty space breathe upon us? Has it not grown colder? Isn't night and always more night approaching? Must not lanterns be lighted in the forenoon? Do we as yet hear nothing of the gravediggers who are burying God. Do we as yet notice nothing of the divine decay?—Gods also decay! God is dead! God will remain dead! And we have killed Him! The most sacred and the most mighty that the world has hitherto possessed has bled to death from our knives—who will wipe this blood from us? With what waters can we be cleansed? What feasts of atonement, what sacred games will we have to invent? Is not the magnitude of this deed too much for us? Will we not ourselves have to turn into gods merely to seem worthy of it? There never was a greater deed—and whoever is born after us because of this will belong to a higher age than all history has been thus far!"—Here the madman was silent and again looked at his audience which also was silent and looked at him strangely. Finally he threw down his lantern so that it broke into pieces and went out. "I have come too early," he said, "it is not yet the time for me. This terrible event is still under way and wandering—it has not yet penetrated to the ears of men. Lightning and thunder need time; the light of the stars needs time; deeds, even after they have been done, need time to be seen and heard. This deed is still further away from them than the most distant stars—*and yet they themselves have done it!*" It is further told that on that same day the madman forced his way into various churches and there had intoned his *Requiem aeternam deo.* When led out and confronted he had nothing to say but this: "What is there still to these churches if they are not the vaults and monuments of God?"

[THE GAY SCIENCE, 125]

THE GREATEST BURDEN

What would you do if one day or night a daemon stealthily crept into the loneliest of your loneliness and said to you: "This life, just as you live it now and have lived it, you will have to live again and innumerable times. There will be nothing new about it, but every pain and every joy, every thought and sigh, and all the unspeakably small and great things of your life must return, and every thing in the same series and sequence. Just so this spider and this moonlight between the trees, and exactly so this moment and I myself. The eternal hour-glass of life is ever being turned over and you with it, you grain of sand." Would you not fall on your face, gnash your teeth and curse the daemon who spoke thus? Have you ever experienced a tremendous moment in which you would answer him: "You are a god and never have I heard anything more divine!" If that thought took control of you, it would transform you and perhaps crush you. The query to each and every thing: "Do you desire this again and an infinite number of times?" would lie upon your acts as the greatest burden! Or how kindly disposed would you have to be toward yourself and life to *have no other desire* than this final eternal confirmation and stamp of approval?

[THE GAY SCIENCE, 341]

It Is Difficult to Understand Us

Have we ever complained because we are misunderstood, misjudged, confused with others, listened to poorly or not at all? Alas, it will be so for a long time to come! It is also our distinction. We would not have sufficient respect for ourselves if we wished it otherwise. We are mistaken for what we are not. That is because we ourselves are growing, are constantly changing. Each spring we still slough off our skin; we are always growing younger, becoming more a part of the future, higher, stronger. We send our roots more and more strongly downward—into evil—and at the same time embrace heaven more and more ardently, more widely, and drink in its light more and more thirstily with all our branches and leaves. We grow like trees—that is difficult to understand, like all life—not merely at one spot but all over, not in one direction but upward as well as inward and downward. Our strength shoots simultaneously into the trunk, branches and roots. We no longer are free to do anything separately, to *be* anything separate. . . . This, as we have said, is our fate. We grow upward; and if that should be fatal—for we dwell nearer and nearer to the lightning—well, then we honor it none the less. It will always be that of which we will give away no part, and will impart nothing, this fate of rising to the heights, *our* fate.

[THE GAY SCIENCE, 371]

[At the end of the third book Nietzsche gives what seems to amount to his creed, though every article of it is essentially a description of his integrity, or the hope for it, and little else:]

What does your conscience tell you?
Thou shalt become what thou art.
[*Amor fati* and sublimation]

Where do your greatest dangers lie?
In sympathy.
[The weakening of the integrity to see things and men as they are]

What do you love in others?
My hopes.
[The courage of loneliness and the determination not to compromise]

Whom do you call mean?
Him who always tries to put to shame.
[The integrity of fairness and absence of pride]

What to you is the most human?
To save others from feeling shame.
[Fairness and mildness]

What is the seal of attained freedom?
No longer to feel ashamed of oneself.
[The dance and joy of the investigator]

6.

Works:
Thus Spoke Zarathustra

In February 1883, Nietzsche wrote the first part of *Thus Spoke Zarathustra*, completed, so he claims, in the incredibly short space of ten days and with extreme exultation —though he was just recovering from a severe attack of influenza. He spent that spring unhappily in Rome, but then returned to Sils-Maria in the Engadine where, so he says, the figure of Zarathustra had been conceived by him two years earlier. In another ten days, between June 26 and July 6, he completed the second part. The winter of 1883-84 he spent at Nice and in another burst wrote the third part. These three parts were first thought of as completing the work, but he went to work at a fourth part at a much slower and less assured pace and completed it at Nice in January 1885.

The reception of this work, even among his friends and acquaintances, was very indifferent. This so confused and troubled him that he had only forty copies of the fourth part printed for private distribution and even then sent out a mere seven. But to Nietzsche himself the *Zarathustra* was not only most important but most original, and his excitement about its accomplishment was literally boundless.

There can be little doubt that it represented a new experience to him, one that he may subconsciously have longed for, but which perhaps the very integrity that was hitherto controlling his experiments had forbidden to him. For in a very real sense the *Zarathustra* suspends the torturous, unending process of experimenting; the procession of new hypotheses, each followed by a courageous attempt at contradiction; even the troublesome vagueness resulting from the fear of a final definition or that an attractive hypothesis become an imperative. All this seems to have been laid aside in the *Zarathustra*, at least for the moment, in a sort of joyous festival of exultation and relieved assurance.

The poet has once again taken precedence over the "thinker," and in the figure of Zarathustra, Nietzsche conceived a dominant metaphor for what the distant future of his search might promise. Zarathustra possesses in full measure the great health and lithesomeness—"stranger, subtler, more daring and joyous than any health has even been." He is the artist, saint, lawgiver, sage, scholar, man of piety, soothsayer, divine recluse as envisioned in *Gay Science*. In a word, Zarathustra is the anticipation of a realization possible only at a very great distance, and, as such, grants a welcome pause to the restlessness and severity of the experimenter of good intellectual conscience and gives him a chance to disport himself.

But he is still a metaphor and not a plastic figure, and in Nietzsche's own sense of the metaphor (On the Virtue of Giving) he does not express but merely "beckons." "A fool," he says, "who insists on final knowlege." Zarathustra appears constantly and speaks in precise terms and yet to everyone about he is still a phantom who cannot be held and is understood better by his animals than by men. He is an anticipation in a very real sense and also a good metaphor, in that, like the best of metaphors, it cannot be stopped—an eidolon of immense proportions. Moreover, Zarathustra himself beckons toward a still more distant figure, not to say phantom: toward the *Uebermensch*, the Overman, the human who points the way beyond all that is now human as its complete sublimation.

It is not difficult to see why a conception like this metaphor of Zarathustra should have caused intense excitement and a sudden burst of clarity and energy in Nietzsche, very much like a hypodermic injection to a haunted spirit. It allowed him under the guise of this figure to speak and act, for a pause, as he wished that he might if all his battles had ended in honest victory and all that was human-all-too-human overcome.

In his autobiographical sketch *Ecce Homo,* which Nietzsche wrote in the last days before his collapse, the memory of this excitement persists as the most unique and original experience of his life. He still makes highly exaggerated claims about it, as indeed he made to Gast at the time of its production. But even these tend to confirm that the *Zarathustra* is in fact a point of rest, a perhaps necessary period of relief in the midst of his struggles, which allowed him at least to stimulate, even though not to acquire permanently, the "great health" out of which the joy of assurance and creation must grow.

He speaks of it as something not only original, but also sacred, conceived "6000 feet beyond man and time" with its leading idea of the Eternal Return as the highest possible formula of affirmation. Indeed, the relief lies in that Zarathustra's "great health" immediately senses what must be denied in life as the mere degeneration of life—what must be extirpated or restored so that life can be made entire and affirmed in its entirety. It is this, so he claims, that makes Zarathustra and him, who has chipped the image out of the crude stone of man's history in which it has been sleeping, so clairvoyant. Suddenly everything becomes clear to him as with a "long-sustained rhythm" by which everything falls into its place. "All life insists on turning into language and all becoming wants to learn to speak from you." In the figure of Zarathustra, he thinks, he has once and for all times and beyond contradiction established a new view of life which seems to him absolutely unique and necessary. "With every word this most affirmative of all spirits contradicts; in him all opposites have been bound into a new unity. The highest and the lowest powers of human nature, the sweetest as well as the most frivolous and terrible flow from one spring with immortal certainty." He will deny all that has hitherto been affirmed and yet be the very opposite of a denying spirit. Zarathustra himself will be the "yes to all things"; the great sublimator in the form of Dionysus. "All that hitherto has been called great in man lies at an infinite distance *below* him. Here man has been surpassed in every instance, the idea of the 'Over-man' has become highest reality."

Most of this is, of course, highly naïve. It expresses the intense joy and excitement of a poet who has discovered a dominant metaphor more than that it describes the actual attainment. Nevertheless, a sustained rhythm has been accomplished which has enabled him to overcome or suspend the physical uncertainties and to clear, for a time, the vagueness of his concepts by virtue of the anticipation offered by the metaphor. The sustained rhythm is the essential characteristic of Zarathustra, the reformer, prophet, and poet; clear to the point of joyous assurance; severe about human frailties, but with concerned tolerance; highly appreciative of every evidence of sublimation in those related enough to approach an understanding of him, but relentlessly prodding them; always admonishing but always kind, even to the hopeless disease that he must pass over rather than attack; affirming with passion and denying severely but without anger. It is all very personal, subjective, and often lyric, addressing groups or individuals, and yet giving the impression of sustained monologues.

Such a person, he says further in *Ecce Homo,* must speak the language of the dithyramb. "I am the inventor of the dithyramb. . . . Such emerald happiness, such divine gentleness never were expressed before me. Even the deep melancholy of such a Dionysus turns into a dithyramb." If the aphorisms of *Thus Spoke Zarathustra* be called dithyrambic, they have none of the wildness of the Greek Dionysus, and Nietzsche's claim merely accents the tenderness of this seemingly dangerous spirit. It is much more to the point to emphasize that in the language of *Zarathustra,* Nietzsche has perfected the aphorism to a degree not attained by a German writer, before or since. It would seem quite safe to agree with the judgment of a recent writer who finds that Nietzsche was the first to elevate the aphorism to an independent, close-knit style, and went far beyond its use merely for an individual thought. "Nietzsche was not satisfied with a collection of loose aphorisms, as Lichtenberg, Fr.

Schlegel, and the French aphorists, La Rochefoucauld, Montaigne, Pascal and others had been. For him one aphorism must clarify, support and round off the other. So Nietzsche presents series of aphorisms artistically, rather than logically or systematically. He tries to establish a certain connection between the separate aphorisms, but so that each aphorism may stand by itself and yet be indispensable to the whole:" [1]

His aphorisms well support the tense, joyous assurance of the physician's insight of man's institutions, as well as the prodding exhortations of the philosopher-teacher. They help to keep the language simple and of familiar sound and yet instill it with suggestions of higher meanings, as though the author were sublimating it as he would man's culture. Purely from the point of view of language, *Thus Spoke Zarathustra* is unsurpassed in its purity and virility and has contributed more than any other writing to whatever simplicity and clarity modern German has been able to reach. To be sure, its sustained rhythm too often reaches an ecstasy, and the preaching too often is reminiscent enough of the Bible to be disturbing. But Nietzsche considered Luther's translation of the Bible the foundation of German prose and quite consciously hoped to complete Luther's work. In a letter to Rohde from Nice, February 22, 1884, he proudly claims: "I am assuming that with this Zarathustra I have perfected the German language. After *Luther* and *Goethe* there still remained a third step—; look and see, dear friend of my soul, whether vigor, suppleness, and euphony have ever been *thus* together in our language. After a page of my book read Goethe—and you will feel that the 'undulating' that clung to Goethe as a pictorial artist is true also of his language. I had the advantage over him because of a more severe and masculine line, without however being crude like Luther. My style is a *dance,* a play of symmetries of all sorts and a neglect and mocking of these symmetries."

Assertions like this result from the extreme excitement under which Nietzsche wrote this book. It still remains true, however, that it is and probably will persist as the classic of modern German writing. On the other hand, the excitement and the brilliancy of the style account also for some of its dangers. It easily carries the reader away and lets him find striking pronouncements for almost any attitude he might want to bolster within himself. He needs only to read it out of context and without keeping in mind either the severe self-examination that the author intended, or even the sly mockery that many seemingly sober statements hide. Consequently the book has been many things for many kinds of people, or in the words of Nietzsche's dedication, "A book for all and none." Perhaps it was a danger to Nietzsche as well. For a time, as least, it hypnotized him into believing that he had arrived at a point far in advance of what was actually a fact, misled by his own brilliant use of language and image.

There are a number of miscellaneous aphorisms in the first collection, called Book One, but the prevailing accent is clearly on what Nietzsche conceived to be the intellectual integrity and courage of the demand for the full acceptance of the autonomy of man and this life and this earth. Indeed, the first evidence of integrity is the full acceptance of life through the rejection of every teaching or belief that contains any element of escape, whether it be the comfort promised by obedience to conventional morality, or the depreciation of life on this earth by the expectation of reward in a future life, or the threat of eternal punishment. The autonomy of this life implies equally the autonomy of man, the "self" that lives and evaluates life, "the creating, willing, evaluating self," whose dominant drive is to create itself into a self beyond what it now superficially and erroneously calls itself. This creating must proceed out of a fullness-to-overflowing of an intellectual, courageous understanding and acceptance of life to the point where its power is so genuine that it cannot but express itself in the "virtue of giving." Zarathustra calls this an honest selfishness which, in order to clear itself of the impurities of old though revered prejudices, must be a "robber of all values." Yet this is very different from the diseased selfishness that steals to increase its enjoyment. "Let your love to share and your understanding serve the meaning of this earth. This I beg and implore of you."

The greater part of the aphorisms, however, is devoted to
an exposition of the initial steps of the sublimation of life
which follow upon its acceptance and which prepare for an
understanding of the goal of sublimation: the Overman of
highest culture.

Sublimation is presented as an unending, ever-watchful,
step-by-step, but severe process of changing what is weak
and diseased, and recreating it into the "great health," guided
by the love and hope for that health. One of the early
addresses is entitled "Joy and Passion" *(Von den Freuden-
und Leidenschaften).* It explains that by making the un-
directed and confusing emotions the concern of the highest
hopes, they can be transformed into joy and virtue. Zarathustra says: "In the end all your passions will be turned into
virtues and all your devils into angels." It is a battle, but a
good one. "Nothing will henceforth proceed from you unless
it be the evil from the battle of your virtues." "But this evil
is necessary, necessary *is* the envy and distrust and the
calumny between your virtues." It is this kind of war that must
accompany the fight for the highest idea as long as the
warrior for sublimation is not, or even perhaps cannot be,
a "saint of understanding." But the characteristics of such
a warrior, if he be honest, must be respect for his enemy
and absence of malice. The distinction of the warrior must lie
in that he will wage only a worthy battle in obedience to
the leading idea that life must be surpassed by sublimation.

Zarathustra makes numerous attempts in this first book to
clarify the idea of sublimation and to warn against an easy
interpretation of it. He calls it, among other things, the "road
to one's self," the attainment of true individuality, a concept
which is the latest value created by man and not yet sufficiently understood. It itself is man's freedom, won by the full
acceptance of life and obedience to the idea. "And as the
world unrolled, so he sees it roll together again in cycles as
the development of the good out of the evil, as the growing of
the purpose out of the accident." [1] In the process of seeking
and clearing the true self, all that one has loved must be
"despised" and a god must have been created out of one's

"seven devils" by the sublimation of all drives and doubts in a severe and lonely struggle. Indeed, the degree of integrity demanded of the process is so severe that it must face not only the danger of the despair of loneliness but equally that of an exhaustion that might breed an indifference to, or even a scoffing at, all such struggle.

Sublimation is a process of continual revaluation, and each revaluation is the experiment to find an interpretation through more thorough integrity and fulness of understanding. As an experiment it has the power of the beckoning metaphor of the evaluator who is a "lover and kind to all things." "Attend, my brethren, to every hour in which your spirit desires to speak in metaphors; there is the origin of your virtue. It is power, this new virtue. A ruling idea, and about it a clever soul; a golden sun and about it a serpent of understanding."

The severity of this process is little relaxed in this first introduction, in spite of the kindly concern which Zarathustra shows for those who honestly try to understand him. If a disciple comes too near to him he warns him off with extreme harshness. In the section entitled "On the Virtue of Giving," page 153, Nietzsche indicates not only that the disciple may have a superficial understanding of Zarathustra's teaching, but also that the teacher himself may not be as clear about his ideas as his enthusiasm indicated, or that he had ventured to disclose as much as his intellectual conscience demanded. Consequently Zarathustra again retires to his hills for months and even years, until his doubts are dissolved and a new clarity and fullness demand a new sharing. He has just had a dream in which a child held a mirror before him reflecting the interpretations of his teachings by his friends and by his enemies. These frighten and anger him and make it all the more necessary that he again descend and speak with more directness, but still with the same kind concern of the teacher as before.

He first seeks out his friends on the "blessed isles" to shake them out of their contentment by reminding them of what they must forego in order truly to uphold the autonomy of man and his power to create life by sublimating it. "God," he

tells them, "is an inference [*Mutmaszung*, which means carrying an inference as far as courage allows,], but I insist that
your inferring reach no further than your creative will."

In the section entitled "In the Blessed Isles," page 160,
Zarathustra insists strongly upon the autonomy of man and
man's actions and upon the earth as his only realm—as he
must to maintain his Dionysian view. Not only the Christian
theological view, but all theism and deism or any metaphysical idealism is to him a denial of his view and consequently
pessimistic, even diseased. "I call it evil and misanthropic; all
this teaching of the One and Complete and Unmoved and
Satiated and Permanent." Faith in man is to him necessarily
the faith in man the creator, constantly attempting to create
himself and his earth into that which he and it most truly are,
fashioning error into health and the beast into culture through
endless transformations. Man must fashion himself and his
life out of the crude block, so his faith dictates, in which
"slumbers an image of him, the image of images." His creating
is the constantly renewed effort to clear that image ever more.
In that process many chips must fly and much suffering be
endured when, with the chips, old fond prejudices and beliefs
are chopped away. But such is the way of the creator and his
integrity as he helps man to emerge. "Alas," he complains,
"that it [the image] must sleep in the hardest, ugliest stone."

This is the "wild wisdom" with which Zarathustra returns
to arouse from their contentment those who would be his
friends, and to impress upon them that sublimation, the recreation of accident into culture, is incompatible with man's
dependence upon a being or value outside himself; that this
wisdom alone will lead to optimism and courage as opposed
to the pessimism, even nihilism, of the theological and idealistic approaches.

After this introduction the addresses of this second book
concern themselves primarily with a description of some of
the larger chips that must fall from the "crude" block that man
is. The more difficult problem of the emerging image is ventured upon with less assurance and almost incidentally. Even
though the final figure does not emerge, still the penetration

toward it, the method and process of sublimation, is more definitely described. It is always a difficult one for Nietzsche, mainly because it demanded an intellectual integrity which must itself constantly be reexamined and extended. The very hammer which he wields at the block is that of intellectual thoroughness and keenness. He even identifies his whole being with it. "Intelligence [*Geist*]," he says, "is life that cuts into its own life and on its own torment increases its own knowledge." [1]

It is meant to be the penetration to one's own real self by sloughing off, or reshaping, all that is found to be unreal because erroneous, superimposed, superstitious, or wrongly applied. If by this cleansing and clearing the reality of the self can be approached, then the true power of the self also is found. In that sense the will to sublimation and culture is also the will to power. In the address on "The Conquering of Self," it says: "And this is the secret that life itself told me: Behold, I am that which must constantly overcome itself. . . . Whatever I create and however fond I may be of it, soon I must be its enemy and of my love." In a broad sense, including psychological acumen, this enmity is intellectual; it is "life that cuts into its own life" to win a clearer understanding and image of itself. The clearer and truer it is, the more genuine and robust it will become and consequently possess the more power.

This idea of life's struggle for the genuineness of itself as its will to power is not so very startling and it follows quite easily from the full acceptance of life and its independence from any outside force, as well as from the autonomy of man as the agent of life's culture. But Zarathustra as the Dionysian prophet seems purposely to make it as startling as possible because he considers that all the established conventions under the protection of the Church, the State, and philosophy make the comprehension of it difficult, and because the only power familiar to society, perhaps even to its freer spirits, is the lust for selfish advantage. Therefore he believes the sublimation of the concept of power itself to be very difficult but indispensable for his approach. Perhaps, if he were clear within himself how sublimation should be reached beyond the preliminary clearing away of the obstacles to it, he would have been less frantic and more joyous about it than he is here.

He finds even much of the preliminary clearing difficult because sublimation always implies more than discarding. In the address "On Redemption," for example, Zarathustra discusses the attitude to be taken toward the historical tradition as the past interpretation of life and its effect upon the present and future. He finds that if history is studied under any aspect other than that of sublimation, it puts an intolerable burden of fragments upon man; creates reverence for some disconnected, separate force and thereby makes man the crippled genius of a single sense; or causes a pessimism about himself by evoking a spirit of vengeance out of which no sublimation can proceed. "The now and the 'once upon a time' on earth, my friends, is what is too hard to bear. I would not know what to do with life if I were not a seer of that which must come. . . . All 'it was' is merely a fragment, a riddle, a gruesome accident—until the creative will says to it: But I wanted it just so!" With that it got rid of vengeance and the gnashing of teeth, and the past could be redeemed by re-creating it into a bold acceptance for the purpose of sublimation. Anything that interferes with this is pessimism to him and that, in turn, leads to a nihilism which is the negation of the creativeness of sublimation.

Insofar as virtue has the meaning of strength, the pursuit of virtue signifies a will to power to Zarathustra. Still, like Nietzsche, he is the anti-moralist, the "immoralist," in that virtue as conceived by conventional morality is not a quality that must be nourished into strength, but something foreign that is acquired for the reward which it brings, and for the transgression of which society avenges itself by the procedure of legal or other punishment. That also is a pessimism to him and intellectually not honest.

The pursuit of strength, the will to power, since it means the sublimation of the native attributes that are by chance any one individual, cannot be a matter of convention which aims at survival or, perhaps, the greatest good to the greatest number—in a word, some sort of contentment: contentment is rather the mark that will appear later as that of "the ugliest man," the mob that by this aim obstructs all sublimation. By definition, sublimation is highly aristocratic and its relations to society that of the spiritual leader serving as the example of what man might make of his crude accidents if he has courage and will assume the torment of alert, endless reformation—if he persists in his will to power in this sense.

However great an obstacle contentment may be and whatever disgust with the mob it may induce because of the latter's lack of regeneration or its degenerating effect, this disgust is still directed upon man and it is, therefore, a basis, in whatever poor fashion, of the process of sublimation. Consequently disgust must avoid pessimism and nihilism, realizing that even the pursuit of contentment is also, at whatever low stage, a will to power. In "The Grave Song," Zarathustra hearkens back to the time when he also sought a kind of contentment, when his early pieties expressed his will for assurance. Later, powered by his intellectual integrity, enlightenment forced him to bury these pieties in spite of the torment which it caused him and the hurt which he had to inflict upon those near to him who failed to understand his urge. But he realizes that the will to sublimation is, after all, related to the early will, the same, in fact, with a clearer direction.

However, Zarathustra has still not clarified the full responsibility connected with his optimism of the acceptance of life. In "The Stillest Hour," it has come to him that the idea which must command this responsibility may be so severe it may even cloud the optimism, and so prove fatal. So he must again leave his friends until he can present the idea as innocently as a child displays a toy.

To face and clarify the idea of Eternal Return, he must go back onto the sea out of which the hills arose where his friends live happily in their partial knowledge. For the sea is the flood of life out of which affirmation must be won and by whose strength he can climb to his highest mountain. It seems to say that however much, up to this time, he may have held to the Dionysian view of life, boldly formulated the idea of the Eternal Return in consequence of that view, eliminated every teleology that denied it, still he had not penetrated it sufficiently in all its implications, particularly those of the crudity and error, the threat of determinism, and the rule of reason in chance. Until he has mastered all these grave things and thereby risen above them and what there is of them in himself, he will not have attained the great health and joy which they promise and out of which he can proclaim the new and, to him, supreme confidence.

So he embarks on the sea to find his new island with his highest hill, still a wanderer, experimenter, and searcher for more clarity not only about his idea, but, with it, also about himself and the dark sea of men. His usual melancholy at sight of the turbulent darkness of this sea, and even pity for it, again overcomes him. But at least he is in the company of adventurous sailors whose daring goes beyond that of the grave scholars of ordinary rational and scientific procedures and who have some relation to his own psychological penetration and divining—who are "not willing with timid touch to follow along a thread, and where they cannot *divine* detest to conclude." He relates a recent vision of his to have them guess at its meaning. In it he is an adventurer climbing up a rough and unused path high above the tree line, defying the usual scholar's spirit of gravity that holds him back at every step. He now calls this gravity his archenemy, though he himself had once accepted it painfully and though it still rides him "half dwarf, half mole." But he throws off this encumbrance by pronouncement of the dangerously daring and irrational idea of the Return: "Was that life? Very well! Once again!" He then gives the idea its extreme formula in the section entitled "On the Vision and the Riddle," page 183.

To accept life in its entirety and to see it forever return in cycles means, however, to know it in all its details, to observe how the weaknesses outnumber the robust, and what an infinite task sublimation must become at this realization. Moreover, sublimation is itself merely the recurrent effort of the few creators within each cycle who are strong enough to face the idea boldly in spite of the disgust which they must feel at the enormity of the task, a task, as the dedication of the book itself says, "for all and no one." It is the affirmation of life out of the robustness of only those who are willing and able constantly to recreate it by the sublimation of all its chances and accidents: "to say no like the storm, and to say yes like the clear sky says yes"—to "dance on the feet of chance."

The acceptance of the idea implies that, just as life recurs with all its chances, accidents, and imperfections, so also its recreators as the potentially sublimated, the Overman, will eternally return to give evidence of the dignity of man and a conception of the individual more severe, but also more complete, than the age of individualism had reached. It demands an endlessly high quality, but also an endless perseverance in the qualified sublimator of life in his endless recurrence. However, this endless recurrence is also a source of joy in that it brings with it a faith in the eternity of man and his earth. The difficulty, however, is that, though this faith is basic and may be held to the point of joyousness, still its only valid demonstration lies in the affirmation expressed in sublimation. But of that Zarathustra is far less an image than he is a preacher of its doctrine. He succeeds far better in clearing away the underbrush so that the path may be discovered, than he does as the pathfinder. In a word, even in this bold metaphor Nietzsche has succeeded in wishing for an answer to his problem more than in building an image of it. His difficulties remain almost as severe as before. He does view them here, however, with less tension because of the tolerance which his courage has given him and because of his "good taste," due to his reluctance to pass judgment and to his alert selectivity in acceptance.

At first Nietzsche thought of these three rapidly written parts of Zarathustra as completing the work. But the lack of understanding that they found even among his friends, and probably even more his own realization that the figure of Zarathustra was far from satisfying the enthusiastic promise of the original conception of the metaphor, compelled him to construct a fourth part. It was written a great deal more slowly

and with less confidence and, when finished, was privately
printed in very few copies, only seven of which he entrusted
to his closest friends. It was not published for the general
public until Easter 1892, two years after his collapse when
every hope for his recovery had been abandoned. The image
of Zarathustra still remains very vague even in this fourth
part, so that Nietzsche planned further parts of which he left
scattered notes.

The fourth book is primarily a review of the original parts
in what would seem an honest effort to disclose to himself the
success or failure of his mission among the best of those whom
it might have reached. It is as though he were turning his
integrity upon himself to see whether and how his early excitement over his metaphor had deceived him.

Thus Spoke Zarathustra

1

When Zarathustra was thirty he left his home and the lake of his home and went into the hills. Here he enjoyed his spirit and his solitude and did not tire of it for ten years. Finally his heart changed—and one morning he arose before dawn, stepped out before the sun and spoke to it thus:

You great star! What would be your happiness unless you had those upon whom you shine!

For ten years you came up here to my cave: you would have tired of your light and your path without me, my eagle and my serpent.

But we waited for you each morning, relieved you of your superabundance and blessed you for it.

Behold, I am satiated with my wisdom like the bee that has gathered too much honey; I am in need of hands that will stretch out to me.

I would like to give and share until the wise among men tire of their folly and the poor once again rejoice in their riches.

To do that I must descend into the depths, as you do in the evening when you set behind the sea and still bring light to the underworld, you over-rich star.

Like you I must *go down*, as the men call it to whom I am about to descend.

113

Then bless me, you calm eye, which can look upon an all-too-great happiness without envy!

Bless the beaker that will overflow that the water may flow forth from it golden and carry the reflection of your happiness everywhere.

Behold! This beaker again wants to empty and Zarathustra wants again to be man.

Thus began the descent of Zarathustra.

2

Alone Zarathustra went down the mountain and no one met him. When he came into the woods, suddenly an old man stood before him who had left his holy hut to gather roots in the forest. And he spoke to Zarathustra thus:

"This wanderer is no stranger to me: many years ago he passed here. His name was Zarathustra; but he is transformed.

At that time you were carrying your ashes into the hills: are you about to carry your fire into the valleys? Don't you fear the penalties of the incendiary?

Yes, I recognize Zarathustra. His eyes are clear and no disgust shows on his lips. Is he not walking along like a dancer?

Zarathustra is transformed, Zarathustra has become a child, Zarathustra is awakened: why do you come to the sleeping?

You lived in your solitude as by the sea, and the sea bore you. Alas, are you about to step on to the land? Alas, do you want again to drag your body yourself?"

Zarathustra answered: "I love man."

"Why," said the saint, "why did I go into the forest and the desert? Wasn't it because I loved men all too much?

Now I love God. I have no love for men. To me man is something too imperfect. Love for man would ruin me."

Zarathustra answered: "Did I say anything about love? I am bringing man a gift!"

"Give them nothing," said the saint, "better take something

from them—that will be best for them; if only it is good for you!

And if you do want to give to them, give them alms, and let them beg for them besides!"

"No," answered Zarathustra, "I give no alms. I am not poor enough for that."

The saint laughed at Zarathustra and spoke thus: "See to it then that they accept your treasures! They are suspicious of hermits and don't believe that they come to make gifts.

To them our steps through the streets sound too lonely. And when at night in their beds they hear a man walking, long before the sun rises, they are apt to ask themselves: where is this thief bound?

Don't go to men, but stay in the forest! Better, go to the animals! Why not be like me—a bear among bears, a bird among birds?"

"And what is the saint doing in the woods?" asked Zarathustra.

The saint answered: "I compose songs and sing them, and as I compose songs, weep, laugh and growl, I praise God.

With songs, weeping, laughter and growls I praise the God who is my God. But what gift are you bringing them?"

When Zarathustra had heard these words he saluted the saint and spoke: "What could I give you? But let me go quickly lest I take something from you." And so they separated, the old man and the man, laughing like two boys.

But when Zarathustra was by himself he spoke thus to his heart: "Could it be! Has this saint in his woods not yet heard that God is *dead!*"

3

When Zarathustra came to the nearest town adjoining the woods he found many people gathered there in the market place, for it had been announced that a tightrope walker was to perform. And Zarathustra spoke to the people thus:

I teach you the Overman. Man is something that must be surpassed. What have you done to surpass him?

Hitherto all beings have created something beyond themselves. Would you be the ebb of this great flood and rather go back to the beast than surpass man?

What is the ape to man? A thing of ridicule and a painful shame. Just that man is to be to the Overman: a laughing-stock and a painful shame.

You have made your way from the worm to man, and much about you still is worm. Once you were apes, and even now man is more ape than any ape.

Even the wisest among you is a mere discord and a mongrel of plant and phantom. But am I asking you to be phantom or plant?

Behold, I teach you the Overman.

The Overman is the meaning of this earth. Let your will say: the Overman shall be the meaning of the earth.

I beseech you, my brethren, *remain true to the earth* and do not believe those who speak to you of hopes beyond this earth. They are poisoners, whether they know it or not. They are despisers of life. They are decaying and poisoned themselves and the earth is tired of them. So let them pass on.

Once to sin against God was the greatest sin, but God died and so the sinners also died. To sin against the earth is now the most terrible of all and to esteem the bowels of the incomprehensible higher than the meaning of the earth!

Once the soul looked with contempt upon the body; then this contempt was the most valued thing of all—it wished to have it wasted and ugly and starved. It believed that thus it could escape the body and the earth.

This soul itself was wasted and ugly and starved and this soul revelled in cruelty!

And you too, my brethren, tell me: what does your body reveal of your soul? Is not your soul poverty and dirt and a miserable comfort?

Forsooth, man is a muddy stream. One must be at least a sea to be able to absorb this muddy stream without becoming unclean.

Behold, I teach you the Overman. He is this sea in which your great contempt can disappear.

What is the greatest experience you can have? It is the hour of your great contempt. The hour in which your happiness turns to disgust and likewise your reason and your virtue.

The hour in which you say: "What is there to my happiness? It is poverty and dirt and a miserable comfort. But my happiness ought to justify life itself!"

The hour in which you say: "What is there to my reason? Does it long for wisdom like the lion for his food? It is poverty and dirt and a miserable comfort!"

The hour in which you say. "What is there to my virtue? Never has it made me rave. I am so tired of my good and my evil! All this is poverty and dirt and a miserable comfort!"

The hour in which you say: "What is there to my justice? I have never noticed that I was aglow and burning. But the just man is aglow and burning!"

The hour in which you say: "What is there to my pity? Is not pity the cross to which He is nailed who loves men? But my pity is no crucifixion."

Did you ever speak thus? Did you ever cry this way? Would that I had heard you cry thus!

It is not your sin—your self-satisfaction cries to heaven, even the way you hoard your sins cries to heaven.

Where is the lightning which might lick you with its tongue? Where is the madness with which you should have been inoculated?

Behold, I teach you the Overman. He is this lightning; he is this madness.

When Zarathustra had spoken thus one of the crowd cried out: "We have listened enough to the tightrope walker, now let us have a chance to see him." And all the people laughed at Zarathustra. But the tightrope walker, who thought that he was meant, got to work.

4

But Zarathustra looked upon the people and was astonished. Then he spoke thus:

Man is a rope, tied between beast and Overman—a rope over an abyss.

A dangerous going over, a dangerous on-the-way, a dangerous looking back, a dangerous shudder and a standing still.

What is great about man is that he is a bridge, and not a goal; what can be loved in man is that he is a *going over* and a *going under*.

I love those who know nothing of life except as going under, for they are passing over.

I love the great despisers, for they are the great reverers and an arrow of longing for the other shore.

I love those who do not look for a reason behind the stars to pass on and be a sacrifice, but who sacrifice themselves for the earth so that the earth may some day belong to the Overman.

I love him who lives in order to know and who seeks knowledge so that the Overman may live. And thus he wills his own passing.

I love him who works and invents in order to build a house for the Overman and to prepare for him the earth, the beasts and plants; for thus he wills his passing.

I love him who loves his virtue; for virtue is the will to pass on and an arrow of longing.

I love him who desires not one drop of virtue for himself, but wants to be wholly the spirit of his virtue; for thus he passes over the bridge as spirit.

I love him who makes his virtue his bent and his fate; then he will live for his virtue's sake and live no longer.

I love him who does not want too many virtues. One virtue is more virtue than two, for it is more of a knot by which his fate depends.

I love him whose soul squanders itself, who wants no thanks

and makes no return, for he is always giving and will not spare himself.

I love him who is ashamed when the dice turn up in his favor and who then asks: am I a cheat? —for he wants to go under.

I love him who sends golden words in advance of his deeds and always fulfills more than he promises; for he wants his passing.

I love him who justifies those about to come and redeems those who have passed; for thus he wants to perish of the present.

I love him who chastises his god because he loves his god; for he must perish of the anger of his god.

I love him whose soul is deep even when wounded and who can go under from a small experience; thus he prefers to pass over the bridge.

I love him whose soul is overfull so that he forgets himself and in him are all things; so all things turn into his going under.

I love him who is of free spirit and free heart; then his head is merely the entrails of his heart; his heart, however, drives him to his going under.

I love those who are like heavy drops falling one by one from the dark cloud which hovers over man; they announce that the lightning is coming and as heralds they go under.

Behold, I am the herald of the lightning, and a heavy drop from the cloud. But the name of this lightning is Overman.

5

When Zarathustra had spoken these words he looked upon the people again and was silent. "There they stand," he said to his heart, "there they laugh. They don't understand me; I am not the mouth for these ears.

Must their ears first be shattered so that they will learn to hear with their eyes? Is it necessary to clatter like kettledrums and revivalists? Or will they only believe the stammerers?

They have something of which they are proud. What do they call this thing that makes them proud? They call it culture; it distinguishes them from the goatherds.

Therefor they dislike to hear the word 'contempt.' Then I will speak to their pride.

Then I will speak to them of that which is most contemptible: but that is *the last man*."

And thus spoke Zarathustra to the people:

The time has come for man to set a goal for himself. It is time that man should plant the seed of his highest hope.

As yet his ground is still rich enough. But this ground of his will some time be poor and tame, and no longer will a high tree be able to grow in it.

Alas! The time is coming when man will no longer throw the arrow of his longing beyond man, and the string of his bow has forgotten how to whirr!

I say to you: one must still have chaos within oneself in order to give birth to a dancing star. I ask you: do you still have this chaos?

Alas, the time will come when man will no longer give birth to a star. Alas, the time of the most despicable man will come, who no longer can despise himself.

Behold! I am showing you *the last man*.

"What is love?" "What is creating?" "What is longing?" "What is star?" —Thus asks the last man and blinks.

The earth will then have become small and upon it there will hop the last man who makes everything small. His kind is as ineradicable as the flea; the last man lives longest.

"We have invented happiness," say these last men and blink.

They have left the regions where life is hard, for one must have warmth. One still loves one's neighbor and snuggles up to him, for one must have warmth.

To be sick or to distrust is rated as sinful: one walks about with care. A fool who still stumbles over stones or men!

A little poison now and then; that promotes pleasant dreams. And in the end, much poison for a pleasant death.

One still works, for work is entertaining. But one is careful not to let the entertainment become a strain.

One is no longer either poor or rich; both are too burdensome. Who still cares to rule? Who still obey? Both are too burdensome.

No shepherd and *one* herd! Everyone wants an equal share, everyone is equal: whoever feels otherwise voluntarily enters the madhouse.

"Once all the world was mad"—so say the finest of them and blink.

One is clever and knows everything that has happened: so there is no end to mockery. One still quarrels but soon comes to a reconciliation—otherwise it spoils digestion.

There is one's little pleasure for the day and a little one for the night; but one respects one's health.

"We have invented happiness" —these last men say and blink.

Here ended the first speech of Zarathustra which is also called "the prologue"; for at this moment a cry and rejoicing of the mob interrupted him. "Give us this last man, oh Zarathustra," —so they cried—"make us into this last man! Then we will let you have the Overman!" Then all the people rejoiced and clicked their tongues. But Zarathustra became sad and spoke thus to his heart:

"They do not understand me; I am not the mouth for these ears.

I probably lived in the hills too long; too long I listened to the brooks and trees. Now I speak to them like a goatherd.

My soul is unmoved and clear as the hills in the forenoon. But they think that I am cold and a mocker in terrible jokes.

Now they look upon me and laugh; and as they laugh they also hate me. There is ice in their laughter."

6

But then something happened that silenced every mouth and made each eye stare. For meanwhile the tightrope walker had begun his work: he had stepped out of a small door and walked along the rope which had been stretched between two towers so that it hung over the market place and the people. But when he had reached the halfway mark, the small door opened again and a gaily clad fellow, similar to a clown, sprang out and hurried after the first performer with nimble steps. "On with you, clubfoot," he cried in a terrible voice, "go on, lazybones, smuggler, pale-face! Or I will tickle you with my heels. What business have you here between towers? Your place is in the tower; you ought to be locked up; you are blocking the way of a better man than you are!" With each word he came nearer and nearer. But when he was but a step behind, the frightful thing happened that silenced every mouth and made each eye stare—he let out a cry like a devil and jumped over him who was in his way. But the latter as he saw his rival winning lost his head and the rope; he threw away his pole and, quicker than this, shot down in a whirl of arms and legs. The market place and the people resembled a sea over which a storm is sweeping; everybody scattered and tumbled over each other, especially there where the body must fall.

But Zarathustra stood still and the body fell right beside him, badly mauled and broken, but not yet dead. After a while the shattered man regained consciousness and saw Zarathustra kneeling beside him. "What are you doing here?" He finally spoke. "I knew long ago that the devil would trip me up. Now he will drag me to hell; do you mean to stop him?"

"By my honor, my friend," Zarathustra answered, "those things do not exist that you are talking about: there is no devil and no hell. Your soul will be dead well before your body. You have nothing to fear."

The man sent him a doubtful glance. "If you are telling the truth," he said, "I am losing nothing when I lose my life. I am not much more than an animal that has been taught to dance by means of beatings and meager bits."

"Not at all," Zarathustra said, "you have made a calling of danger; that is not to be despised. Now you are perishing of your calling; for that I will bury you with my own hands."

When Zarathustra had said that, the dying man did not answer; but he moved his hand as though he were seeking Zarathustra's hand to thank him.

7

When Zarathustra had said this to his heart, he packed the body on his back and started on his way. Before he had taken a hundred steps a fellow crept up to him and whispered into his ear—and behold; the man who was speaking was the clown of the tower. "Turn away from this city, oh Zarathustra," he said, "there are too many here who hate you. The good and the just hate you and call you their enemy and despiser; you are hated by the faithful of the true faith and they call you a danger for the people. It was lucky for you that they laughed at you; and forsooth, you did speak like a jester. It was your good fortune that you consorted with the dead dog; when you humbled yourself you saved yourself for the nonce. But go away from the city—or tomorrow I will spring over you, the living over the dead." When he had said this the fellow disappeared; but Zarathustra walked through the dark streets.

At the city gate the gravediggers met him: they shone their torch into his face, recognized Zarathustra and mocked him. "Zarathustra is carrying off the dead dog; brave of Zarathustra to turn gravedigger! Our hands are too clean for this roast. Is Zarathustra trying to steal the devil's morsel? Good enough! We hope that you enjoy it! If only the devil is not the better thief than Zarathustra! —He will steal them both and devour them both!" And they put their heads together and laughed.

Zarathustra said not a word and continued on his way. When he had walked for two hours, past woods and swamps, he found that he had heard too much of the hungry howling of wolves and he too felt the pangs of hunger. So he stopped at a lonely house in which a light was burning.

"Hunger is attacking me like a robber. In woods and swamps my hunger attacks me, and in deep night.

My hunger has strange moods. Often it comes upon me after meals, and today it did not come all day long: where can I have been?"

With that he knocked at the door of the house. An old man appeared; he carried a light and asked: "Who is coming to me and my poor sleep?"

"A living and a dead man," said Zarathustra. "Give me something to eat; I forgot it during the day. He who feeds the hungry, refreshes his own soul; so says wisdom."

The old man went out but came right back and offered Zarathustra bread and wine. "A bad region for those that hunger," he said, "that is why I live here. Beast and man come to me, the hermit. But bid your companion also eat and drink; he is more tired than you."

Zarathustra answered: "My companion is dead; I will hardly be able to persuade him."

"That is not my affair," the old man grumbled. "Whoever knocks at my door must take what I offer. Eat and fare you well!"

Thereupon Zarathustra walked for another two hours, trusting to the path and the light of the stars, for he was used to walking at night and loved to face all that slept. But with the dawn Zarathustra found himself in a dense forest and there was no longer a path to guide him. So he placed the body into a hollow tree—for he wanted to protect it against the wolves—and he himself lay down on the ground and the moss. He fell asleep immediately, tired of body but with his soul unmoved.

8

Zarathustra slept for a long time and not only the dawn but also the forenoon passed over him. Finally his eyes opened. In amazement he gazed into the woods and the silence; in amazement he looked into himself. Then he arose quickly like a seafarer who suddenly spies the land, and he rejoiced, for he saw a new truth. Then he spoke to his heart thus:

"I see a light: I need companions and living ones—not dead companions and bodies that I carry about with me wherever I please.

But I need living companions who will follow me because they wish to follow themselves—and whither I decide.

I saw the light: Zarathustra is not to speak to the people but to companions! Zarathustra is not to be the shepherd and sheepdog of a herd!

To entice many away from the herd—for this I came. I am to be a curse to the people and the herd. Zarathustra wants the shepherds to call him robber.

I say shepherds but they call themselves the good and the just. I say shepherds but they call themselves the faithful of the true faith.

Behold these good and just men! Whom do they hate most? Him who breaks the tables of their values, the breaker, the lawbreaker—but that is the creator.

The creator is looking for companions and not bodies, nor herds and believers. The creator seeks fellow creators, such as will write new values on new tables.

The creator seeks companions and fellow harvesters, for in him all is ready for the harvest. But he lacks the hundred sickles; so he plucks the ears and is disgruntled.

The creator seeks companions and those who know how to whet their sickles. They will be called destroyers and despisers of good and evil. But they are the harvesters and those who celebrate.

Zarathustra seeks fellow creators who harvest and celebrate with him. What concern has he for herds and shepherds and dead bodies!

And you, my serious companion, fare you well! Well did I bury you in this hollow tree; well did I hide you from the wolves.

But I am leaving you, the time is up. Between dawn and dawn a new truth came to me.

I am not meant to be a shepherd nor a gravedigger. Nor will I again speak to the people; for the last time I spoke to a corpse.

I will join the creators, the harvesters, the celebrants. I will show them the rainbow and all the steps of the Overman.

I will sing my song to those who live alone or by twos; and whoever still has ears for the unheard-of, his heart I will make heavy with my happiness.

I am pursuing my goal, going my path; I will leap over those who hesitate or lag behind. My pace shall be their decline."

9

Zarathustra had said this to his heart when the sun was at the zenith. Then something made him look up, for above he heard the shrill call of a bird. And behold! An eagle drew large circles through the air and a serpent clung to it, not like a prey but like a friend, for it had coiled itself about its neck.

"They are my animals," said Zarathustra, and rejoiced heartily.

"The proudest animal under the sun and the cleverest under the sun.

They have been reconnoitring.

They wish to explore whether Zarathustra is still alive. Verily, am I still alive?

I encountered more danger among men than among animals. Zarathustra's ways are dangerous. May my animals lead me!"

When Zarathustra had said this he recalled the words of the saint in the forest, sighed and spoke thus to his heart:

"Would that I were more clever! Would that I were wholly clever like my serpent.

But that is asking the impossible. So I will beg my pride always to go with my cleverness.

And if ever my cleverness forsakes me—alas, it loves to fly away! —may my pride at least fly with my folly."

Thus began Zarathustra's down-going.

The Address of Zarathustra

Part One

ON THE THREE TRANSFORMATIONS

I am calling your attention to the three transformations of the spirit: how the spirit becomes a camel, the camel a lion, and, finally, the lion a child.

There are many weighty things for the spirit that delights in its burden and is reverent; its strength longs for that which is weighty and most difficult.

What is hard to bear? So asks the spirit that delights in its burden. It kneels down like a camel that wants to be well laden.

What is hardest to bear, you heroes? So asks the spirit that delights in its burden, that I may take it upon myself and rejoice in my strength.

Is it not this: to humble oneself in order to hurt one's pride? To let one's folly shine in order to mock at one's wisdom?

Or is it this: to part from your cause when it is celebrating its victory? To ascend high hills in order to tempt the tempter?

Or is it this: to feed on the acorns and grass of knowledge and for the sake of truth to suffer the hunger of the spirit?

Or is it this: to be sick and to turn away the comforter, and to make friends with the deaf who cannot hear what you want?

Or is it this: to descend into muddy water if it is the water of truth and not to avoid cold frogs and hot toads?

Or is it this: to love those who despise us and reach out your hand to the specter if it tries to frighten us?

All these most weighty things the spirit that loves its burden takes upon itself like the camel that hurries with its burden into the desert. Thus the spirit hurries into its desert.

But in the loneliest of deserts the second transformation takes place: here the spirit becomes a lion; it will capture its freedom and be the master in its own desert.

Here it seeks its last master; it will contend with him and its last god, it will fight for victory with the great dragon.

What is this great dragon that the spirit will no longer call master and god? "Thou shalt," the great dragon is called. But the spirit of the lion says, "I will."

On the path lies "Thou shalt," a scaly animal, its gold sparkling, and on every scale the golden "thou shalt."

Thousand-year-old values sparkle on these scales and the mightiest of all dragons says: "The value of all things glows on me.

Every value has long since been created and I am every created value. Verily, there shall be no more 'I will'!" Thus speaks the dragon.

My brothers, why does the spirit have need of the lion? Why does not the animal suffice that loves its burden, renounces and is reverent?

Create new values—that not even the lion can do. But to win freedom for new creation—that the power of the lion can accomplish.

To win freedom and a holy "No" even to duty: for that, my brethren, there is need of the lion.

To assume the right to new values—that is the most terrible assumption for a reverent spirit that loves its burdens. Verily, this a robbing and the affair of a beast of prey.

Once it loved the "Thou shalt" as most sacred. Now it must see delusion and whim even in the most holy, so that it may win freedom from its love. For this kind of prey there is need of the lion.

But tell me, my brethren, what can the child do that even

the lion was not capable of? Why must the preying lion still become a child?

The child is innocence and forgetting, a beginning anew, a game, a wheel rolling by itself, a new motion, a holy "Yes."

Yes, for the game of creating, my brethren, there is need of a holy "Yes." Now the spirit wants *its* will; being lost to the world it wins *its own* world.

I am mentioning to you three transformations of the spirit: how the spirit becomes a camel, the camel a lion, and, finally, the lion a child.

Thus spoke Zarathustra. And at that time he dwelt in the city which is called The Spotted Cow.

ON THE ACADEMIC CHAIRS OF VIRTUE

Zarathustra heard praises of a sage who was said to expound well on sleep and virtue and was greatly honored and well paid for it.

All the young men sat before his chair. Zarathustra went and also sat before him. The wise man spoke thus:

Honor and respectful regard for sleep. That is the first thing. Avoid all who sleep badly and lie awake at night!

Even the thief respects sleep; he always steals softly through the night. But the watchman of the night has no regard; shamelessly he carries his horn.

To sleep is not a mean art; one must stay awake all day in anticipation of it.

Ten times a day you must practice restraint; that produces a good exhaustion and is opium for the soul.

Ten times you must again reconcile yourself; for renunciation is better and the unreconciled sleep badly.

During the day you must find ten truths; otherwise you will search for truth at night, this father of melancholy.

Few know it, but you must have all virtues in order to sleep well. Will I bear false witness? Will I commit adultery?

Will I covet my neighbor's maid? All this would agree badly with a good sleep.

Even if one had all virtues, one thing still would be

necessary, namely, to put the virtues to sleep at the proper time.

Otherwise they will fight each other, the pretty damsels, and over you, poor wretch.

Good sleep requires peace with God and your neighbor. And peace, too, with the devil of your neighbor: or he will haunt you at night.

Honor and obedience to the authority, and even the crooked authority. Good sleep demands it. Can I help it if power walks about on crooked legs?

I shall always call him the best shepherd who leads his sheep into green pastures; that agrees best with good sleep.

I do not desire many honors nor great treasures, for that inflames the spleen. But it is difficult to sleep without a good name or modest treasure.

I like a small company better than an evil one; but it must come and go at the proper time. That is most conducive to good sleep.

Also, I like the poor in spirit; they promote sleep. Blessed are they, especially if one always agrees with them.

Thus passes the day of the virtuous. But when the night approaches, I am careful not to implore sleep. Sleep, this master of virtue, does not want to be called.

Instead I review what I have done and thought during the day. Regurgitating like a cow I patiently ask myself: what were your ten restraints?

And what were the ten reconciliations, the ten truths and the ten chuckles with which you delighted your heart?

Thinking such things and cradled by forty thoughts, sleep, the master of virtues, suddenly overtakes me without being called.

Sleep knocks on my eye and it gets heavy. Sleep touches my mouth and it stays open.

Verily, it comes to me on soft soles, the dearest of thieves, and steals my thoughts. I stand there as dumb as this academic chair.

But I do not stand long and down I go. . . .

When Zarathustra had heard the sage speak thus he

laughed to himself, for a light had come to him. And he spoke thus to his heart:

I consider this sage a fool with his forty thoughts, but I do believe that he is an expert on sleep.

Anyone even near this sage is fortunate. A sleep like that is contagious even through a thick wall.

There is magic even in his chair. And the young people did not gather in vain before this preacher of virtue.

His wisdom is this: stay awake in order to sleep well. And truly, if life had no sense and I had to choose nonsense, then this would be the most desirable nonsense for me too.

Now I understand clearly what was desired above all things when teachers of virtue were in demand. Good sleep was sought, and opiate virtues along with it.

For all these much-praised sages of academic chairs, dreamless sleep was wisdom. They knew of no better meaning of life.

And even today there are a few like this preacher of virtue, and they not always as honest. But their time is up. And they will not stand long, and down they will be.

Blessed are these who are sleepy, for soon they will drop off.

Thus spoke Zarathustra.

ON THE WORLD BEYOND

Once Zarathustra also let his delusion roam beyond man like all who trust in a world beyond. At that the world seemed to me to be the work of a suffering and tortured god.

A dream it seemed to me and a fiction of a god, the motley smoke before the eyes of one divinely dissatisfied.

Good and evil, joy and sorrow, and I and you—motley smoke it seemed before creative eyes. The creator wished to look away from himself and so he created the world.

For those who suffer it is an intoxicating joy to look away from their suffering and lose themselves. Once I also imagined the world to be drunken joy and losing of self.

This world, the eternally imperfect, the image of an eternal contradiction and an imperfect image—a drunken joy of an imperfect creator—thus this world once seemed to me.

In this fashion I once cast my delusion beyond man like all who trust in a world beyond. Truly beyond man?

Alas, my brethren, this god whom I created was the work and madness of man, like all gods!

He was man and only a poor fraction of man and of myself. Out of my own ashes and glow this specter came to me, and certainly not from beyond! What happened then, my brethren? I overcame my suffering self; I carried my ashes up a mountain and discovered a brighter flame. And behold, at once the specter vanished!

Now after my recovery it would be a suffering and a torment to believe in such specters. Now it would be disease and a humiliation. This I say to all who trust in a world beyond.

Suffering it was and impotence that created all the worlds beyond, and that short madness of bliss which only those experience who suffer most. It was exhaustion that wants to reach the ultimate in a *single* leap, a leap of death, a poor ignorant exhaustion that no longer even wants to will: this created all gods and worlds beyond.

Believe me, my brethren, it was the body that despaired of the body—that groped with the fingers of the deluded spirit at the ultimate walls. Believe me, my brethren, it was the body that despaired of the earth—it heard the bowels of being speak to it.

It wished to ram its head through the ultimate walls—and beyond into "yonder world."

But "yonder world" is well hidden from man: that dehumanized, inhuman world which is a heavenly naught; and the bowels of being do not speak to man at all unless it be as man.

Truly, all being is hard to prove and to induce to speak. Is not the most miraculous of all things proved best?

This I, and the contradiction and confusion of this I, still speaks most honestly of its being, this creating, willing, evaluating I, which is the measure and worth of things.

This most honest being, this I, speaks of the body even when it revels in poetry and flutters with broken wings.

This I learns to speak more and more honestly, and the more it learns the more it finds words and honors for the body and the earth.

My I taught me a new pride and I am teaching it to men: no longer to bury one's head in the sand of heavenly things but to carry it freely, an earth-head that creates the meaning of the earth.

I am teaching men a new will: to will this path that man has gone blindly, to call it good and not to steal aside like the diseased and dying.

They were the sick and dying who despised the body and the earth and invented heaven and the redemptive blood-drops. But even these sweet and gloomy poisons they took from the body and the earth.

They wished to escape their misery, and the stars were too far off. So they sighed: "Would that there were heavenly ways to steal into another life and joy!" —At that they invented their sly dodges and blood-drops. These ingrates believed they had escaped their body and the earth. But to what did they owe the ecstatic joy of their escape? To their bodies and the earth.

Zarathustra is gentle with the sick; he is not angry with their kind of comfort and ingratitude. Would that they might recover and overcome their sickness and create a higher body for themselves!

Nor is Zarathustra angry with the convalescent when he fondles his delusion and at night steals about the grave of his god. But to me even his tears are sickness and a sick body.

There always were many sickly among those who revel in poetry and long for God. Furiously do they hate the search for knowledge and that newest of all virtues, which is called integrity.

They are always looking back toward the dark ages. Then,

to be sure, delusion and faith were a different thing; the raving of reason was godlike and doubt was sin.

All too well do I know these godlike people: they want faith in themselves and doubt to be sin.

Surely, they also do not believe best in worlds beyond and redemptive blood-drops, but in the body, and their own body is the thing *per se* to them.

But it is a sickly thing and gladly would they shed their hide. That is why they listen to the preachers of death and why they themselves preach worlds beyond.

I would rather, my brethren, that you listen to the voice of the sound body. It is a more honest and purer voice.

The sound, perfect and four-square body speaks more honestly and purely; it speaks of the meaning of the earth.

Thus spoke Zarathustra.

On Those Who Despise the Body

I have my word to say to those who despise the body. I am not asking them to learn better or teach better, but merely to say farewell to their body—and so be silent.

"I am body and soul" —so speaks the child. And why not speak like children? But the awakened, the enlightened man says: I am body altogether and nothing besides; and soul is merely a word for an aspect of the body.

Your body is a great reason, a plurality with *one* meaning, a war and a peace, a herd and a shepherd.

Also your small reason, my brother, which you call mind, is a tool of your body, a small tool and toy of your great reason.

"I," you say, and are proud of the word. But the greater thing—in which you refuse to believe—is your body and its great reason. That does not say I but does I.

What your senses feel and your mind learns, that never has its end in itself. But the senses and the mind would like to convince you that they are the end of all things; so vain are they.

Sense and mind are tools and toys; behind them there still lies the Self. The Self searches even with the eyes of the senses, it listens with the ears of the mind.

The Self is always listening and searching; it compares, uses force, conquers, destroys. It rules and is the ruler also of the I.

Behind your thoughts and feelings, my brethren, there stands the mighty commander, an unknown sage: its name is Self. It dwells in your body; it is your body.

There is more reason in your body than in your best wisdom. Who can possibly know why your body has need of this very best wisdom?

Your Self laughs at your I and its proud leaps. "Just what are these leaps and flights of thought?" it says. "A detour toward my purposes. I am the leading strings of the I and the prompter of its ideas!"

The Self says to the I: "Feel pain here!" And then it suffers and ponders how to suffer no more—and that is just what it *should* think.

The Self says to the I: "Rejoice!" Then it rejoices and ponders how to rejoice often—and that is just what it *should* think.

I have this to say to those who despise the body: the fact that they disregard constitutes their regard. What is it that created regard and disregard and worth and will?

The creative Self created regard and disregard; it created pleasure and pain. The creative Self created its spirit as an organ of its will.

Even in your folly and despising, you despisers of the body, you serve your Self. I say to you: your Self itself is about to die and is turning away from life.

It can no longer do what it wants most to do—to create beyond itself. That is what it wants most to do, that is its whole urge.

But now it proves to be too late for that. Therefor your Self wants to perish, you despisers of the body.

Your Self wants to perish and therefor you turned into

despisers of the body! For you are no longer able to create beyond yourselves.

And so you now inveigh against life and the earth. There is an unknown envy in the askance looks of your despising.

I do not go your way, you despisers of the body! To me you are no bridges towards the Overman!

Thus spoke Zarathustra.

On Violent and Joyous Emotions

My brother, if you have a virtue and it is your virtue, then you have it in common with nobody.

To be sure, you want to give it a name and fondle it; you want to pinch its ears and sport with it.

And behold, you have its name in common with the mob and you yourself have become mob and herd with your virtue!

It would be better for you to say: "Inexpressible and nameless is that which produces the torment and sweetness of my soul and even the hunger of my bowels."

Let your virtue be too lofty for the familiarity of names, and if you must speak of it do not be ashamed to stammer.

Speak and stammer thus: "You are my good which I love; just so you please me wholly; I want my good to be just so.

I do not want it as the command of a God; I do not want it as a regulation and need of men; it shall not be a signpost to earths and paradises in the beyond.

The virtue which I love is a mundane virtue. There is little wisdom in it and least of all common reason.

But this bird built its nest with me; that is why I love and fondle it—now it sits on its golden eggs."

Thus you should stammer and praise your virtue.

Once you had violent passions and called them evil. But now you only have your virtues. They grew out of your violent passions.

You entrusted your highest goal to your passions. Then they turned into your virtues and joyous passions.

And if you should be of the choleric or the voluptuous or the fanatic or the vengeful; in the end all your passions became virtues and all your devils angels.

Once you had wild dogs in your cellar. But in the end they changed into birds and lovely songsters.

Out of your poisons you brewed your balm; you milked your cow, melancholy—now you drink the sweet milk of its udder.

Henceforth nothing evil will proceed from you unless it be the evil resulting from the battle of your virtues.

My brother, you are fortunate if you have but *one* virtue and no more. In that way you will pass more easily over the bridge.

It is distinguishing to have many virtues, but a hard lot. Many a man went into the desert and killed himself because he tired of being the battle and battlefield of his virtues.

My brother, are war and battle evil? But this evil is necessary, necessary is the envy, the distrust and the calumny among your virtues.

Behold, how each of your virtues is desirous of the highest. It wants the whole of your spirit in order to be its herald; it wants all the power of your anger, hatred and love.

Each virtue is jealous of the other and jealousy is a terrible thing. Even virtues can perish of jealousy.

He whom the flames of jealousy surround will, at last, like a scorpion, aim the poisonous sting against himself.

My brother, did you ever see a virtue slander and stab itself?

Man is something that must be overcome, and for that reason you must love your virtues—for you will perish of them.

Thus spoke Zarathustra.

ON THE TREE AT THE FOOT OF THE HILL

Zarathustra had noticed that a young man was avoiding him. One evening when he was walking alone through the hills which inclose the city which is called The Motley Cow, he found a young man who was sitting with his back against a tree and looking into the valley with tired glances. Zarathustra took hold of the tree against which the young man was sitting and spoke to him thus:

"If I tried to shake this tree with my hands I would not be able to do it. But the wind which we do not see worries and bends it at will. We are bent and worried most by invisible hands."

At that the young man rose in fright and said: "I hear Zarathustra and I was just thinking of him." Zarathustra answered:

"Why are you frightened? —But it is the same with man as with this tree. The more he strives up into the height and the light, the stronger his roots strive earthward, downward, into the dark, the depth—into evil."

"Yes, into evil!" cried the young man. "Is it possible that you have discovered my soul?"

Zarathustra smiled and said: "Many a soul will never be discovered unless it be invented first."

"Yes, into evil!" the young man repeated.

"You spoke truly, Zarathustra. Since I strive for the height I no longer trust myself and no one trusts me any more. Why is that?

I change too fast: my today contradicts my yesterday. Often I skip steps as I climb—and no step forgives that.

When I am above I always find myself alone. No one speaks to me, the frost of the loneliness makes me shiver. What is it that I seek in the height? My contempt and my longing grow at the same time; the higher I climb the more I despise him who climbs. What is he seeking in the height?"

Here the young man was silent. Zarathustra contemplated the tree at which they stood and spoke thus:

"This tree stands alone on the hill; it grew high beyond man and animal. If it wished to speak there would be no one to understand it, so high did it grow. Now it waits and waits. What is it waiting for? It dwells too near to the seat of the clouds; probably it is waiting for the first lightning!" When Zarathustra had said this, the young man gestured wildly and cried out: "Yes, Zarathustra, you speak the truth. When I strove for the height I was longing for my destruction and you are the lightning for which I was waiting. What am I now that you have appeared? It was *envy* of you that has destroyed me!" So the young man spoke and wept bitterly.

But Zarathustra put his arm about him and led him away.

And when they had walked together for a while Zarathustra began to speak thus:

"It rends my heart. Better than your words, your eye tells me your whole danger.

As yet you are not free; you are still *seeking* freedom. Your searching has left you sleepless and over-alert. You want the free heights, you thirst for stars. But your evil drives are also thirsting for freedom.

Your wild dogs want to be released; lustily they bark in their cellar while your spirit plots to open all prisons.

To me you are still a prisoner who is dreaming of his freedom. The soul of such prisoners turns clever but also deceitful and evil.

Even the freed spirit still must purify himself. There is much prison and mold remaining in him: his eye must still become clear.

Yes, I know your danger. But by my love and hope I beseech you: do not throw away your love and hope!

You still feel you are noble; and the others too, who dislike you and cast angry glances at you, still believe you to be noble. Remember, a noble man is in everybody's way.

A noble man is in the way even of the good man; and when they call him a good man they try to get rid of him by doing so.

The noble man wants to create the new and a new virtue. The good man wants the old and that the old be preserved.

But the danger for the noble man is not that he may turn into a good man, but that he becomes insolent, a mocker and destroyer.

Alas, I knew noble men who lost their highest hope. Now they slander all high hopes.

Insolently they followed fleeting lusts and their goals were barely beyond the day.

'Spirit also is voluptuous' —they said. With that they broke the wings of their spirit and now it barely crawls and soils whatever it gnaws.

Once they hoped to be heroes; now they are voluptuaries. The hero is to them a grief and a horror.

But by my love and hope I beseech you: do not throw away the hero in your soul! Keep holy your highest hope!"

Thus spoke Zarathustra.

ON WAR AND WARRIORS

We do not want to be spared by our best enemies, nor by those whom we wholly love. So let me tell you the truth!

My brothers in war! I love you with all my heart; I am and was of your kind. And I am also your best enemy. So let me tell you the truth!

I know about the hatred and envy in your hearts. You are not big enough not to know hatred and envy. Then be great enough not to be ashamed of it! If you cannot be saints of knowledge, then at least be its warriors. They are companions and forerunners of such saintliness.

I see many soldiers; would that I saw many warriors! "Uniform," they call what they wear. I hope that it is not uniformity that they hide with it! You should be one whose eyes always are looking for an enemy—*your* enemy. Some of you hate at the very first glance.

You should look for your enemy, carry on your war, and for your ideas! And if your idea loses you should be honest enough to call it a victory! You should love peace as means for new wars; and the short peace more than the long one.

I am not advising work but battle. I am not advising peace but victory. Let your work be a battle and your peace a victory!

One can only be silent and sit still when he has bow and arrow; otherwise one chats and quarrels. Your peace should be a victory!

You say that a good cause hallows even war? I say that it is the good war that hallows every cause.

War and courage have done more great things than love of neighbor. Not your pity but your bravery has hitherto saved the unfortunate.

"What is good?" you ask. To be brave is good. Let the little girls say: "To be good is to be pretty and touching at the same time."

They call you heartless, but I love the hesitation of your heartiness. You are ashamed of your flood, but others are ashamed of their ebb.

You are ugly? Very well, my brethren! Clothe yourself in sublimity, the mantle of ugliness!

And when your soul becomes great, it turns haughty, and there is malice in your sublimity. I know you.

In malice the haughty meets with the weakling. But they misunderstand each other. I know you.

You may have enemies only whom you hate, but not enemies whom you despise. You must be proud of your enemy; then the successes of your enemy are your successes also.

Revolt—that is the distinction of a slave. Let your distinction be obedience! Let even your commanding be obedience!

To a good warrior, "thou shalt" is more pleasant than "I will." Every thing that you love must first have been given to you as a command.

Let your love of life be love of your highest hope; and your highest hope should be the highest idea of life!

But you must permit your highest thought to be commanded by me—and it reads: man is something that must be overcome.

Thus live your life of obedience and war! What is there to a long life? What warrior wishes to be spared!

I am not sparing you; I love you wholly, my brothers in war!

Thus spoke Zarathustra.

ON THE NEW IDOL

Somewhere there still exist peoples and herds, but not with us. Here there are states.

The state? What is it? Very well! Open your ears, for now I will give you my message of the death of peoples.

The state means the coldest of all cold monsters. Its lie is cold; and this lie crawls from its mouth: "I, the state, am the people."

That is a lie! Creators created the peoples and suspended over them a faith and a love: thus they served life.

It is the destroyers who set traps for the many and call them state. They suspend a sword and a hundred greeds over them.

Where there still is a people, it does not understand the state and hates it like an evil eye and a sin against customs and rights.

I give you this sign: every people speaks its own language of good and evil which the neighbor does not understand. In its customs and rights it invented its own language.

But the state lies in all languages of good and evil; it lies whatever it says—and whatever it has it has stolen.

Everything about it is false; it bites with stolen teeth, the wild dog. Even its bowels are false.

Confusion of tongues of good and evil: this is the sign which I give you as the sign of the state. Verily, this sign signifies the will to death; it beckons the preachers of death.

Many too many were born; the state was invented for the superfluous!

Look how he lures them, these many-too-many! How he gobbles and masticates them!

"On earth there is nothing greater than I; I am the directing finger of God" —so howls this monster. And not only the long-eared and short-sighted sink to their knees!

Alas, to you too, you great souls, he whispers his gloomy lies! Alas, he divines the rich hearts that gladly spend themselves!

Yes, he finds you out also, you conquerors of the old God! You became exhausted in battle and now your exhaustion serves the new idol!

He would like to have the heroes and honored men about him, this new idol! He likes to sun himself in the sunshine of your good conscience, this cold monster!

The new idol will give *you* everything if you worship him; thus he acquires the splendor of your virtues and the look of your proud eyes.

With you he would bait the many-too-many! Yes, thus he invented a devilish trick, a horse of death, tinkling with the adornment of divine honors!

A dying for many was thus invented which boasts of being life itself; surely, a precious gift for all preachers of death!

I call it the state where all are addicts of poison, good and bad; the state, where all lose themselves, good and bad; the state, where the slow suicide of all passes as "life."

Take a look at these superfluous people! They steal the products of the inventors and the treasures of the wise, and call their theft culture—and with them everything turns to disease and woe!

Look at these superfluous people! They are always sick, they vomit their gall and call it newspaper. They devour each other and cannot even digest themselves.

Look at these superfluous people! They win riches and become all the poorer in doing so. They want power, and, to begin with, the lever of power, much money—these impotent people.

See them climb, these swift monkeys! They climb over each other and so drag each other into the slime and the depths.

They are all aiming at the throne; it is their madness—just

as though good fortune sat on the throne! Often the slime sits on the throne—and often, too, the throne on the slime.

They are all mad and climbing apes and overheated. Their idol, this cold monster, has a foul odor; all of them, these idolators, spread a foul odor. My brothers, do you want to choke from the breath of their mouths and lusts? I would rather that you broke the windows and escaped into the open.

Avoid the foul smell! Avoid the idolatry of the superfluous! Turn away from the steam of these human sacrifices!

The earth is still there for great souls to choose freely. For the lonesome and the twain there still are many seats free, about which the breeze of quiet oceans wafts.

A free life is still there for great souls. Truly, he who posses-ses little is least possessed. Praised be the small poverty!

Only where state ends does the man who is not superfluous begin; there begins the song of necessity, the unique and ir-replaceable melody. There where the state *ends*—take a good look, my brothers! Don't you see it, this rainbow and bridge of the Overman?

Thus spoke Zarathustra.

On The Flies of the Market Place

Escape into your solitude, my friend. You seem deaf-ened by the noise of the great men and stung by the stings of the small men.

The woods and crags can preserve a dignified silence. Be like the spreading tree that you love: quietly and attentively it hangs over the sea.

Where solitude ends the market place begins; and where the market place begins there the noise of the great actors also begins, and the buzzing of the poisonous flies.

In the world even the best things count for nothing unless someone makes a show of them. The people call these pro-ducers great men.

The mob comprehends little of greatness, that is to say, of

creativeness. But it has a feeling for all impresarios and actors of great things.

The world revolves about the inventors of new values—invisibly it revolves. The people and reputation revolve about the play actor. That is the course of the world.

The actor has intelligence but little integrity. He always believes in that which causes the strongest belief: belief in *himself*.

He has a new belief tomorrow, and the day after tomorrow another. Like the people he has nimble senses and is changeable like the weather.

To overthrow means to prove; to excite means to convince. And blood is for him the best reason of all.

A truth that will slip into fine ears only he calls a lie and nothing. Truly, he believes only in gods who make a big noise in the world!

The market place is full of solemn jesters—and the people are proud of these great men! They are the lords of the day.

But time presses and so they press you. From you also they want a Yes or No. Woe to you, if you place your stool between For and Against.

Do not be envious of these people with absolute convictions and these impatient men, you lover of truth! Truth never went arm in arm with an absolute.

Because of these impatient people go back to your security. Only in the market place are you attacked by a Yes or No.

Experience is a slow thing for all deep wells; they must wait a long time before they know what fell into their depths.

Every great thing takes place aside from the market place and glory. The inventors of new values always lived aside from the market place and glory.

Escape into your solitude, my friend; I see you stung by poisonous flies. Escape into the cold, strong air.

Escape into your solitude! You have lived too near to the puny and miserable men. Flee from their hidden revenge! Toward you they feel nothing but revenge. Do not raise your arm against them! They are innumerable and it is not your lot to be a flyswatter.

These puny and miserable men are numberless; and raindrops and weeds have destroyed many a proud edifice.

You are not a stone, but many drops have already made a hollow. The many drops may yet break and shatter you.

I see that the poisonous flies have exhausted you and drawn blood in a hundred places, and your pride will not even let you resent it.

In all innocence they want your blood, their bloodless souls long for blood—so they bite in all innocence.

But you are profound, you suffer too deeply even from small wounds, and before they are healed the same poisonous worm crawled over your hand.

You are too proud to kill these pilferers. But do not let it be your fate to bear all their poisonous guilt.

They buzz about you with their praise, but their praise is an intrusion; they want the nearness of your skin and blood.

They flatter you as they would a god or a devil; they whine in front of you as before a god or a devil. What is that to you! They still are flatterers and whiners and nothing more.

Often they are very charming toward you. But that was always the trick of cowards. Yes, the cowards are clever!

Their puny souls ponder much about you—you constantly are questionable to them. Everything that is pondered much becomes questionable.

They will find fault with every one of your virtues. They really pardon only—your mistakes.

Because you are kind and just you say: "They cannot be blamed for their puny lives."

But their puny souls say: "Every great life is culpable."

Even when you are kind to them they feel themselves despised by you; and they will return your kindness with hidden unkindness.

Your quiet pride goes against their taste; they rejoice if you are ever modest enough to be vain.

That which we recognize in a person we also kindle in him. So be on your guard against the little people!

They feel themselves small in your presence, and their lowliness glimmers and glows in hidden revenge against you.

Didn't you notice that often they became silent when you approached them and that their strength left them like the smoke from a dying fire?

Yes, my friend, to your neighbors you are this bad conscience, for they are unworthy of you. So they hate you and would like to suck your blood.

Your neighbors will always be poisonous flies. That which is great in you—that necessarily makes them more poisonous and more like flies.

My friend, escape into your solitude and into the cold, strong air. It is not your lot to swat flies.

Thus spoke Zarathustra.

ON THE THOUSAND GOALS AND ONE

Zarathustra saw many lands and many peoples and so he discovered the good and evil of many peoples. No greater power did he find on earth than good and evil.

No people could live without evaluating. If, however, it wishes to preserve itself it must not evaluate in the same way as its neighbor.

Many a thing that was called good by one people was a mockery and shame to another: so I discovered. Much that was considered bad in one place was decked with purple honors in another.

One neighbor never understood the other; always he was astounded by the neighbor's delusion and malice.

A table of values is suspended over every people. Behold, it is the table of their conquests over self; it is the voice of their will to power.

They call praiseworthy that which they consider difficult; they call good that which is indispensable and difficult. And that which frees them in their highest distress, namely what is rare and most difficult—that they praise as holy.

That which enables them to rule and conquer and shine forth to the horror and envy of their neighbors, that they call the lofty, the first, the standard of values, the meaning of all things.

Truly, my brother, once you have discovered a people's needs and land and climate, and its neighbor, then you will be able to divine the law of its conquests over self and why this is the way it ascends to its hope.

"You must always be the first and excel over the others; your jealous souls shall love no one unless it be your friend" —this made the heart of the Greek tremble, and was his path to greatness.

"Speak the truth and be expert with the bow and arrow" —that seemed precious and difficult for the people from which my name comes—the name both dear and difficult for me.

"Honor father and mother and obey them with all your heart" —this table of self-control another people suspended over itself and because of it became mighty and lasting.

"Be loyal, and for the sake of loyalty risk your honor and blood even for evil and dangerous causes": with that self-control another people became pregnant and heavy with great hopes.

Truly, men gave all their good and evil to themselves. Truly, they did not take it, they did not find it, it did not come to them as a voice from heaven.

It was man who put value upon things in order to preserve himself—he was the first to create the meaning of things, a human meaning. That is why he calls himself "man," that is, the evaluator.

To evaluate is to create. Hear this, you creators! To evaluate is itself the value and most precious of all treasured things.

Treasuring alone produces value, and without treasuring life would have no kernel. Hear this, you creators!

Change of values—that is the progress of creators. He who is destined to be a creator must always destroy.

Peoples were the first creators, and much later the individual; truly, the individual himself is still the newest creation.

Once peoples set up a table of values over themselves. Love

that wishes to rule and love that wishes to obey together created such tablets.

The joy in the herd is older than the delight in the I; and as long as the good conscience says herd, the bad conscience says: I.

Truly, this tricky I, the loveless, which seeks its advantage in the advantage of the many, that is not the origin of the herd, but its downfall.

Always it was the lovers and creators who created good and evil. The fire of love glows in the names of all virtues, and the fire of anger.

Zarathustra saw many lands and many peoples. No greater power did he find on earth than the works of the lovers: "good" and "evil" are they called.

Truly, the power of this praise and censure is a monster. Who will tame it, brothers? Who will throw the yoke over the thousand necks of this beast?

Hitherto there were a thousand goals, for there were a thousand peoples. Only the yoke for the thousand necks is still missing, the *one* goal still is missing. As yet mankind has no goal.

But tell me, my brothers: if the goal is missing for mankind, is not then mankind itself still missing?

Thus spoke Zarathustra.

ON THE LOVE OF NEIGHBOR

You crowd around your neighbor and have beautiful words for it. But I say this: Your love of neighbor is your poor love of self.

You fled to your neighbor from yourself and would like to make a virtue of it. But I see through your "selflessness."

The You is older than the I; the You is hallowed but not yet the I. So man crowds about his neighbor. Am I advising love of neighbor? I would rather advise you to flee the nighest and to love the highest!

Higher than the love of neighbor is the love of the farthest

and the future. Higher than the love of man is the love of
things and specters.

This specter that runs along ahead of you, my brother, is
more beautiful than you. Why do you not give it your flesh
and bones? But you are afraid and run to your neighbor.

You cannot tolerate yourself and do not love yourself
enough. So now you try to tempt your neighbor to love, and
gild yourself with his error.

I wish that you could not bear all these nearest things and
their neighbors; you would then be obliged to be a friend of
yourself and your overflowing heart. When you wish to speak
well of yourself you invite a witness, and after you have
traduced him to think well of you, you too think well of yourself.

Not only he who speaks against his better knowledge lies,
but he lies most of all who speaks without knowledge. In that
manner you speak of yourself to others and deceive your
neighbor.

The fool says: "Association with others spoils one's character, especially when one has none."

One person goes to his neighbor because he is seeking himself, another because he wishes to lose himself. Your deficient
love for yourself turns your solitude into a prison.

It is those who are distant who pay for your love of neighbor, and when five of you are gathered a sixth must always
die.

Nor do I love your festivals. I found too many play actors
present, and often even the audience behaves like actors.

I am not recommending the neighbor to you, but the friend.
Let the friend be for you the festival of the earth and an
anticipation of the Overman.

I am teaching to you the friend and his overflowing heart.
But one must know how to be a sponge if one wishes to be
loved by an overflowing heart.

I am teaching the friend in whom the world is complete, a
chalice of good—the creative friend who always has a
complete world to give away.

And just as the world unrolled for him, so he sees it roll

together again in cycles, and the evolving of the good from the evil, as the evolving of purpose from chance.

May the future and the farthest things be the purpose of your today; in your friend you must love the Overman as your purpose.

My brothers, I do not advise love of the nighest; I advise love of the highest.

Thus spoke Zarathustra.

ON THE BITE OF THE VIPER

One day Zarathustra had fallen asleep under a fig tree because it was hot, and had thrown his arms over his face. Then a viper came and bit his neck so that the pain made Zarathustra cry out. When he had put down his arms he saw the snake. It in turn recognized the eyes of Zarathustra, writhed awkwardly and tried to get away. "Please stay," said Zarathustra, "as yet you have not accepted my thanks! You awoke me in time. I still have a long way to go." "Your way is very short," the viper answered sadly, "my poison kills." Zarathustra smiled and said: "When did a dragon ever die from the poison of a snake? But take back your poison! You are not rich enough to give it to me." Then the viper fell about Zarathustra's neck and licked the wound.

Once, when Zarathustra told his disciples about this, they asked: "What, O Zarathustra, is the moral of your story?" Zarathustra answered: "The good and just call me the destroyer of morality; my story is amoral.

But if you have an enemy do not repay evil with good, for that would put him to shame. Rather prove to him that he has done you a good turn.

It is better to be angry with him than to put him to shame! And I do not like to see you bless when you are cursed. It is better to curse a little yourself.

And if a great wrong has been done you then quickly add five little ones of your own. It is terrible to see a man all alone oppressed by guilt.

Do you know this? A shared wrong is half a right. Only he who is able to bear it should assume the wrong.

A small revenge is more humane than no revenge. And unless punishment is also a right and an honor for the offender, I do not like your punishments. It is more distinguished to take the blame than to insist on being in the right, especially when one is right. Only one must be rich enough to do so.

Also, I do not like your cold justice; in the eyes of your judges there always lurks the hangman and his cold iron.

Tell me, where can justice be found which is love with seeing eyes?

You must discover a love which will bear not only punishment but all guilt as well! You must discover a justice which will acquit every one excepting the judge!

Do you wish to hear this also? For him who wishes to be wholly just, even the lie becomes a human kindness.

But what chance is there to be wholly just! How can I give each man that which is his! Let this be enough: I will give each man what is mine.

And finally, my brothers, take heed not to wrong any hermit! How could a hermit forget! How requite!

A hermit is like a deep well. It is easy enough to throw a stone into it; but tell me: when it has sunk to the bottom who will bring it up again? Take care and do not insult the hermit! But if you do, well, then kill him also!"

Thus spoke Zarathustra.

ON THE VIRTUE OF GIVING

1

When Zarathustra had taken his farewell from the city that he loved and which called itself The Motley Cow, many who called themselves his disciples came to see him on his way. When they came to a crossroads Zarathustra told them that he now wished to go alone, for he liked to be alone. As a farewell gift his disciples gave him a cane with a golden head in the form of the sun about which a serpent coiled itself. Zarathustra was delighted with the staff and leaned upon it. Then he spoke thus to his disciples:

Tell me, how did gold get to be the highest value? Because it is uncommon and impractical and shining and mild in its splendor. It always spends itself. Only as an image of the highest virtue did gold attain the highest value. The eye of the giver shines like gold. The light of gold makes peace between sun and moon.

Uncommon is the highest virtue and impractical, its light is brilliant and mild; the highest virtue is the virtue of giving.

I understand you well, my brothers: like me you are in search of the virtue of giving. What would you have in common with cats and wolves?

You thirst to become sacrifices and gifts yourselves; and therefore you thirst to heap all riches upon your soul.

Insatiably you long for treasures and gems because your virtue is insatiable in its desire to give.

You force all things to come to you and become yours so that they may flow back from your treasure-trove as gifts of your love.

Verily, such love of giving must be a robber of all values; but I call such selfishness hale and holy.

There is another selfishness, one all-too-poor, a greedy one, which wants always to steal, the selfishness of the diseased, a sick selfishness.

With the eye of the thief it examines all things that shine; with the greed of hunger it measures him who has much to eat; and it always steals about the table of the givers.

I call this greed disease and a hidden degeneration; the thievish greed of such selfishness tells of a diseased body.

Tell me, my brothers, what is rated bad and worst? Is it not *degeneration*? And we always suspect degeneration where the giving soul is missing.

Our path is upward, from the genus upward to the over-genus. But the degenerate mind, which says, "All for myself," is a horror to us.

Our senses fly upward; so they are a metaphor of our body, a metaphor of our elevation. The names of virtues are metaphors of such elevation.

Thus the body, evolving and struggling, goes through history. But the mind, what is its function? It is the companion, herald and echo of the battles and victories of the body.

All names of good and evil are metaphors; they do not express, they merely beckon. He is a fool who would want definite knowledge from them.

Heed, my brothers, every hour in which your spirit would speak in metaphors. There is the origin of your virtue.

There the body is uplifted and resurrected; with its delight it enthralls the spirit so that it becomes a creator, an evaluator, a lover, and a benefactor of all things.

When your heart surges wide and full like a stream, a blessing and a danger to those living near it: that is the origin of your virtue.

When you are above praise and censure and your will wants to command all things as the will of a lover: that is the origin of your virtue.

When you despise comfort and the soft bed and cannot bed yourself far enough from the weaklings: that is the origin of your virtue.

When you will but a *single* will and you call this cessation of all need your necessity: that is the origin of your virtue.

Truly, it is a new good and evil! Truly, a new surging and the voice of a new spring!

It is power, this new virtue; a ruling idea, and around it a clever soul; a golden sun, and around it the serpent of knowledge.

2

Here Zarathustra was silent for a while and looked upon his disciples with affection. Then he continued to speak —and his voice was transformed.

My brothers, remain true to the earth with the power of your virtue!

Let your love of giving and your knowledge serve the meaning of the earth! So I beg and beseech you.

Let it not fly away from earthly things and beat its wings against eternal walls! Alas, there was always so much virtue gone astray!

Like me, lead this strayed virtue back to earth—yes, back to the body and life so that it may give meaning to the earth, a human meaning!

Both mind and virtue have hitherto gone astray in a hundred ways. Even now there still dwell in our body all these delusions and error and there they have become body and will.

In a hundred ways both mind and virtue have hitherto experimented and gone astray. Yes, man was an experiment. Alas, much nonsense and error has been incorporated in us.

Not only the reason of millenniums—its madness also breaks forth in us. It is dangerous to be an heir.

We are still fighting step by step with the giant named chance, and hitherto nonsense, the non-sense, still ruled.

Your mind and your virtue should serve the meaning of this earth, my brothers; and the value of all things shall be set anew by you! Therefore you must be warriors! Therefore you must be creators!

With knowledge the body purifies itself; experimenting with knowledge it elevates itself; for the man of knowledge all drives become holy; for the elevated the soul becomes gay.

Physician, help yourself; thus you will also help your patient. Let that be his best help, namely that he turns his eyes upon him who heals himself.

There are a thousand paths which have not yet been traversed, a thousand healths and hidden islands of life. Unexhausted and undiscovered still is man and the earth of man.

Watch and listen, you lonely ones! Winds with mysterious wing-beats are coming from the future, and there are glad tidings for fine ears.

You solitary ones of today, who have set yourselves apart, some day you will be a people; from you who have chosen yourselves there shall grow a chosen people—and out of it the Overman.

Truly, the earth shall yet be a place of recovery! Already a new fragrance lies over it, one that brings health—and a new hope!

3

When Zarathustra had spoken these words he grew silent, like one who had not yet spoken his last word. For a long time he hesitatingly balanced his staff in his hand. Finally he spoke thus—and his voice was transformed:

I am going alone now, my disciples! You also go along and alone. Thus do I will it. Verily, I advise you: go away from me and be on your guard against Zarathustra! Better yet, be ashamed of him! Perhaps he has deceived you. The man of understanding must not only be able to love his enemies but to hate his friends as well.

One repays a teacher badly by always remaining a pupil. And why should you not pluck at my wreath?

You revere me; but what if one day your reverence topples? Take care lest a statue crush you.

You say that you believe in Zarathustra? But what is there to Zarathustra? You say that you are my believers? But what is there to any believers? You had not yet sought yourselves when you found me. That is the way of all believers and therefore there is so little to any belief.

Now I am asking you to lose me and to find yourselves; not until you have all denied me will I return to you.

Truly, with other eyes will I then seek my lost friends; with a different love will I then love you.

And at some time you will have become my friends, and children of *one* hope. Then I will be with you a third time so that we may celebrate the great noon together.

The great noon is the time when man stands in the middle of his course between beast and Overman and so celebrates his highest hope, for it is the path toward a new morning.

Then as he goes down he will bless himself because he is going further on; and the sun of his knowledge will have reached its zenith.

"Dead are all gods. Now we want the Overman to live!" Let this be our last will at the great noon!

Thus spoke Zarathustra.

Part Two

THE CHILD WITH THE MIRROR

Zarathustra returned to the hills and the solitude of his cave and withdrew from men, and waited like a sower who had scattered his seed. But his soul was full of impatience and a longing for those whom he loved, for he still had much to give. But this is the hardest thing of all: to close your open hand out of affection and to preserve your modesty as giver.

So he passed months and years in solitude, but his wisdom grew and the fullness of it pained him.

But one morning he awoke even before dawn, lay on his bed in thought for a long time, and finally spoke to his heart:

"What was it that frightened me in my dream so that I awoke? Did not a child with a mirror approach me? Oh, Zarathustra, said the child, look at yourself in the mirror! But when I looked into the mirror I cried out in distress, for I did not see myself in it but the grimace and mockery of a devil. Truly, I understand the sign and the warning of the dream only too well: my *teaching* is in danger; weeds try to pass as wheat!

My enemies have become mighty and have distorted the image of my teachings so that those dearest to me must be ashamed of the gifts which I gave them. My friends have been lost to me; the hour has come to seek those who are lost." With these words Zarathustra arose quickly, but not like one who is frightened and gasping for air: rather like a seer and a singer upon whom the spirit has fallen. His eagle and his serpent looked upon him in astonishment, for happiness shone from his eyes.

"What has come over me, my animals?" said Zarathustra. "Am I not transformed? Did not bliss come to me like a storm?

My happiness is foolish and will say foolish things; it is still too young. So be patient with it.

My happiness has wounded me. All those who suffer shall be my physicians! I am again allowed to go down to my friends, and to my enemies! Again Zarathustra is allowed to speak and give and expend his best on those whom he loves.

My impatient love overflows in streams, downwards toward the dawn and the setting. My soul rushes into the valleys out of the reticent hills and storms of pain.

For too long a time have I longed and looked into the distance. I belonged to solitude too long and so I forgot how to be silent. I have become mouth wholly, and the rushing of the brook from a high rock; my soul longs to roar downward into the valleys.

And should the stream of my love fall upon difficult ground, what can keep the stream from finally finding its way to the sea!

To be sure, within me there is a sea that is alone and self-sufficient; but the stream of my love will carry it down— into the sea!

I am going new paths; a new speech comes to me; like all creators I have grown tired of the old ways of speaking. My spirit will no longer go on well-worn soles. All speech seems too slow to me. Storm, I will spring onto your wagon! And even you I will whip with my malice!

I will sweep over the wide seas like a cry and a rejoicing until I find the blessed isles where my brothers dwell. And my enemies among them! Oh, how I now love everyone to whom I am permitted to speak! My enemies also belong to my happiness.

And when I want to mount my wildest horse, my spear will always be my best help; it is always the best servant of my foot—the spear which I hurl against my enemies! How grateful I am to my enemies who finally give me the chance to hurl it!

The tension of my cloud was too great. Between the bright flashes of the lightning I will throw hailstorms into the depths.

Then my chest will expand mightily, mightily it will blow its storm over the hills, then relief will come.

Truly, my bliss and my freedom come like a storm! But I want my enemies to think that the devil is raging over their heads.

You also, my friends, will be frightened at my wild wisdom and perhaps you will run away together with my enemies.

Oh, that I knew how to entice you back with the flutes of shepherds! Oh, that my lioness, my wisdom, had learned to roar gently! Many things we have learned from each other!

On the lonely hills my wisdom became pregnant; on rough stones it gave birth to its young, its youngest.

Now it runs foolishly through the hard desert and searches and searches for soft grass, this old, wild wisdom of mine. That which is dearest to it it would like to bed on the soft turf of your hearts, on your love, my friends!"

Thus spoke Zarathustra.

IN THE BLESSED ISLES

The figs fall from the trees and are good and sweet; and as they fall their red skin bursts. I am the north wind to ripe figs.

Like ripe figs my teaching also falls for you, my friends. Now enjoy its juice and sweet meat! Autumn is about us, and clear heavens, and afternoon. See, what a fullness is about us! From this fullness it is beautiful to look out upon distant seas.

Once, when one looked out upon distant seas, one said God; but now I have taught you to say: Overman.

God is an inference, but I insist that your inferring reach no further than your creative will.

Could you *create* a god? —Very well, then stop speaking of gods! But surely you could create the Overman. Perhaps not you yourselves, my brethren! But you could make yourselves into fathers and ancestors of the Overman. Let this be your best creating.

God is an inference, but I insist that your inferring have its limit in that which can be thought through.

Could you *think* a god? But let this be your will to truth: that everything be translated into that which can be thought, seen and felt by man! You should think your senses through to the end.

What you called world must first be created by you; it itself shall become your reason, your image, your will and your love.

How could you endure life without this hope, you men of intellect? You would not want to have been born into the incomprehensible, nor into the unintelligible.

But to reveal my heart wholly to you, my friends: if there were gods how could I bear not to be a god! *Therefore* there are no gods.

To be sure, I drew this conclusion. Now it draws me.—

God is an inference. But who could drain all the torment of this inference without dying? Should he who creates be robbed of his faith, and the eagle of its soaring into the proud heights?

God is a thought that makes all that is straight to be crooked, and all that stands to whirl. Do you mean to say that time is done away with and all that is transitory is a lie?

To think this, is a whirl and a vertigo for the human frame

and nausea for the stomach. Truly, I call it a dancing sickness to infer such a thing. All this teaching of the One and the Complete, the Unmoved Satiated and Eternal, I call evil and inimical to man!

All that is intransitory—that is but a simile! And poets lie too much. The best metaphors should speak of time and change; they should be a praise and justification of all that is transitory!

To create—that is the great redemption from suffering and the easing of life. However, much suffering and much change is needed to produce the creator. But that is why you advocate and justify that which is transitory.

But in order that the creator be a child and be born, he must be willing also to be the mother and bear the pains of childbirth. Verily, my path was through a hundred souls and through a hundred cradles and pains of childbirth. Many a farewell I have taken and I know the last, heart-breaking hours.

But my creative will, my fate, wants it thus. Or, to speak more frankly, my will wants just this fate.

All my senses suffer and are imprisoned; but my will is always ready to bring freedom and joy. Willing sets free! That is the real teaching of will and freedom—this Zarathustra teaches.

No longer to will, no longer to evaluate, no longer to create! I hope that this great exhaustion will never come upon me!

Also in my search for knowledge I feel only my will's joy in begetting and becoming; and whatever innocence there is in my knowledge results from the presence of the will to beget in it.

This will of mine enticed me away from God and gods. What would there be to create if gods—existed!

But my fervent will to create constantly impels me anew toward man. So the hammer is impelled toward the stone.

In the stone, you men, I see an image sleeping, the image of my images! Alas, that it must sleep in the hardest, ugliest stone!

Now my hammer rages cruelly against its prison. Chips fly from the stone; but why should that concern me?

I will finish it, for a shadow came to me—the stillest and lightest of all things once rose before me!

The beauty of the Overman came to me as a shadow. What interest can I still have in gods!

Thus spoke Zarathustra.

ON THE TARANTULAS

Behold, this is the hiding place of the tarantula! Do you wish to see it? Here is its web; touch it and it will tremble. There it comes; welcome, tarantula!

On your back is your mark, the black triangle. And I know, too, what is in your heart.

Revenge is in your soul. Black scurf develops wherever you bite; your poison makes the soul whirl with revenge!

In this parable I am speaking to you who make the soul whirl, you preachers of *equality!* To me you are tarantulas and secretly vengeful!

But I will bring your ambushes to light; my laughter of the heights will laugh straight at you. I will tear at your web so that your rage will lure you from your cave of lies and your revenge pop out from behind your word "justice."

That man be redeemed from revenge: that is to me the bridge to the highest hope and the rainbow after long storms.

Tarantulas, to be sure, have very different intentions. "This is what justice is to us, namely that the world be covered by the storms of our revenge." So they tell each other.

"We will wreak revenge and heap abuse on everybody who is not like us"—thus runs the pledge of these tarantula-hearts.

"Henceforth the name for all virtue shall be 'will to equality'; and we will raise up our cry against all that has power."

It is the tyrant's madness of impotence, you preachers of equality, that makes you cry thus for "equality"; your hidden tyrannic lusts thus disguise themselves in terms of virtue!

Disappointed conceit and secret envy, perhaps the conceit and envy of your fathers, thus burst forth as the flame and madness of revenge.

What the father concealed finds expression in the son; and often I found the son to be the revealed secret of the father.

They resemble enthusiasts; however, it is not the heart that enthuses them but—revenge. And when they are subtle and cold, it is not their spirit but envy that makes them subtle and cold.

Their envy also leads them on the paths of the thinker and this is the mark of their envy: they always go too far, so that finally their exhaustion must lie down and sleep on the snow.

Revenge speaks out of every complaint, and in every praise there is malice, and their bliss is to act as judge.

Therefore I advise you, my friends, distrust all those in whom there is a strong impulse to judge! They are poor, miserable people; their eyes betray the hangman and the bloodhound.

Mistrust all those who like to speak of justice! Verily, more than honey is lacking in their souls.

And when they call themselves "the good and the righteous," do not forget that they lack nothing of the pharisee excepting—power.

My friends, I do not want to be confused or mistaken.

There are those who preach my teaching of life, and yet they are preachers of equality, and are tarantulas.

They speak in favor of life even though they sit in their holes, these poisonous spiders, and are inimical to life. They want merely to harm. They want to harm those who are in power for the time being; for among them the teaching of death is best understood.

If it were otherwise, these tarantulas would teach differently, for once they were the foremost at maligning the world and at burning heretics.

I do not want to be confused with these preachers of equality or mistaken for them. Justice tells *me*: "Men are not equal."

Nor shall they become so! What would my love for the Overman mean if I spoke otherwise?

They shall throng toward the future on a thousand bridges and paths, and there shall be more and more war and inequality among them; thus my great love makes me speak!

Their enmities shall make of them inventors of images and specters, and with their images and specters they shall wage the highest of battles with one another!

Good and evil, rich and poor, high and lowly, and all the names of values—all these shall be weapons and clashing marks of distinction to indicate that life must again and again overcome itself!

This life itself wishes to build itself up into the heights with pillars and stages; it wishes to have a view into far distances and towards blissful beauties. *For that* it must have height!

Because there is need of heights, steps and contradiction of the steps and of those ascending, are also necessary! Life wishes to ascend and in ascending overcome itself.

Take a look, my friends! Here where you see the cave of the tarantula rise the ruins of an old temple. Look at them with enlightened eyes!

Whoever it was who once let his thoughts tower high in stone here, knew about the mystery of all life like the wisest of men!

Here he teaches us in the plainest metaphor that even in beauty there must be conflict and inequality, and a struggle for power and mastery.

How divinely vault and arches meet as though in conflict; how their light and shadows strive with each other, these divine contenders.

With equal assurance and beauty let us also be enemies, my friends! Let us strive divinely with each other!

Alas, at this point my old enemy, the tarantula, bit me. With assurance and beauty it bit my finger!

"So punishment and justice are necessary," it thinks. "These songs in honor of enmity shall not have been sung in vain!"

Yes, it has avenged itself! Alas, it will make even my soul whirl with revenge! But to keep me from whirling, my friends, tie me fast to this pillar! It is better to be a saint at the pillar than a whirl of vengefulness!

Be assured, Zarathustra is not a whirlwind; and if he is a dancer, he still never will be a tarantula dancer!

Thus spoke Zarathustra.

ON THE FAMOUS SAGES

All you famous sages, you have served the people and the superstition of the people—and *not* the truth! And yet, it is just that for which you were revered.

So, too, your lack of belief was tolerated because it was amusing and a roundabout way to interest the people. So the master lets his slaves have their way and even takes pleasure in their impertinence.

But hated by the people as the wolf by dogs is the free spirit; the enemy of all fetters worships nothing and lives in forests.

To hound him out of his retreat—that is what the people have always called "sense of righteousness"; they still set their fiercest dogs upon him.

"Truth is established, as firmly as the people! Woe to him who still would search!" That has always been the cry.

You wanted to prove the people right in their reverence. That is what you called their "will to truth," you famous sages!

Your heart always made you say: "I am of the people; the voice of God came to me from there."

Stubborn and clever like a donkey, you were always the advocates of the people.

And many a man in power who wished to fare well with the people has had his horses led by—a donkey, a famous sage.

But now, you famous sages, I wish that you would throw off the lion's skin altogether! —the motley skin of the beast of prey and the shaggy hide of the investigator, searcher and conqueror.

Alas, you first would have to break your revering will if I am to believe in your "truthfulness."

To me that man is truthful who goes into godless deserts, and has broken his revering heart.

On the yellow sands and burned by the sun, he may, in his thirst, cast oblique glances towards islands rich in wells and where living things rest under dark trees. But his thirst cannot persuade him to become like these contented people, for where there are oases there also are idols.

Hungry, violent, lonesome, godless: thus the lion's will desires to be. Free from the bliss of slaves, redeemed from gods and adoration, fearless and fearful, great and lonely is the will of the truthful man.

The truthful, the free spirits have always dwelt in the desert as lords of the desert; but the well-fed, famous sages—the draught-animals—live in the cities. As donkeys they always draw the *people's* wagon.

I do not chide them because of it, really; but to me they still are servants and in harness even when the harness sparkles with gold.

Often they are good, praiseworthy servants; for virtue says: "If you must be a servant, then find the one to whom your service is of most use."

"By being his servant the spirit and the virtue of your master shall grow. Then you also will grow together with his spirit and virtue!"

It is true, you famous sages and servants of the people, you did grow with the spirit and virtue of the people—and the people because of you! I say this to your credit. Still, with all your virtues, you remain people, people with dull eyes, people who do not know what intelligence is! Intelligence is life that cuts into its own life and by its own torment increases its own knowledge. Did you know that?

And the bliss of such intelligence is this: to be anointed with tears and to be consecrated for the sacrifice. Did you know that?

And even the blindness and the searching and groping of the blind shall testify to the power of the sun into which he looked.

You know only the spark of the intellect, but you do not see the anvil which it is also, nor the cruelty of its hammer!

Truly, you do not know the pride of the intellect! Even less would you be able to bear its modesty if ever it wished to speak to you!

Never yet were you able to cast your intellect into a pit of snow; you are not hot enough for that! Nor do you know the ecstasies of its chill.

In all things you are too familiar with the spirit; and of wisdom you often make a sanitarium and a retreat for bad poets.

You are no eagles and therefore you never have experienced the joy in the terror of the intellect. He who is not a bird should not soar over abysses. I find you lukewarm; but the stream of deep intelligence is cold. Cold as ice are the deepest wells of the spirit, refreshing for hot hands and creators. I see your pose as honorable men, stiff and with a straight back, you famous sages! —neither a strong wind nor will impels you.

Did you never see a sail passing over the sea, rounded, bellowed and trembling because of the violence of the wind?

Like the sail, trembling from the violence of the spirit, my wisdom passes over the sea—my wild wisdom!

But you servants of the people, you famous sages, how would you *be able* to go with me!

Thus spoke Zarathustra.

THE SONG OF THE DANCE

One evening Zarathustra was walking through the woods with his disciples, and when he was looking for a spring, behold, he came upon a green meadow which was shut in by trees and bushes, and girls were dancing on it. As soon as the girls recognized Zarathustra they interrupted the dance. But Zarathustra approached them in a friendly manner and said:

"Do not stop your dance, you beautiful girls! I am no spoilsport with an evil eye, nor an enemy of girls.

I am God's advocate before the devil, and he is the spirit of gravity. Why would I disapprove of divine dances, you light-footed girls, or of maidens' feet with pretty ankles?

To be sure, I am a forest and a night of dark trees. But those who are not afraid of my darkness will find the roses under my cypresses.

Also, they will find the little god whom girls like most. He will lie beside the well, still and with his eyes closed. He went to sleep in bright daylight, the idler; perhaps he was chasing butterflies too much.

Do not be angry with me, you pretty dancers, if I discipline him a little. He may cry out and weep but even then he is laughable. I will have him beg you for a dance with tears in his eyes and I myself will sing a song to accompany the dance; a song of the dance and a mockery of the spirit of gravity, my most high and mighty devil, of whom they say that he is the 'lord of this earth.'"

And this is the song that Zarathustra sang when Cupid and the girls were dancing together.

Not long ago I looked into your eyes, oh life! And I seemed to sink into the unfathomable. But you drew me out with a golden rod; you laughed at me and mocked when I called you unfathomable.

"All fishes speak that way," you said; "that which they do not fathom they call unfathomable. But I am merely changeable and wild and in all things a woman, and not a virtuous one, even though you men call me 'the depth' or 'loyalty,' 'the eternal,' 'the mysterious.' But you men always endow us with your own virtues —oh, you virtuous ones!"

Thus life laughed, the incredible one; but I never believe her laughter when she speaks evilly of herself.

And when I confronted my wild wisdom, it said to me angrily: "You will, you desire, you love. For that reason alone do you praise life!"

I had almost given her a wicked answer and told the angry one the truth. One cannot be more wicked than to tell one's wisdom "the truth."

For that is the way things are among us three: really and thoroughly I love only life, and, indeed, most when I hate it!

But that I am fond of wisdom, and often too fond, is merely because it reminds me so very much of life! It has its eye, its laughter and even its golden fishing rod. Can I be blamed because the two look so alike?

And once when I asked life: What is this wisdom? —it answered eagerly: "Oh, yes, wisdom! One thirsts for it and never has enough; one looks through veils and gropes through nets. Is it beautiful? How can I tell! But it is a lure for even the oldest carps. It is changeable and stubborn; I have often seen it bite its lips and draw a comb through its hair the wrong way. Perhaps it is evil and false and in all things a woman. But when it speaks ill of itself, just then it seduces most."

When I said this to life it laughed scornfully and closed its eyes. "Are you perhaps speaking of me? And what if you are right, does one say these things so boldly? But now speak to me of your wisdom."

Now you again opened your eyes, beloved life! And at that I seemed to sink into the unfathomable.

Thus Zarathustra sang. But when the dance was at an end and the maidens had gone, he became sad.

"The sun has long since set," he said at last; "the meadow is damp and a cool breeze comes from the woods.

There is an unknown presence about me and it is looking at me thoughtfully: How is it that you still are living, Zarathustra?

Why? Wherefor? Whereby? Whither? Where? How? Is it not a folly to go on living?—

Oh, my friends, it is the evening that makes me ask thus. Forgive my sadness. The evening has come. Forgive me that it has turned evening!"

Thus spoke Zarathustra.

ON IMMACULATE PERCEPTION

Yesterday as the moon rose it seemed to me that it was about to give birth to a sun, so broad and pregnant did it lie at the horizon. But I saw that its pregnancy was a lie; and I would sooner believe in the man in the moon than the woman.

To be sure, there is little of the man about this timid reveller of the night. Indeed, it wanders over the roofs with a bad conscience. For it is lustful and jealous, this monk in the moon, lustful for the earth and the pleasures of lovers.

No, I do not like this tomcat on the roofs! I am disgusted with all those who steal about half-closed windows!

Piously and softly it wanders along on carpets of stars: —but I dislike the softly treading feet of men without the ring of a single spur.

The step of every honest person talks, but the cat steals along. Like a cat the moon goes along and with no honesty.

This parable is for you sentimental hypocrites, you of "pure perception"! I call you—lecherous!

You, too, love the earth and what is of this earth: I saw through you well! But in your love there is shame and a bad conscience, for you are just like the moon. These things have persuaded your mind but not your bowels to despise all that is of this earth; they, however, are the strongest thing about you! And now your mind is ashamed that it obeys the bowels and because of this shame takes the path of stealth and lies.

Your deceptive mind says to you: "The highest thing to me would be to look upon life without desire and not with the tongue hanging out like a dog. To be happy in contemplation, with the will at rest, without the grasp or greed of selfishness—the whole body cold and grey as ashes, but with the drunken eyes of the moon!

"This I would like best"—thus the deceiver deceives himself—"to love the earth as the moon loves it and to touch its beauty with the eyes only. And this shall be for me the *immaculate* perception of all things: that I desire nothing of things excepting that they shall lie before me like a mirror with a hundred eyes."

Oh, you sentimental hypocrites, you lechers! There is no innocence in your desires and so you slander desire itself!

Verily, not as those who create, beget, or delight in the process of becoming do you love the earth!

Where is innocence to be found? There where there is the will to beget. And that person has the purest will who desires to create beyond himself.

And where is there beauty? Where I *must will* with all my will; where I will to love and perish so that an image may not remain a mere image.

To love and perish: that has forever rhymed. The will to love: that meant also to be willing to die. This I say to you cowards!

And now you want your emasculated squints to be taken for "contemplation"! And what cowardly eyes can touch should be named "beautiful"! Oh, you defilers of noble names.

But this shall be your curse, you immaculate ones, you of pure perception: that you shall never give birth, even though you lie at the horizon broad and pregnant!

Verily, you fill your mouths with noble words and we are supposed to believe that your heart is overflowing, you liars.

But my words are simple, despised, crooked words; I gladly pick up whatever falls under the table at your meals. With them I can always—tickle the nose of hypocrites!

There is always a bad atmosphere about you and your meals; your lies and secrets poison the air!

Have the courage to believe yourselves—yourselves and your bowels! The man who does not believe himself always lies.

You held the mask of a god before yourselves, you "pure" ones; into the mask of a god your horrible worms crawled.

Truly, you are deceivers with your "contemplation"! Zarathustra himself once was fooled by your godlike skins and had no suspicion of the coiled worms with which you were filled.

He once believed that the soul of a god was playing in your

games, you of pure perception! He could imagine no better art than your arts! Distance from you hid from him the filth of the snakes and the evil odor, and that the lustful cunning of a lizard was crawling about you.

But when I came *near* it became day for me; and now your day has come—the love-making of the moon has come to an end! Take a look! There he stands, pale and caught in the act—by the dawn!

There it comes, the glowing ball—*its* love for the earth is rising.

All love of the sun is innocence and longing to create!

Look at it as it rises over the sea impatiently! Do you not feel the thirst and hot breath of its love? It wants to suck at the sea and draw its depth into the heights, and then the longing of the sea rises with a thousand breasts. It wants to be kissed and sucked at by the thirst of the sun; it wants to become air and height and the path of light and light itself!

Verily, like the sun I love all life and all deep seas. And this shall be my meaning of perception: all depth shall rise up—to my height!

Thus spoke Zarathustra.

On Great Events

There is an island in the sea, not far from Zarathustra's Blessed Isles, on which there is a fire-mountain that constantly smokes. The people, and especially the old women of the people, say of this mountain that, like a granite block, it stands before the gate to the underworld; but that through this fire-mountain there is a narrow path downward, leading to this gate of the underworld.

It came to pass at the time when Zarathustra dwelt in the Blessed Isles that a ship dropped anchor at the island on which the fire-mountain stands, and its crew went on land to shoot rabbits. Toward noon, when the captain and crew were together again, they suddenly saw a man coming towards them through the air, and a voice said clearly: "It is time. It is high time!" But when the figure was very close to them, it suddenly flew past them like a shadow in the direction of the fire-mountain. Then with greatest consternation they realized that it was Zarathustra; for all, with the exception of the captain, had already seen him and loved him in the manner of the people's love, that is to say, half love and half shyness. "Look!" said the old helmsman, "Zarathustra is going to hell!"

About the same time that the sailors landed on the fire island, there was a rumor about that Zarathustra had disappeared; and when his friends were questioned they said that he had taken ship by night without saying where he was going. This caused an uneasiness, and three days later the story of the sailors added to this unrest. Now all the people said that the devil had taken Zarathustra. His disciples laughed at this kind of talk, and one of them even said: "I would sooner believe that Zarathustra had gone to take the devil." But at the bottom of their hearts they were all filled with worry and longing. Consequently they rejoiced greatly when, on the fifth day, Zarathustra appeared among them.

This is the report of Zarathustra's conversation with the fire dog: The earth has a hide, he said, and this hide has diseases. One of these diseases, for example, is called "man." Another disease is called "fire dog," about which men have told, and listened to, many a lie.

I took to the sea to fathom this secret, and I have seen the truth of it naked, indeed, barefoot up to the neck.

I now know what there is to this fire dog, and, at the same time, to all devils of wreckage and revolution, of whom not only old women are afraid. "Out with you, fire dog, out of your depths!" I cried, "and admit how deep this depth of yours is! Where did you get this stuff that you snort up?

You drank abundantly of the sea; your salty speech shows that. Verily, for a dog of the depths you took too much of your nourishment from the surface! At most I will take you for the ventriloquist of the earth; always when I heard devils of wreckage and revolution speak I found them to be like you: salty, lying and superficial.

You understand how to growl and obscure things with ashes! No one is better at being loudmouthed, and you are expert at the art of making slime to boil! Wherever you are there must always be slime nearby and much that is spongy, pock-marked and forcibly compressed. All this wants to be free.

All of you love to howl 'Freedom,' but I have learned not to believe in 'great events' when there is much howling and smoke.

You had better believe me, friend noise-of-hell! The greatest events—they are not our loudest but our most quiet hours. The world does not revolve about the inventors of new noises but about the inventors of new values; it revolves *inaudibly*.

You must admit: little had happened after the noise and smoke had cleared away. What does it matter that a city has become a mummy and that a statue lies in the mud!

This word also I am giving all overthrowers of statues: probably the greatest of all follies is to throw salt into the sea and statues into the mud. The statue lay in the slime of your contempt; but the general rule is that out of contempt life and living beauty grow again! It will rise with more godlike features and will be seductive because of its suffering. Indeed, the time will come when it will thank you for having overthrown it, you revolutionaries! This is my advice to kings and churches and to everything that is afflicted with the infirmities of age and virtue: have yourselves overthrown so that you may return to life—and virtue return to you!"

This was my speech to the fire dog. Then he interrupted me and said crossly: "Church? What is that?"

"Church," I answered, "is a kind of state and, indeed, the most deceitful of all. But be silent, you dog of a hypocrite! You surely know your kind best of all! Like you, the state is a hypocritical dog; like you, it likes to speak with smoke and growls—to make people believe that, like you, it speaks from the very bowels of things. For it, the state, wants to be the most important beast on earth. And people believe it, too."

When I had said that, the fire dog acted as though insane with envy. "What," he cried, "the most important beast on earth? And people believe it?" And so much hot air and horrible sounds issued from his throat that I thought he would choke with anger and envy.

At last he became more quiet and his gasping lessened, and I laughed and said: "You are angry, fire dog. So I am right about you! To show you how right I am, hear about another fire dog; he does really speak from the heart of the earth. His breath is gold and golden rain. What are ashes and smoke and hot slime to him! Laughter flutters from him like a gay cloud; he has no use for your gurgling and spewing and the rumbling of your bowels. But he takes his gold and his laughter from the heart of the earth.

Remember this: *the heart of the earth is of gold.*"

When the fire dog heard this he could not bear to listen any longer. He drew in his tail for shame, gave a timid "bow-wow," and crawled down into his cave.

This is the story Zarathustra told. But his disciples barely listened to him because of their great desire to tell him of the sailors, the rabbits and the flying man.

"What am I to think of that!" said Zarathustra. "Am I a ghost? But it probably was my shadow. Perhaps you have already heard of the wanderer and his shadow? But it is clear that I must restrain it. Otherwise it may spoil my reputation."

Again Zarathustra shook his head and speculated: "What am I to think of that? Why did the specter cry, 'It is time! It is high time!' High time for *what?*"

Thus spoke Zarathustra.

ON REDEMPTION

One day when Zarathustra was crossing the bridge, the cripples and beggars surrounded him, and one cripple spoke thus to him: "Look, Zarathustra! Even the people are learning from you and beginning to believe in your teaching. But you still must do one thing before they will believe you wholly:

you must also convince us cripples! Here you have a fine selection and, indeed, an opportunity with more than one forelock. You can heal the blind and help the lame to walk; you might also relieve the person who has too much behind him. That, it seems to me, would be the real way to make the cripples believe in Zarathustra!"

Zarathustra answered the speaker thus: "When you deprive the hunchback of his hump you take away his spirit—so the people teach. And when you give eyes to the blind man, he sees too many bad things, so that he curses the person who has healed him. But the greatest harm is done to the lame man who is made to walk. For as soon as he can walk his vices run away with him—so the people teach about the cripples. But why should not Zarathustra learn from the people, if the people learn from Zarathustra?

Since I have been among men this is the least important thing that I have seen: that this person lacks an eye, another an ear, and a third a leg; and that there are others who have lost a tongue or a nose or the head. I see and saw worse things and many a thing so horrible that I hesitate to mention it, even a few things that I even dislike to be silent about. I am thinking of people who lack everything, excepting that they have one thing too much, people who are nothing at all excepting a big eye or a big mouth or a big belly or some other big thing—I call them inverted cripples.

When I left my solitude and crossed the bridge for the first time, I did not believe my eyes, and looked and looked again, and said finally: 'That is an ear, as big as a man.' Nevertheless I looked more closely and, indeed, under the ear something did move that was miserably small and insignificant and weak. And, indeed, the immense ear was attached to a small, thin stalk, and this stalk was a man! By using a magnifying glass one could even see a small, envious face, and also that a bloated little soul was dangling from the stalk. The people, however, told me that the big ear was not only a man but a great man, a genius. But I never did believe people when they talk about great men, and I held to my belief that it was an inverted cripple who had too little of all things and too much of one thing."

When he had said this to the hunchback and to those for whom the hunchback was mouthpiece and advocate, Zarathustra was greatly dismayed and said to his disciples:

Truly, my friends, I walk among men as among fragments and parts of men! This is the most terrible thing to observe: that I find man fragmented and scattered as on a battlefield or a butcher's bench. When my eye escapes from the now to the once-upon-a-time, it always finds the same: fragments and limbs and gruesome accidents—but no men!

The now and the past on earth—oh, my friends—that *to me* is hardest to bear. I would not know how to stay alive if I were not also a seer of those things that still must come. A seer, a man of will, a creator, a future and a bridge to the future—and, alas, also, so to speak, a cripple on this bridge. Zarathustra is all these things.

You also have often asked yourselves: "What is Zarathustra to us? What meaning should he have for us?" And your answers were questions, as is my habit. Does he make promises or does he fulfill? Is he a conqueror, or is he an inheritor? A harvest or a plowshare? A physician or a convalescent? Is he a poet or a soothsayer? A liberator or a tamer? A good man or an evil man? I wander among men as among fragments of the future, of the future that I see before me.

And whatever I compose and gather, I do so in order to compose and gather into one whole that which is fragment and riddle and gruesome accident. How could I bear to be a man if man were not also a composer and solver of riddles and redeemer of chance! To redeem the past and recreate the "it was" into "thus I willed it"—that alone I would call redemption!

The will alone is the liberator and bringer of joy. This is what I taught you. Now learn this also: the will itself is still a prisoner. Willing frees; but what do you call the thing that puts even the liberator in chains?

"It has been": this is the gnashing of teeth and the most forsaken sadness of the will. Being impotent in the face of all

that has been done, it is an angry observer of all that is past.
The will cannot will backwards. Its most forsaken sadness is
that it cannot break time and the desires of time. Willing
frees. But what does the will contrive in order to rid itself of
sadness and to mock at its prison?

Every prisoner is a fool! And in a foolish manner the imprisoned will frees itself. The fact that time does not go backwards makes it angry. "That which once was" is the stone that
it cannot roll back. Therefore out of anger and discontent it
simply rolls stones and takes revenge on all things which, like
itself, feel anger and discontent.

Thus the will, this liberator, became malicious, and now,
because it cannot go backwards, it takes revenge on everything that is capable of suffering. This is what revenge itself
is: the will's ill will against time and its "it was." Indeed, a
great folly dwells in our will; and the fact that this folly acquired intelligence became a curse for all mankind!

The spirit of revenge, my friends, has hitherto been man's
best reflection, and wherever there was suffering one wanted
it also to be called punishment.

"Punishment" is what revenge calls itself, and with this
deception it takes on the pretense of a good conscience. And
because there is suffering in merely willing, because one cannot will backwards, therefore willing itself and all life was
said to be—punishment!

Now cloud upon cloud rolled over the mind until at last
madness preached: "All things pass away, therefore all things
deserve to pass away!—And justice itself is the very law of
time: that it must devour its children" —so madness preached.

"Morality is the order according to law and punishment.
Oh, where is there a redemption from the course of things and
the punishment 'existence'?" So madness preached. "Can there
be redemption if there is an eternal law? Alas, the stone 'it
was' cannot be rolled away; and all punishment also must be
forever!" This madness preached.

"No deed can be made undone; how could it be made undone by punishment! This is what there is eternal about the
punishment 'existence': that existence must eternally be ac-

tion and guilt! Unless the will redeems itself and turns into non-willing—" But, my brothers, you know this fairy song of madness.

I led you away from all such fairy songs when I taught you that the will is a creator. All "it was" is a fragment, a riddle, a gruesome chance, until the creative will adds: "But I wanted it thus!" Until the creative will adds: "But so do I will it! So shall I will it!"

But has it already spoken thus? And when will it happen? Is the will already relieved of its own folly? Has the will become its own redeemer and bringer of joy? Has it forgotten the spirit of revenge and all gnashing of teeth? Who has taught it to reconcile itself with time, and with that which is higher than all reconciliation?

The will must desire something higher than all reconciliation, namely the will to power. But how will it arrive at that? Who would teach it even to will backwards?

At this point of his address, however, something happened that made Zarathustra stop suddenly and be highly terrified. He looked upon his disciples in terror, and his eyes bored through their thoughts and afterthoughts as though with arrows. But after a while he was again smiling and calmed, and he said to them: "It is hard to live among men because silence is so hard, especially for one who is garrulous."

Thus spoke Zarathustra. The hunchback had covered his face while he listened to Zarathustra. But when he heard Zarathustra laugh he looked up curiously and said slowly: "Why does Zarathustra speak differently to us than to his disciples?"

Zarathustra answered: "What is marvellous about that? It is quite proper to speak to hunchbacks in a humpy manner!"

"Very well," said the hunchback, "and with pupils it is proper to tell tales out of school. But why does Zarathustra speak differently to his disciples than—to himself?"

THE STILLEST HOUR

What has happened to me, my friends? You see me distraught, restless, unwilling to stay, ready to go—alas, to go away from you!

Yes, once more Zarathustra must return into his solitude; but this time the bear goes back to his cave reluctantly. What has happened to me!

Who is demanding this? —Alas, my angry mistress desired it; she spoke to me. Have I ever told you her name? Last night *my stillest hour* spoke to me, for that is the name of my terrible mistress. This is what happened; for I must tell you everything, so that your hearts will not harden against me for leaving you so suddenly.

Do you know the terror of the moment when one falls asleep? You are terrified to the toes because the ground gives way under you and the dream begins. I am giving you this as a parable. Yesterday, at the stillest hour, the ground gave way under me; the dream began. The hand moved, the clock of my life took a deep breath. Never did I hear such stillness about me; so that my heart was terrified.

Then something spoke without voice: "You know it, Zarathustra?" —I cried out in fear at this whisper; the blood left my face. But I was silent. Then something again spoke to me without voice: "You know it, Zarathustra, but you are not telling."

Finally I answered like a stubborn person: "Yes, I know it well enough, but I do not want to tell it!"

Then again something spoke without voice: "You do not want to, Zarathustra? Is that really true? Do not hide behind your stubbornness!"

I wept and trembled like a child and said: "I would like to do so, but how can I? Do not demand this from me; it is beyond my power!"

Then something spoke again without voice: "What do you matter, Zarathustra? Speak out and be shattered."

And I answered: "Am *I* the one to speak? Who am I? I am

awaiting someone more worthy; I am not worthy even to be shattered because of him."

Then something again spoke to me without voice: "What do you matter? You are as yet not humble enough. Humility has the toughest hide."

And I answered: "What has not the hide of my humility already borne! I dwell at the foot of my height. No one has told me as yet how far it may be to the peak. But well do I know my valleys."

Then something again spoke without voice: "Oh, Zarathustra, the one who is to move mountains also removes valleys and depressions."

And I answered: "As yet my word has removed no mountains, and when I spoke it did not reach men. I did go to men, but I did not get through to them!"

Then something again spoke without voice: "What do you know about *that*? The dew falls upon the grass when the night is most still."

And I answered: "They mocked at me when I found and went my own way; and in truth my legs trembled at that time. So they said to me: 'You have forgotten the way; perhaps you have also forgotten how to walk!'"

Then something again spoke without voice: "What does their scorn matter? You are a person who has forgotten how to obey; now you are to command! Do you not know what kind of person is most needed? The one who commands great things. It is hard to carry out a great thing, but it is harder still to command a great thing. This is what is most unforgivable in you: you have the power and yet do not want to rule."

And I answered: "I lack the voice of the lion for commanding."

Then again something like a whisper spoke to me: "It is the stillest words that bring on the storm. Thoughts that approach on the feet of doves direct the world. Oh, Zarathustra, you are destined to walk as the shadow of that which is to come. Therefore you must command and with your commands lead the way."

And I answered: "I am ashamed."

And again something spoke to me without voice: "You must still become a child, and be without a sense of shame. The pride of youth is still upon you; you grew up slowly. But any one who wants to turn into a child must first overcome his youth."

I thought this over for a long time and trembled. Finally, however, I repeated what I had said at first: "I do not want to."

At that there was a laughter about me. Oh, how this laughing tore my bowels and cut into my heart! For the last time something spoke to me: "Zarathustra, your fruits are ripe, but you are not ripe for your fruits! You must return to your solitude, for you must still become mellow."

Then the laughter returned, and it fled. Thereupon it grew still about me as if with a double stillness. But I lay on the ground and the sweat poured from my limbs. —Now you have heard everything, and why I must return to my solitude. I have concealed nothing from you, my friends. But hear this also from me who is the most taciturn of all men—and wants to be so! Alas, my friends, I might have something more to say to you, something more to give! Why is it that I am not giving it to you? Can it be that I am stingy?—

When Zarathustra had spoken these words, the power of his sorrow and the approach of his farewell from his friends overcame him so much that he wept aloud, and no one knew how to comfort him. But that night he went away by himself and left his friends.

ON THE VISION AND THE RIDDLE

When it was rumored among the sailors that Zarathustra was on board—for a man from the Blessed Isles had embarked with him—there was great curiosity and anticipation. But for two days Zarathustra remained silent, for he was so cold and deaf from sadness that he answered neither in response to glances nor questions. But on the evening of the second day he again opened his ears, though he still remained silent, for many strange and dangerous things could be heard on this ship which had come from far off and still had a long way to go. Zarathustra was a friend of all those who go on long journeys and who like to live with danger. And as he listened, his tongue also was loosened, and the ice of his heart broke. Then he began to speak thus:

To you bold searchers, researchers and whoever ventures out upon terrible seas with cunning sails, to you who are drunk with riddles, who delight in the twilight, and whose souls are enticed toward every swirling abyss—for you are not willing with timid touch to follow along a thread, and where you cannot *divine* you detest to conclude—to you alone will I tell the riddle which I saw, the vision of the most lonely of men.

Not long ago I walked gloomily through the colorless twilight, gloomy and hard, with compressed lips. More than one sun had set. A path which rose defiantly through the rolling stones, a malicious, lonely path, friendly to neither weeds nor bush, a mountain path crunched under the defiance of my foot. Walking along silently over the mocking tinkling of the pebbles and crunching the stone that would have me slip, I forced my feet upwards. Upwards—in defiance of the spirit that would drag me down into the abyss, the spirit of gravity, my devil and archenemy. Upwards, though this spirit sat upon me, half dwarf, half mole; lame himself and making me lame; dripping lead into my ears and thoughts like drops of lead into my brain!

"Oh, Zarathustra," he whispered as he mocked me with every syllable. "You philosopher's stone! You threw yourself up high, but every stone that is thrown must—fall! Oh, Zarathustra, you philosopher's stone, you hurling stone, you smasher of stars! You threw yourself up high but every stone that is thrown—*must* fall! Condemned to be yourself, and to your own stoning, oh, Zarathustra, you did throw the stone out far—but it will fall back upon *you*." Thereupon the dwarf was silent and remained so for a long time. His silence oppressed me, for when two are together in such a manner, they are much lonelier than when alone. I climbed and climbed, I dreamed and thought, but everything oppressed me. I was like a sick person whom severe torture has exhausted, and, then, a worse dream has awakened. But there is something in me that I call courage; that has hitherto slain every discouragement. This courage finally bade me stand still and say: "Dwarf! You or I!"

Courage is the best slayer—courage which *attacks;* for in every attack there is joyous music.

Man, however, is the most courageous animal; with his courage he has conquered every beast. With joyous music he has conquered even every woe. But man's woe is the deepest woe. Courage kills even the dizziness at an abyss, and at what point has man not stood at an abyss? Is not seeing itself —seeing abysses?

Courage is the best slayer, courage slays even pity. Pity is the deepest abyss. However deeply man looks into life, at every depth he also will look into suffering.

Courage is the best slayer, courage that attacks. It slays even death, for it says: "Was *that* life? Very well! Once again!"

In such a saying there is joyous music. He that has ears to hear, let him hear.

"Stop, dwarf!" I said. "I! Or you! But I am the stronger— you do not know my most abysmal thought! You would not be able to bear it!"

Then something happened to relieve me, for the dwarf, becoming inquisitive, jumped from my shoulder and crouched down on a stone in front of me. But at that very spot was a gateway.

"Look at this gateway, dwarf! It has two fronts. Two paths meet here, the ends of which no one has yet reached. This long path backwards; it lasts an eternity. And this path onward—that is another eternity. They contradict each other, these paths; they bump their heads right here—it is here at this gateway that they meet. The name of the gateway is inscribed above: "This Moment." But if one of the paths were pursued farther and to an ever greater distance, do you believe that these paths would eternally contradict each other?"

"All that is straight, lies," the dwarf murmured contempt-uously. "Every truth is crooked; time itself is a circle."

"You spirit of gravity!" I cried angrily, "don't make things too easy for yourself, or I will leave you crouching there where you are, you lamefoot! It was I who held you high!"

I went on to say: "Behold this moment! From this gateway Moment, a long eternal path runs *backwards:* behind us lies an eternity. Must not whatever of all things *can* run, once before have run this path? Must not whatever of all things *can* happen, once before have happened, been done, passed by? And if everything has already been, then what about this moment, dwarf? Must not this gateway already—have been?

Are not all things so tightly intertwined that this moment must draw on all coming things? *Therefore*—itself also?

For whatever of all things can run, even *out* into this long path—*must* run it again! And this slow spider crawling in the moonlight, and this moonlight itself, and you and I at the gate-way whispering together of eternal things—must we not all have been here before? —and return and run along that other path before us, in this long gruesome path—must we not re-turn eternally?"

Thus I spoke more and more softly, for I was afraid of my own thoughts and afterthoughts. Then, suddenly, I heard a dog *howling* nearby. Have I ever heard a dog howling thus? My thoughts ran back. Yes! When I was a child, in the most distant childhood, then I heard a dog howl thus. And I saw him too, bristling, his head held high, trembling, in the stillest midnight when even dogs believe in ghosts, so that I was sorry for him. Just then, you see, the full moon was over the house, deadly silent; just then it stood still, a round glow, si-lent on the flat roof, as though on a strange property.

This terrified the dog, for dogs believe in thieves and ghosts. And when I heard him howl again in this way I again pitied him. What had now become of the dwarf? The gate-way? The spider? All the whispering —Was I dreaming? Had I awakened?

Suddenly I was standing between wild cliffs, alone, bleak, in the bleakest moonlight.

But there lay a man. Then the dog, springing, bristling, whimpering—he now saw me coming—howled again; he *cried.* Have I ever heard a dog thus cry for help? And, indeed, I have never seen the like of this. I saw a young shepherd writhing, choking, in spasms, his face distorted, and from his mouth hung a big, black snake.

Have I ever on *anyone's* face seen such loathing and pale horror? Perhaps he had been asleep when the snake had crawled into his throat and bit itself fast. My hand tore and tore at the snake, but in vain! I could not tear the snake from the throat. Then came a cry from me: "Bite! Bite hard! Off with the head! Bite hard!" Thus my horror, my hatred, my disgust, my pity, all that which was good or bad in me cried this *one* cry.

You bold men about me! You searchers and researchers and those of you who ventured out upon unexplored seas with cunning sails! You who delight in riddles! Solve this riddle that I saw; give me the solution of this vision of the most lonely of men. For it was a vision and a sight of the future. What was it that I saw in this parable? Who is this person who still is to come? Who is the shepherd into whose throat the snake was crawling? Who is the man into whose throat all that is hardest and blackest will crawl?

The shepherd, however, bit as my cry had advised him; he took a good bite, and spat the head of the snake far away —and jumped up. No longer shepherd, no longer man, but a person transformed, transfigured, who *laughed.* Never on earth did a man laugh as he laughed!

Oh, my brothers, I heard a laughter that was not the laugh of a human being— and now a thirst gnaws at me, a longing which will never be satisfied. My longing for this laughter gnaws at me. How can I bear to go on living? And how could I bear to die now!

Thus spoke Zarathustra.

BEFORE SUNRISE

Oh, heaven above me, so pure and deep! You abyss of light! When I behold you I shudder with godly desires. *My* depth is to throw myself into your height! *My* innocence is to hide within your beauty.

As his beauty envelops a god, so you hide your stars. You do not speak and yet you reveal to me your wisdom. Today you rose for me over the roaring sea in silence, but your love and your sensitiveness still brought revelation to my roaring soul. How could I help but to divine all the sensitiveness of your soul when you came to me so beautifully, enveloped in your beauty; when you spoke to me by your silence, revealed by your wisdom! *Ahead* of the sun you came to me, the loneliest of men.

We have been friends from the beginning: grief and awe and origin we have in common; we have even the sun in common. We do not speak together because we know too many things— our silence communicates, we smile our knowledge at each other. Are you not the light of my fire? Have you not the sister-soul to my insight? We learned everything together; together we learned to rise above ourselves to ourselves and to smile with no obscuring clouds. Cloudlessly we smile down with bright eyes and from faraway distance, while beneath us lies the heavy fog of compulsion, purpose and guilt.

And when I wandered alone, what did my soul hunger for in the night and on wrong paths? And when I climbed mountains, whom was I looking for if not you? All my wandering and mountain climbing was a mere necessity and an expedient for my awkwardness.

My whole will is intent only upon *flying*, upon flying up into *you*? What did I hate more than drifting clouds and everything that stained you? Even my own hatred I hated because it stained you! I detest the drifting clouds, those cats that are stealing along after their prey; they are taking from you

and me that which we have in common: the immense, unlimited Yes and Amen.

I do not like these mediators and mixers, these drifting
clouds. They are neither one thing nor the other, and have
learned neither to bless nor to curse thoroughly. I would rather
sit in a cask under an obscured sky, or in a crevice without a
sky, than see you, the heaven of light, tainted with drifting
clouds!

Often I had the desire to fasten them down with the jagged
golden wires of the lightning, so that, like the thunder, I
might beat the kettledrum on their diaphragm:—an angry
drummer because they were robbing me of your Yes and
Amen, you heaven above me, so pure and bright, you abyss
of light! I much prefer noise and thunder and the curses of
the storm to the contemplative, doubting calm of these cats;
among men also my best hatred is for those who step softly,
the half and half, and the doubting, hesitating, drifting clouds.

"He who cannot bless should *learn* to curse!" This clear
teaching came to me out of the clear sky; even on black
nights this star is seen in my heavens. Yes, I am one who
blesses and am a sayer of Yes as long as you are about me,
you pure, bright heaven, you abyss of light! With you I will
carry my blessing Yes even into every crevice. I have become
a sayer of Yes and one who blesses; for a long time I have
wrestled so that my hands might be free to bless. This has
been my blessing: to stand over each thing as its own heaven,
as its round roof, its azure dome and eternal security; and he
who blesses thus, is himself blessed.

For all things have been baptized at the fount of eternity
and beyond good and evil; good and evil themselves are
merely interfering shadows, damp obfuscations and drifting
clouds. Surely, it is to bless and not to blaspheme that I
teach: "Over all things there stands the heaven of accident,
the heaven of innocence, the heaven of chance and the heaven
of playfulness."

"By chance"—that is the oldest nobility of the world: that
I have restored to things and thereby freed them from slavery
under Purpose. This freedom and cheerfulness of heaven I

placed over all things like an azure dome when I taught that over them and through them no "eternal will" functions. This caprice and this playfulness I put in place of that will when I taught: "In all things *one* thing is impossible—rationality!"

To be sure, a little reason, a germ of truth is scattered from star to star—this leaven is mixed in with all things; for the sake of caprice there is wisdom mixed in with all things! To be sure, a little wisdom is possible; but in all things I found this blessed assurance: that they like best of all to *dance* on the feet of chance.

Oh, heaven above me, you pure, high heaven! For me your purity lies in the fact that there is no eternal spider and spider-web of reason; that you are the dance floor for divine chances, that you are the table of the gods for divine dice and throwers of dice!

But you blushed? Did I say something that cannot be expressed? Did I blaspheme in my effort to bless you? Or is it the sense of shame when only two are together that has caused you to blush? Did you bid me go and be silent because now—the *day* is approaching?

The world is deep—and deeper than the day has thought. It is not proper to put everything into words before the day has come. But the day is approaching, so let us part!

Oh, heaven above me, you sensitive, glowing heaven. Oh, you my happiness before sunrise! The dawn is coming; so let us part!

Thus spoke Zarathustra.

THE CONVALESCENT

1

One morning, not long after his return to his cave, Zarathustra jumped up from his couch like a madman, let out a terrible cry, and behaved as though there were another person on his couch who would not leave it. Zarathustra's cry made his animals run up to him in fright, and from all the caves and hiding places near Zarathustra's cave all kinds of beasts scuttled away, flying, fluttering, crawling, springing, each in its way. Zarathustra then spoke these words:

"Up, abysmal thought, out of my depth! I am your cock and break of day, you sleepy worm. Up! Up! My voice shall crow you awake! Unbutton your ears and listen! For I want to hear you! Up! Up! Here is thunder enough to make graves learn to listen! Wipe the sleep and all heaviness and blindness from your eyes!

Listen to me with your eyes too; my voice is a good cure even for those born blind. Once you are awake you shall stay so forever. I am not the kind who will awaken great-grandmothers only to bid them—sleep on!

You are moving, stretching, groaning? Up! Up! Don't groan —I want you to speak. Zarathustra, the godless, is calling you! I, Zarathustra, the advocate of life, the advocate of suffering, the advocate of the cycle—I call upon you, my most abysmal thought!

Hail to me! You are coming; I hear you! My abyss speaks; I have made my deepest depth turn to the light! Hail to me! Come up! Give me your hand. Ah, turn away! —Horrible, horrible—woe is me!"

2

Zarathustra had hardly spoken these words when he fell down as though dead and remained so for a long time. When he recovered he was pale and trembled, and lay for a long time, and would neither eat nor drink. This condition lasted seven days; but his animals did not leave him, day or night, excepting when the eagle flew out to look for food. Whatever he collected or robbed he laid on Zarathustra's couch so that Zarathustra finally lay among red berries, grapes, rose apples, fragrant herbs and pine cones. At his feet, moreover, two lambs lay which the eagle had robbed from their shepherd. Finally after seven days Zarathustra sat up on his couch, took the rose apple and delighted in its fragrance. At that they believed that the time had come to speak to him.

"Zarathustra," they said, "you have been lying this way for seven days; are you not about ready to stand on your feet? Come out of your cave. The world awaits you like a garden. The wind is playing with heavy fragrance in expectation of you, and all brooks would like to follow your course. All things were longing for you while you stayed by yourself for seven days. Come out of your cave. All things want to be your healer! Like a leavened dough you lay; your soul rose and spilled over its rims."

"Oh, my animals," said Zarathustra, "chatter away and let me listen to you! Your chatter refreshes me; the world looks like a garden to me whenever there is chatter. How lovely words and sounds are! Are not words and sounds rainbows and phantom bridges between things that are separated eternally? A distinct world belongs to each soul; for each soul every other soul is an after-world.

It is of things that are most alike that illusion tells the most beautiful lies; the smallest cleft is hardest to bridge. For me—how could there be an outside-me? There is no outside! But tones make us forget all this. How pleasant it is that we do forget! Have not names and tones been given to things in order that man might take pleasure in things? Speech is a beautiful whimsey; with it man dances over all things. How pleasant all speech is and all the lies of tones! With the tones our love dances on gay rainbows!"

"Oh Zarathustra," answered the animals, "for those who think as you do all things dance of themselves; they come, join hands, laugh and retreat—and return. Everything goes, everything returns; eternally the wheel of existence rolls. Everything dies and blossoms again; the year of existence goes on eternally. Everything breaks and is put together anew; the identical house of existence is built eternally. Everything parts and meets again; the ring of existence remains true to itself forever. At every *Now* existence begins; the sphere *There* rolls around every *Here*. The center is everywhere. The path of eternity is not a straight one."

"Oh, you buffoons and barrel organs!" answered Zara-thustra, and smiled. "How well you know what had to be ful-filled in seven days—and how that monster crawled into my throat and choked. But I bit off its head and spewed it out far from me. And you—you have made a street song out of it? Here I lie, still exhausted from biting and spewing, even sick because of my own salvation.

And you have been watching all this? Are you cruel also? Did you have a desire to witness my great pain as men do? Man, you must know, is the most cruel animal. His greatest delight on earth has always been at tragedies, bullfights and crucifixions, and when he invented hell, behold, it became his heaven on earth.

When the great man cries, the little man quickly runs to see, and his tongue hangs out from lustfulness. He, however, calls it 'pity.' The little man, especially the poet, how eager he is to accuse life! Listen to his words, but do not fail to hear the lust which is part of all accusations! Life gets the better of such accusers of life with a wink of the eye. It teases him and says: 'You love me? Wait a bit, I have no time for you just now.'

Of all animals man is the most cruel towards himself; in all who call themselves 'sinner,' 'cross-bearer' and 'penitent,' do not fail to hear the lustfulness in such complaints and accu-sations!

And I myself, am I accusing men with these words? Oh, my animals, this one thing alone have I learned thus far: that for his best man needs his most evil; that all that is most evil supplies his *best energy* and is the hardest stone for the high-est kind of creator; that man must become better *and* more evil. The fact that I know that man is evil is not the cross to which I was nailed. But I cried as none has cried before: Alas, that man's greatest evil is so very small! And his best is so very small!

This great disgust it was that choked me and crawled into my throat; and when the soothsayer preached: 'It is all the same; nothing is worth while; knowledge chokes.'

A long twilight limped along ahead of me, an exhaustion

tired unto death and drunken with death, which spoke with yawning mouth. 'Man, of whom you are so tired, the little man, returns eternally.' Thus my exhaustion yawned and dragged its feet and could not go asleep. The earth of man seemed changed into a cave, its chest sunken, all life turned into human mold and bones and musty past; my sighs and questions croaked and choked and gnawed and wailed by night and day: 'Alas, man returns eternally! The little man returns eternally!'

Once I had seen both naked, the greatest man and the smallest man, both all-too-alike, all-too-human, even the greatest! All-too-small the greatest! This was my disgust with man! Eternal return even for the smallest! This was my disgust with all existence! Loathing! Loathing!"

Thus spoke Zarathustra and sighed and shuddered, for he was reminded of his sickness. But his animals would not let him go on. "Say no more, you convalescent! But go out into the world which awaits you like a garden.

Go out to the roses and to where the bees and doves gather, but especially to the songbirds in order that you may learn to *sing* from them. Singing, you see, is for convalescents; leave speaking to the healthy. And if the healthy also should want songs, their songs would still be different from those of the convalescent."

"Silence! you buffoons and barrel organs!" answered Zarathustra, and smiled at his animals. "How well you know of the comfort which I invented for myself during those seven days. That I must sing again, that was the comfort and *that* the recovery which I invented; why should you straightway make a popular song of it?"

"Say no more," his animals answered again. "Rather, now that you have recovered, fashion a new lyre! You need a new lyre for your new songs. Sing and let your songs rush forth; heal your soul with new songs, now that you bear your great fate such as was never yet the lot of man! For your animals know very well, oh, Zarathustra, who you are and who you must become:

Behold, *you are the teacher of the eternal return*—that is your lot! But this great destiny, that you must be the first to teach this doctrine, how can it avoid also being your greatest danger and disease!

We know what you are teaching, namely that all things return eternally and we with them, and that we already have been here an infinite number of times and all things with us. You teach that there is a great year of becoming, a monster of a year; this, like an hourglass, must turn about again and again so that it may run down and out; and thus all these years must be alike in the smallest and greatest detail. We also know what you would say to yourself if you should want to die right now. But your animals beg you not to die as yet! You would speak to yourself without a tremble but rather with a sigh of happy relief, for a great weight and depression would be lifted from you, you most patient of men!

You would say: Now I am dying and disappearing and in a trice I am a nothing. Souls are as mortal as bodies. But the knot of causes in which I am entangled returns and that will create me again! I myself am part of the causes of the eternal return. I shall return, together with this sun, this earth, this eagle and this serpent—*not* to a new life or a better life or a similar life. I shall return eternally to this selfsame life, in order to teach again the eternal return of all things; in order to pronounce again the word of the great noon of the earth and man, and to proclaim again the Overman to man.

I have spoken and shall perish of my word. Thus my eternal lot decrees—as the proclaimer I am perishing. The hour has come for me as the proclaimer to bless myself. Thus *ends* Zarathustra's down-going."

When the animals had said this they were silent and waited for Zarathustra to say something to them. But Zarathustra did not notice that they were silent. He lay still with his eyes closed, similar to one asleep, even though he was not asleep, for he was just then conversing with his soul. But when the serpent and the eagle found that he was reticent they honored the great silence about him and carefully stole away.

THE OTHER DANCING SONG

1

Lately I looked into your eye, oh life, and I saw gold blinking in your dark eye, and my heart stood still with desire. On the dark waters I saw a golden boat blinking, a sinking, drinking, beckoning golden rocking-boat! At my foot, mad for the dance, you cast a glance, a laughing, questioning, melting rocking-glance. With your little hands you twice shook your castanets; at which my foot at once rocked with the eagerness to dance.

My heels reared, my toes listened to understand you. Does not the dancer wear his ear in his toes! I leaped toward you. You retreated from my leap and the tongue from between your fleeing, flying curls flashed at me! I leaped away from your serpents and immediately you stopped, half turned away but with your eye full of longing!

With crooked glances you teach me crooked ways; on crooked ways my foot learns—mischief! I fear your nearness, I love your distance; your retreat entices me, your seeking stops me. I suffer, but what have I not gladly suffered because of you!

You, whose coldness fires, whose heat entices, whose flight ties me down, whose mockery—moves me: who would not hate you, the great binder, encircler, tempter, searcher, finder! Who would not love you, you innocent, impatient, swift sinner with the eyes of a child!

Whither are you luring me now, unruly madcap? And now you flee again, you sweet tomboy and ingrate: I am dancing after you, I follow even your slightest trail. Where are you? Give me your hand—or merely a finger! Here are caves and thickets; we will get lost! Stand still! Don't you see the owls and bats flying about?

You owl! You bat! Are you mocking me? Where are we? You learned this howling and barking from the dogs. You are baring your white teeth so prettily at me, your evil eyes leap at me from out of your curly mane! This dance is a wild chase; I am the hunter; will you be my hound or my chamois? Here you are next to me, you swift, malicious jumper! Now up, now down! Now I have fallen! See how I lie here and beg for mercy. How gladly would I walk on more pleasant ways with you! —on the paths of love through still, blossoming bushes; or there along the sea where goldfish swim and dance!

Are you tired? Over there are sheep and the glow of evening. Isn't it beautiful to sleep to the flutes of the shepherds? You are so very tired? I will carry you; let down your arms! Or are you thirsty? I have something for you, but your mouth will not drink it!

Oh, this cursed, swift, subtle snake and elusive witch! Where are you? On my face I feel two drops and red spots from your hand! Really I am tired of always being your sheepish shepherd! You witch, I have sung to you so far; now you shall—cry for me!

To the beat of my whip you shall dance and cry! Surely I have not forgotten the whip? —No.

2

Then life answered me thus while it stopped its pretty ears:

"Oh, Zarathustra, do not crack your whip so terribly! You know well enough: noise murders thought, and just now such tender thoughts are coming to me. We are two who do no real good nor any real evil. Beyond good and evil we found our island and our green meadow—we two alone! For that reason alone we must be kind to each other! Even if we do not love each other wholly, must we necessarily quarrel? You know well enough that I like you, and often too well; and the reason for it is that I am jealous of your wisdom. Oh, this mad, old folly of wisdom! If ever your wisdom should leave you, alas, my love also would desert you quickly."

Then life looked back and around thoughtfully and said

softly: "Oh, Zarathustra, you are not true enough to me! You do not love me nearly as much as you say. I know that you are thinking of leaving me soon. There is an old, very heavy, growling bell; at night it growls toward your cave. When you hear this bell striking the hour at midnight, then you are thinking, between the hour of one and twelve—Zarathustra, I know it, you are thinking that soon you intend to leave me!"

"Yes," I said slowly, "but you know it too—" And I whispered something into her ear, right between the tangled, yellow, foolish curls.

"You know that, oh, Zarathustra? Nobody knows that."

And we faced each other as we looked upon the green meadow over which the cool evening just then was passing, and we wept together. Just then life was dearer to me than my wisdom ever has been.

Thus spoke Zarathustra.

3

One!

Oh man, attend!

Two!

What has the deep midnight to say?

Three!

"I slept, I slept—

Four!

"I have awakened from a deep dream.

Five!

"The world is deep,

Six!

"And deeper than the day has thought.

Seven!

"Deep is its woe—

Eight!

"Joy—deeper still than any ache:

Nine!

"Woe says: Pass on!

Ten!

"But all joy wants eternity—

Eleven!

"—wants deep, deep eternity!"

Twelve!

THE SEVEN SEALS
(OR THE YES AND AMEN SONG)

1

I am a soothsayer and filled with that soothsaying spirit which wanders on a high ridge between two oceans, as a heavy cloud between the past and the future; an enemy of all sultry valleys and of all that is tired and can neither die nor live; my dark bosom ready for the lightning and its redeeming flashes, heavy with the lightning that says Yes! that laughs Yes! to soothsaying flashes of lightning. Such pregnancy is a bliss; he who at some time is to light the light of the future must hang onto the mountain for a long time as a heavy weather! If this is what I am, how should I not be passionate for eternity and for the nuptial ring of rings, the ring of return! Never yet have I found the woman to present me with children, unless it be this woman whom I love: for I love you, O eternity!

For I love you, O eternity!

2

If my anger has ever shaken graves, moved boundary stones, broken and rolled old tablets into steep depths; if my scorn ever blew away moldy words, was a broom to cross-spiders and a sweeping wind for old, musty mausoleums; if ever I rejoiced to see where the old gods are buried, or in blessing the world and loving the world, to see the monuments of old deniers of this world—for I love even the churches and the graves of the gods, when the heavens with a clear eye look through their broken roofs—then how should I not be passionate for eternity and for the nuptial ring of rings, the ring of return! Never yet have I found the woman to present me with children, unless it be this woman whom I love: for I love you, O eternity!

For I love you, O eternity!

3

If ever a breath of the creative breath came to me, or of that heavenly necessity which forces even chance to join the dance of the stars; if ever I laughed the laughter of the creative lightning upon which there follows the thunder of the deed, obedient, though it grumbles; if ever I rolled the divine dice at the divine table of this earth so that the earth trembled and burst and spewed forth rivers of fire—for the earth is a divine table, and it trembles with new words and dice-casts of the gods—then, how should I not be passionate for eternity and for the nuptial ring of rings, the ring of return! Never yet have I found the woman to present me with children, unless it be this woman whom I love: for I love you, O eternity!

For I love you, O eternity!

4

If ever I drank heartily from that spicing and mixing mug in which all things are well blended; if ever my hand poured what is most distant into what is nearest: fire into spirit, joy into woe, and the most troublesome into the kindest; if I myself am a grain of that solvent salt by means of which all things blend well in the mixing mug—for there is a salt which blends good and evil, and even the most evil is fit to use as spice and for the final foaming—then, how should I not be passionate for eternity and for the nuptial ring of rings, the ring of return! Never yet have I found the woman to present me with children, unless it be this woman whom I love: for I love you, O eternity!

For I love you, O eternity!

5

If ever I was fond of the sea and of everything related to the sea, and fondest even when it angrily contradicts me; if ever the desire for searching is in me which drives my sails toward unexplored things; if the joy of the seafarer is my desire; if ever my rejoicing cried: "The coast has disappeared, now the last chain has fallen from me: —the boundless is rushing around me, I see time and space blinking in the far distance —then, how should I not be passionate for eternity and for the nuptial ring of rings, the ring of return! Never yet have I found the woman to present me with children, unless it be this woman whom I love: for I love you, O eternity!

For I love you, O eternity!

6

If my virtue is the virtue of the dancer, and if I often
have leaped with both feet into golden emerald ecstasy; if my
malice is a laughing malice, at home among rose arbors and
hedges of lilies—for in laughter all that is evil is at hand but
is hallowed and absolved by its own bliss—and if this is my
alpha and omega, that all that is weighty should become
light, all body a dancer, all spirit a bird; and, verily, that is
my alpha and omega! —then, how should I not be passionate
for eternity and for the nuptial ring of rings, the ring of return! Never yet have I found the woman to present me with
children, unless it be this woman whom I love: for I love you,
O eternity!

For I love you, O eternity!

7

If ever I stretched quiet skies over myself and flew on
my own wings into my own heaven; if ever I playfully swam
into deep distances of light and the bird-wisdom of my freedom came to me; thus speaks my wisdom-bird: "Behold, there
is no above, no below! Throw yourself about, out, back, you
who are weightless! Sing! No longer speak! Are not words
made for the weighty? Do not all words lie for him who
is weightless? Sing! No longer speak!" —How should I not be
passionate for eternity and for the nuptial ring of rings, the
ring of return! Never yet have I found the woman to present
me with children, unless it be this woman whom I love: for
I love you, O eternity!

For I love you, O eternity!

7.

Works:
Beyond Good and Evil:
A Prelude to a Philosophy
of the Future

Since *Thus Spoke Zarathustra* did not fulfill the hopes which the initial view of the metaphor of Zarathustra had promised, Nietzsche undertook a more sober attempt to justify his point of view, or, as he called it, to develop his philosophy. To this end he made preparatory notes even during the writing of *Zarathustra* and, when the latter met with little understanding and much misunderstanding, he planned to publish a treatise which would present those principles which he thought necessary for a proper interpretation. It was begun in the spring of 1885 with a foreword written in June 1885, after completion of the first draft. It appeared in August 1886 under the title *Beyond Good and Evil*. The title implies that judgments and evaluations are presented, not under conventional moral aspects which are stated as being prejudiced and outworn, but under one beyond such limitations and in accordance with what is taken to be a more scientific basis and of bolder intellectual activity. It is accordingly a resumption and an attempt at further clarification of the investigations preceding *Thus Spoke Zarathustra*.

The foreword gives the program of the treatise quite succinctly as a strong plea for his continuously perspective or experimental philosophy as against all former philosophies, which are without exception taken to be in some form dogmatic. He considers them all influenced by Plato's idealism and in the service of Christian religion and theology, which he calls "the popular Platonism." He expresses appreciation for this idealism as a necessary error, in that the struggle against it had furnished the entire energy of modern thinking by "the good Europeans and the free, *very* free spirits" who refuse to be lulled by the quietism of Jesuitism and democracy.

"Good and Evil," by which is meant the hitherto universally accepted morality in its various forms—whether it be the Decalogue and the institutional Christian morality taught by the Church, or the ethical systems of the philosophers, especially that of Kant and his categorical imperative—all are treated as perspectives or hypotheses which fail to satisfy the fundamental fact of the Dionysian character of life, the Eternal Return, and the will to power through sublimation. Consequently a new perspective outside and beyond this morality is proposed and experimented with to test its validity and power.

If Nietzsche had been primarily a scholar or a philosopher, such a perspective would have been examined quite calmly. Instead he might be called a tortured moralist in this attempt to establish a super-morality. The demand of a fully honest acceptance of the Dionysian view and the Eternal Return produces in him, or his followers, the torments of an ecstatic. The psychologist claims to reach the joy of the confident genius in divining souls, but protests too much. The aristocratic sublimator suffers too painfully from the belief that he must be a "fate" and establish a new order of rank in which life's will to power is expended only on producing the effective sublimators, whom the less creative but still enlightened must accept as their lawgiver and obey intelligently and proudly; while the unenlightened are content, because they must be, to act merely as the nourishing humus. The great health and joy that Nietzsche had sought before *Thus Spoke Zarathustra*, and that the latter was meant to establish firmly, is still hidden under a strained struggle.

In the second chapter Nietzsche describes his kind of psychology as the experimenting with perspectives which are based on a deep penetration of the forces of life, with no other object in view than to proceed with interpretations based on the greatest possible intellectual integrity and a freedom from every kind of self-deception.

The worth of any act, or the lack of it, he claims, has always been a matter of perspective anyway, though not admitted to be. In pre-historic times, he insists, the worth of an act was judged solely by its results and should consequently be called pre-moral. Later, enlightenment led to the study of the sources of an act but translated the source into intent and thus introduced the system of morality. The new method interprets intent as a mere surface phenomenon which is in need of a new investigation and should therefore be called extra-moral. He calls this psychology a system of experiments by "the finest, most honest, though also the most malicious consciences of today—as living touchstones of the soul." [1]

This psychology is based upon the right to his primary assumption, or indeed his faith, that life is, in the sense described above, will to power and nothing besides. Upon this assumption all his experiments are made, and his right to the assumption he establishes by the following argument. If we assume that the only "given" reality to which we can penetrate, upward or downward, is the reality of our drives, why should we not then be permitted to experiment with the question whether this given reality is not sufficient to serve as the explanation even of the mechanistic world as a kind of primitive activity of the drives—the simplest original synthesis as a "pre-form" of life, which later in the organic processes branches out and takes on various forms. [2] His method demands that this experiment be carried to its extreme, to accept no causality other than the causality of the drives until the experiment is reduced to an absurdity.

Hypothetically, then, the causality of the will is taken to be the only one. The assumption is "risked" that will is effecting will wherever effects are recognized, and wherever an active force is found it proves to be an effect and force of the will. This is the primary experiment that Nietzsche pursued all his life. In this book, at any rate, it is no more than an experimental basic hypothesis to be tested to the utmost, with the meaning of power in society and the individual to be restlessly examined as to its organization, development, and sublimation. He insists that he is not stating a "truth," since that would be mere "moral naïveté," but rather a dominant fiction which he considers to be far more mature than what is called truth, and is consequently more valuable.

He realizes that power is a dangerous word, but he likes the danger of the experiment. He seeks, however, to keep the unwary away by warning that it is only for those who have the insight to know power honestly and the quality to possess it. He demands caution and skepticism, but he discards the cynic who betrays his shallowness by his delight in biting and barking and is wholly immune to the sadness and disgust of the thorough psychologist at the sight of man's ordinary conception of power. He not only excludes the ordinary man from viewing any part of his experiment, but he will wear a mask also before the half-prepared for fear of what their interpretations might signify for them. He wants to guard himself against popularity lest his results be too readily taken, made the fashion, and so become false. He also suggests that youth had better be excluded because it is too uncompromising and lacking in fine distinctions. Youth will consequently be endangered by the boldness of the experiment and not realize its subtlety and stern demands on integrity. For these new philosophers, he says, are "attempters," perhaps "tempters" also; and this designation is also merely an attempt, if one will, a "temptation." [1] It is in their nature, in some respect or other, to desire to remain an enigma.

Nietzsche undertakes to examine the attitudes and institutions within, rather than beyond good and evil, in order to establish their antithesis to his aristocratic philosophy. All these attitudes he gathers under the Christian attitude toward life, since he finds it dominant even among the so-called enlightened of modern thinkers and leaders. In this Nietzsche is very much the propagandist who rather violently sweeps clear the path for his new approach. His sweeping statements about the beginnings of Christianity and his brusque suspicions of the integrity of all philosophy submitting to Christian values makes his own intellectual integrity suspect, except that he would claim the right to this violence as being necessary in order to put his primary hypothesis to the most honest test.

He makes the origin of Christianity a revolt against and a reversal of the subtlety of the aristocratic Greco-Roman liberalism and naturalism, executed by the "Oriental slave" with his fear and hatred of uncertainties. Since his life in itself held no promise, he had to hate the proud, aristocratic attitude toward its problems and difficulties and was willing to sacrifice all freedom, pride, self-confidence of the intellect to find comfort in an absolute faith that promised dignity to and reward for his sufferings.[1] In a word, the will to faith in God and a future life took the place of the will to the faith in life and the will to power as the sublimation of life. The Northern barbarian, as he characterizes the Germans particularly, then turned this originally genuine but painful revolt into that "loyal and offensively crude faith in obedience to authority," which Nietzsche makes responsible for the absence of culture in modern times.

This sharp strained antithesis is indeed a frank and open statement of the difference between the Christian democratic principle with its submission to God, and Nietzsche's reliance on man's sublimation of himself on the basis of his own autonomy and this life. In that respect it is honestly stated and its vehemence an expression of the pain he experienced because of his need to divorce himself from the faith to which he once had been devoted and which he knew all thorough disciples would also experience. The attack is sometimes bitter, at times lighthearted and with a touch of humor, especially when he can call upon his beloved Greeks as allies; but it is never frivolous or cynical. Its integrity does not lie on a scholarly basis, but wholly on the completeness of a new faith in the autonomy of life.

Nietzsche also finds the cruelty that accompanies the recreation and sublimation of life attending all religious development, which he defines in three historical steps: in the earliest stage humans were sacrificed to a god; in Puritan times ascetic, religious men, particularly the saint, sacrificed their nature to God; in modern materialism and skepticism man sacrifices God to fate or nothingness, and arrives at a nihilism. This last stage he calls wholly futile and a stark betrayal of life. But he finds the same to be true of the more honest and, in some respects, beneficial sovereign religions of Christian Puritanism and Jesuitism, in that they, too, are pessimistic about life and teach the denial of it. He therefore demands a complete reversal in the basic faith and finds it in the Dionysian acceptance of the Eternal Return with its affirmation of all of life and the discipline and steady training of its constant recreation by sublimation. That brings a "deeper world, new problems and new games for man, 'the eternal child.'"

He demonstrates that the basic elements of the struggle for culture were reversed and distorted at the very start of the Christian era through the influence of what he calls "the revolt of the slaves," organized by the Jews. He makes the Jews responsible for a revolution in morals out of resentment and fear whereby the virile and vital drives of man were declared to be evil. He credits them with introducing into the vocabulary of moral sentiments the concept of "world" as equivalent to evil, thereby changing the direction of culture from the battle of the sublimation of human drives to their submersion in obedience to prohibitions—from a positive battle to a negative obedience.

He emphasizes, however, that sublimation also makes a great demand on obedience. Since it is the battle for the victory of those drives and powers which will give to life its greatest worth and dignity and thus command the conduct of life, its morality must require a high degree of obedience. Each stage of the adventure requires that the attained value be obeyed loyally and for a long time in order that its victory be consolidated before it be used in a renewed battle with a possibly higher value as a worthy contestant. Indeed, Nietzsche asserts that this battle of life, however high its aim, contains elements of cruelty like all battles, as though nature violated itself but still maintained itself and its cultural aim by the imperative to man that he guard his self-respect by long and loyal obedience to the value which was last won, until the new victory is complete.

This interplay of battle and obedience, victory and renewed battle, is to him the process of sublimation for the free spirits. Those persistent and successful at it are the new philosophers and commanders of the future. Even everything in the past that was prized as culture, though the process was incomplete and misunderstood, is nevertheless the product of the discipline and training through obedience. It is a *"willful restriction of perspective,"* [1] that produced as its virtues, art, music, dance, reason, and intellectualism, in the struggle for which the strength, bold inquisitiveness, and elasticity of European culture developed.

This is the picture which modern Europe presents to Nietzsche. In it he sees the end of all development and the futile contradiction of the law of life as the will to culture by sublimation. To him it is the belittling and degeneration of man. It is a Europe that desires no morality except that of the herd, which no longer has need of "rights," when the only right is that common to all and whose ruling drive is sympathy for all.

In this very cause for the modern ebb, however, he also finds hope for the renewal of the struggle for culture. He believes that the modern admixture of races and peoples of the present Europe introduced, by the loss of its purity, a great battle of values which proved to be so exhausting that a hatred of conflicts ensued and out of it a desire for passive obedience. However, he says, there will always remain a few who are more robust and still sense the battle of values as the extreme stimulus.

These bold and free spirits are the new philosophers who will resume the battle for sublimation by means of a transvaluation of all the prevailing descending values. They prepare the great adventures and experiments of disciplining, training, and breeding by which they hope to overcome the prevailing trend of history.

The final chapter attempts to draw a conclusion from the preceding investigations and to outline the character of the new commander of culture, the standards that he must establish beyond those of good and evil, and his attitude toward those who attempt to understand and follow him.

He repeats that his commander is, above all, the sublimator of life and of every phase of it. His sole devotion is to life and to man as its master. He would learn to know life with the greatest possible thoroughness and the highest intellectual and spiritual honesty, in order to extract from it those values that will fashion life and man into the highest inherent power and purity. It is a superlatively, perhaps impossibly audacious conception of intellectual and spiritual aristocracy, entirely foreign and inimical to all democratic institutions, or to society as commonly understood. But as an exclusively intellectual value it may have the power of a corrective, even though Nietzsche meant to make it constitutive and generally commanding.

His philosopher, then, is the man who has freed himself from all preconceptions and all metaphysical precepts and has instead sought and progressively succeeded to create the crude matter of life into its highest quality. He believes himself a man wholly of quality with the sure and ready sense for the differences between man and man, the order of rank. His distinguishing characteristic is this "pathos of distance" as the instinct which searches for and protects quality against compromise and useless contacts. He is himself the product of the discipline, training, and breeding of generations of aristocrats—not of particular physical ancestors, but of generations of intellectual and spiritual searchers for distinction. A democratic society, however, cannot produce this philosopher unless he be the rare exception of the violent dissenter. Yet within the large society the aristocratic commander is always the exception who rises above the broad base which has so little sense for quality, that it does not, and cannot live by its own value, but must be given standards appropriate to its lesser powers and to its function as the supporting base.

Nietzsche calls this broad base of society the slaves, because their lack of the sense for quality enslaves them to crude matter and therefore enables them to serve only as the substructure and soil for the higher rank. They follow a morality suitable to their experiences and to their preservation within life as they know and understand it, very distinct from the values of the masters of culture and in apposition to them. Nietzsche claims to discover varying degrees of this difference between slave and master morality, in spite of attempts at compromise or the more frequent admixture and mutual misunderstanding of the two, even in the same person.

The moral code of the masters, the commanders of culture, he defines as the expression of their consciousness of quality, of its richness and fullness that desires to expend itself. "Good" is what is distinguished, as well as the person who reveres what is distinguished and, therefore, possesses a deep but unassuming sense of the order of rank. He is very severe about the genuineness of his quality as he is generally severe about himself and others. Lack of self-interest is to him the denial of his search for distinction, and sympathy the weakening of the severity of his judgment of quality. He avoids and despises what impedes this search, such as the timid, slavishly suspicious, narrowly utilitarian, the sycophant and liar. He sets the value "good" upon what is distinguished, and calls that which he finds contemptible, "bad." Because of his gratitude to those related to him in the past and to the more experienced co-fighters of his own time, his reverence for quality sets him apart from the modern worshipper of progress. Reverence is indeed part of his integrity, as it is also the pathos of distance by which he will learn only from those related to him and reject all others. He will seek his friends, but also the most worthy of his foes, among his equals.

Contrariwise, slave morality is dictated by a lack of quality and power. The slave is bound to crude matter and so unfree, exhausted, and suffering. He therefore develops a pessimism toward life and the suspicion that the distinguished values, because they make his life intolerable, are evil. He cherishes as good only that which will relieve his misery, such as sympathy, patience, humility, and friendliness. His ideal of good is that of the innoxious man to whom power and struggle, even though spiritual and intellectual, is evil. To the philosopher, however, the innoxious is weak, naïve, stupid, and bad. To Nietzsche the distinguished do not exist primarily for the sake of society. The fact that they have the quality and ability to be something higher is justification enough to set them apart. If the few succeed in making themselves commanders of values, a larger few will be found to interpret them, while the large mass remains content with its harmless values.

But even if an aristocratic society should at last eventuate by means of the severest discipline in a continuous struggle with adverse circumstances, Nietzsche gives it a poor chance to persist. When favorable circumstances have been won, he believes that the tension will relax and the former intellectual severity will no longer continue as the justice it first was. When the majority no longer see the need for struggle, a few will renew the fight on the basis of an individual morality of power without the former restraint of severe integrity, and then degenerate to "explosive aristocrats and monsters." As a result, the new moral philosopher will again preach mediocrity in order to combat the danger of such excesses and be caught in the web of a renewed pessimism, though under the guise of restraint, dignity, duty, and love of neighbor. "It will be difficult," Nietzsche concludes, *"to hide the irony of it."* [1]

from:

Beyond Good and Evil

Hitherto all psychology has been obstructed by moral prejudices and fears; it has not dared to plumb the depths. No one has as yet even touched upon the idea of taking psychology as I do, namely as the morphology and the *theory of the development of the will to power*, if, to be sure, it is permitted to recognize in everything that has been written thus far a symptom of what has hitherto been concealed. The force of moral prejudices has penetrated deeply into the intellectual world,—seemingly the coldest and least prejudiced world—and, of course, has caused harm, hindrance, obscurity, and false interpretations. A real physio-psychology must contend with unconscious obstacles in the heart of the investigator; the "heart" is opposed to it. Even the theory of the interrelation of "good" and "bad" drives, as a subtler form of immorality, is a distress and disgust to the still hardy and hearty conscience—, far more so a theory of the derivation of all good drives from the bad. But suppose that someone goes to the length of taking the affects of hatred, envy, greed, dominance as life-conditioning effects, as something that must basically and as a matter of principle be part of the household of life and which consequently must be sublimated if life itself is to be sublimated. He will suffer from such a direction of his judgment as from a nausea. And yet, even this hypothesis is by far not the most painful and strangest in this immense, still new realm of dangerous discoveries;— and there are indeed a hundred good reasons why everybody should stay away from them—who *can!* On the other hand, if one's ship once has been tossed hither, then have the teeth tightly clenched, the eyes open! the hand firmly at the helm!— we will sail right over morality; thereby stifling, perhaps wrecking our own remainder of morality, as we pursue and risk our direction—but what matter *we!* Never has a *deeper* world of insight been opened to bold travelers and adventurers. And the psychologist who thus makes "sacrifices"—it is not the *sacrifizio dell' intelleto*, quite the opposite!—will at least be permitted to demand that psychology again be recognized as the mistress of the sciences for whose service and preparation the other disciplines exist. For now psychology is again the way to the basic problems.

[23]

Assuming that it should be possible to explain the whole activity of our drives as the organization and expression of one basic form of the will, that is, the will to power according to my principle; assuming that all organic functions can be reduced to this will to power—then one would have acquired the right to designate clearly all active forces as *will to power*. The world viewed from within, the world defined and described on the basis of its "intelligible character"— would be will to power and nothing besides.

[36]

But when the contrasts and wars in such natures [Nietzsche's Philosopher] act as one *more* stimulus and incitement to life, and if, together with their powerful and implacable drives, they have also inherited and developed the real mastery of warring—that is self-control and self-outwitting—then there arise those marvellous, incomprehensible, and unfathomable mystery men who are predestined to victory and enticement.—They appear at the very same time when that weaker type with its desire for peace comes to the fore: both types belong together and arise from the same causes.

[200]

[Nietzsche continues the description of his new Philosopher:]

A transvaluation of values under whose pressure and hammer a conscience would be steeled, a heart would be changed to steel sufficient to bear the weight of such a responsibility. On the other hand, the necessity for such leaders, the terrible danger that they may not appear, or could fail in their task, or themselves degenerate—those are the real worries and dark clouds; as you know, you free spirits.

[203]

[Nietzsche describes the moral skepticism of his new Philosopher:]

This skepticism despises and yet attracts; it undermines and yet takes possession; it is without faith but is not lost; it gives a dangerous freedom to the spirit but keeps the heart stern; a *German* form of skepticism.—It may be fearlessness of the eye, bravery and severity of the dissecting hand, a

tough will to dangerous voyages of explorations, to intellectual
North Pole expeditions under bleak and dangerous skies.

[209]

[The tools of his new Philosopher:]
  With creative hand they seize upon the future; all that is
and was turns into means for them; a tool, a hammer. Their
"cognition" is creating; their creating a lawgiving; their will
to truth is—*will to power*.

[211]

[He would flatter the "good" people, Nietzsche says, by
explaining to them that a high intellectuality is after all a]
synthesis of all those conditions claimed for the "merely
moral," after each condition has been acquired by long discipline and exercise, perhaps by a whole chain of generations; that it is the spiritual sublimation of justice and of that
thoughtful severity which knows that it is commissioned to
maintain the *order of rank* in the world, even among things—
and not merely among men.

[219]

[Growth is taken to mean the sublimation of the beast in
man. According to the nature of growth it is painful and attended by cruelty.] Almost everything that we call "higher
culture" rests upon what we call a spiritualizing and deepen-
ing of *cruelty*—this is my proposition. The well-known "wild
beast" in man has not been mortified; it lives, flourishes; it
has merely—divinely sublimated itself.—Consider, that in his
search for knowledge even the scholar, by forcing his intellect
to know *against* the inclination of his mind, and often also
against the wishes of his heart—that is to say No where he
would prefer to affirm, love, and worship—is acting as an
artist and transformer of cruelty. . . . In every desire to know
there is a drop of cruelty.

[229]

The discipline of suffering, the *great* suffering—do you not realize that this very discipline has produced all sublimation of man thus far?

[225]

[In the proud historical training of the Nineteenth Century Nietzsche sees a danger. To be sure, he calls it the "sixth sense" of the Nineteenth Century and in itself of great importance as] the ability quickly to divine the order of rank of all evaluations according to which a people, society, and man have lived; the "divinitory instinct" for the relationship of these evaluations, for the relation of the authority of values to the authority of active forces. [But instead of being used as a fine tool for the fashioning artist of culture working at the distinction and perfection of his native powers, it has turned into plebeian curiosity with wide but impartial interests which tries to digest many things that cannot possibly be assimilated. Instead of growth, it promotes a "half-barbarian" mediocrity and, therefore, is a danger to sublimation.]

[224]

[Not only is it the task of the Nietzschean philosopher to know himself with progressive thoroughness, but also there is no possibility for him to know beyond that.] An immutable "this I am" has a voice in every basic problem; about man and woman, for example, a thinker can learn nothing radically new, he can only think through to the end what already is implanted in him.

[231]

The distinguished soul has reverence for himself . . .

[287]

[At the end of the book Nietzsche engages in a dithyrambic celebration of Dionysus as the god who initiated him into his complete faith in life. He calls himself the] last disciple and initiate [of this] great ambiguous and alluring god, [the inciter and enticer to the sublimation of life, the original psychologist] that great enigma and tempter-god and born ratcatcher of the conscience; whose voice knows how to penetrate into the underworld of every soul; who never says a word nor casts a glance that does not contain some hint or fold of enticement; part of whose mastery it is that he knows how to give an illusion, not of what he is, but what is one more compulsion to those who follow him to approach ever nearer to him in order to pursue him more and more intimately and thoroughly. . . . Should I not at last be permitted to give you, my friends, a slight taste of this philosophy as far as I am allowed. With half a voice, as is proper; for it contains much that is mysterious, new, strange, wondrous, and uncanny.

[295]

[Once, Nietzsche reports, Dionysus said to him] "To me man is a pleasant, brave, inventive beast who has no equal on earth and can find his way out of every labyrinth. I like him; I often contemplate how I can help him on and make him stronger, more evil, and deeper than he is. "Stronger, more evil, and deeper?" I asked in horror. "Yes, I will repeat: stronger, more evil, and deeper; and also more beautiful." At that the tempter-god gave me his halcyon smile as though he had made a charming witticism.

[295]

8.

Works:
Toward a Genealogy of
Morals:
A Polemic

In November 1887, about a year after the appearance of *Beyond Good and Evil*, Nietzsche published a series of three essays under the title *Toward a Genealogy of Morals: A Polemic*, and stated that it was to serve as a supplement and interpretation to *Beyond Good and Evil*.

It is no more a polemic than the previous collections of aphorisms. Indeed, the very form suggests rather a quieter mood, though what calm there is results from the self-confidence of his outlook, rather than from a lessening of his aggressive fervor. The friends of his ideas were becoming fewer because they found him uncomfortably demanding in intellectual things and too unbending. His publisher would not take the risk of finding a sufficient public for his books and Nietzsche had to supply the cost himself.

But he seems to have felt a strong urge not only to clarify his ideas on morality, in which he found himself most at variance with friends and public, but, as lay in his nature, to examine once again his own depth and the integrity of his findings. The book is a claim of depth and honesty of investigation, a description and exposure of his psychological insight, as much as a polemic against the established morality. It was written within a few weeks between the middle of June and the early part of July 1887, and appeared in November of that year, after the second essay had been revised and re-written. It contains the Foreword and the essays entitled "Good and Evil, Good and Mean"; "Guilt, Bad Conscience and the Like"; and "What Do Ascetic Ideals Signify?"

A. *The Need of a Critique of Moral Values*

The Foreword, which he dates July 1887, immediately after the completion of the first draft of the book, is devoted primarily to the statement that the problem of the origin and meaning of morality had occupied him even as a child, due to his doubting nature which, though he dislikes to admit it, asserted itself "so unsolicited, so irresistibly, so in contradiction to my surroundings, age, example and family that I might almost justly call it my *a priori.*" It was therefore quite natural, he says, that his intellectual curiosity and suspicions should make him halt before the question of what really is the origin of our "good and evil." However, as he continues to explain by referring back to *Human, All-Too-Human* and *Gay Science,* his historical investigation is not an investigation in the usually accepted sense, but rather a psychological examination of the values of life sought by morality—or what is accepted as morality. This investigation, in turn, is directed by his basic faith in life as the will to power through sublimation, which is ruling him more and more and, therefore, sharpening his opposition to the sacrosanct morality which tolerates this life for the sake of an ideal, metaphysical life. Consequently, his primary investigation will be into the *value of* morality inspired by a skeptical attitude towards all moral codes. "We need a *critique* of all moral values; the *worth of these values themselves must first be questioned.*" [1] This, he believes, is the particular contribution that he has long been attempting, but which now, he hopes, is maturer, clearer, stronger, and more complete.

B. *"Good and Evil, Good and Mean,"*
The Morality of Resentment

At the very beginning of this first essay, in which he undertakes to draw a sharp distinction between the prevailing social (in his terminology, democratic) morality and his aristocratic values, the method of his procedure becomes very clear. He is very certain of his basic premise that there is no true approach to life except through its Dionysian nature; that it transmutes and incarnates itself in man, who has the power to penetrate it by virtue of his disciplined intellectual curiosity and sharpened instinct of psychological probing, and finally to express, and thus create, the values of nature and man's power as it sublimates itself. Any other approach is certain to be mistaken and worthless. To him it constitutes a lack of integrity and a blindness to follow any premise but his own or any other goal; or even, in the course of psychological insight, to see what by the premise cannot be there. When that happens the investigator is either directed by a false premise, or misled by the authority of names that have grown out of false premises. So honesty here more than ever means loyalty to the Dionysian faith and the acceptance of the will to power through sublimation. It escapes being an arid dogma only in that the goal remains in the very vague distance of an unending but severely disciplined search. At the same time, however, it progressively widens the distance between the non-participating masses and even the erroneously participating scholars and philosophers; makes the new philosopher more and more exacting and almost completely alone, consoling himself with his pride in the pathos of distance. Aristocratic signifies true; democratic means non-participating or false, and so untrue to life. However, every evaluation is on the lofty plane of sublimation and has little direct relation to practical social living and institutions. When Nietzsche, nevertheless, puts them into such relations, he is often awkward or even naïvely distorting.

At the opening of the essay Nietzsche professes a curiosity about the English utilitarian moralists. He finds that they possess some psychological acumen and have even made brave attacks upon certain prejudices. But he considers the whole of their investigations wrong and with a complete absence of historical sense, because they start from a false premise and decree their moral values out of it. He attacks them in a very cavalier fashion, merely stating that they are wholly mistaken, not troubling to say, for example, that if Bentham's "the greatest good of the greatest number" were a proper value, then his own approach would be completely wrong.

Because he was a trained philologist and had reason to consider himself an expert in the ancient classics, he felt quite confident as he engaged in etymologies and semantics of the moral terms that were to prove his contentions. But they all start from his own premise and he decrees his values out of it in the very fashion that he decries in the English psychologists. Moreover, rather than in etymologies, he is engaging in semantics of his own sort which he describes and recommends in a note appended at the end of this first essay. He suggests that the philosophical faculty of some university advertise a prize essay on the subject: What indications does philology, especially etymological investigations, offer for the history of the development of moral concepts? He then goes on to say that such investigations demand the participation of psychologists and physiologists because all moral evaluations must be interpreted physiologically and medically, even more than psychologically. The crucial question must be made that of worth more than meaning, and consequently the point of view must be adjusted to it.

Thus he decrees that etymologically "good" has always meant "distinguished," as opposed to *schlecht* which, somewhat like "mean," still carries the meaning simple, uncomplicated, average, as well as bad. But according to Nietzsche, it merely means plebeian, simple, low, and mean, and contained no moral value until after the Thirty Years War and the growth of a democratic spirit, or else because of English influence. He allows himself all kinds of dubious etymologies under his system, suggesting boldly that the Latin designation *malus*, for bad, may be derived from the Greek μελας, or dark, by which the Italians characterized the low pre-Arian strain in contrast to the Arian conquerers—just as German democracy may be a throw-back to the pre-Arians who were getting the better of the blond race of monsters. His final excess in this direction is his suggestion that the German word for good, *gut*, may even signify "the godly," the man of divine origin and be "identical with the popular (originally noble) name of the Goths." [1]

This kind of reasoning makes all that follows subject to definite reservations, particularly his claim to severe intellectual integrity. It illustrates clearly that to him it was intellectually blind and therefore false to see any premise but his own Dionysian will to power through sublimation. That was his only problem; a very delicate one, he thought, and meant only to be pondered and solved by the select few, and "*still*," [2] without fanfare, as though to most it were monstrous, dangerous, or unnecessarily disturbing. However, having prepared by such etymologies for what he seemed to consider a necessary shock, he proceeds directly to his attack upon modern Christian democratic culture and upon the foundation on which he makes it rest: namely, his favorite discovery of the moral revolution of the slaves, the main subject of this essay.

First, he establishes as the general law of sublimation that a political superiority concept regularly tends to sublimate itself into an intellectual and spiritual one, either of a genuine, honest, and healthy character, or of one consciously false, cunning, and diseased. He then maintains that the superiority of the priests has at all times been of the latter type and in no instance more thoroughly so than in the case of the Jews who became the founders of our Christian-Judean culture.

He attributes to the Jews an intense feeling of frustration because of their defeat by the Roman masters, and out of it an intense hatred of the masters. This they were able to turn into a spiritual power with great cunning, and by virtue of it succeeded in reversing the aristocratic values of their masters and called them "evil," as against the "good" of their own weakness. The powerful resentment out of which the priest organized this revolution was applied with so great a cunning and intelligence, and with so complete a success, that its revolutionary character was unnoticed. Though it failed to be the opposite, it was in reality a will to power by sublimation, though deceitful.

The culminating enticement of this Jewish revolt is to Nietzsche the principle of charity by means of which the Jewish priests completed a victory so secure that it maintained itself in Christianity without serious challenge for two thousand years. He calls the crucifixion of Christ, as the symbol of the love of mankind, the culminating propaganda ruse and the last instrument of Jewish resentment which, instead of a denial of Jewish values, is in reality their crown and thus the very opposite of redemption.

Nietzsche permits himself such extremes out of his desperate faith in Dionysian nature and out of his drive towards a consistency within it that he calls intellectual integrity. His passion in dealing with this subject is the best indication of the struggle with his integrity. He is often more emotional than reflective.

None of this should be construed as merely anti-Semitic, a prejudice of which Nietzsche kept himself free except for a fleeting moment, but as his attack upon the destructive nature of resentment and the pessimistic denial of man's autonomy. He is very serious, yet reluctant about the discussion of Christ. "There are many things about which to be silent on this subject." [1] Resentment, however, he considers basically a negative drive destructive of genuine sublimation. In an aristocrat, he says, it is either entirely absent or at most explosive and quickly forgotten, so that he keeps himself free of its debilitating and poisonous effects.

As resentment morality evaluates the weakness, passivity, and denial of man as the good, so it teaches that the distinquished, the original good, is the evil enemy and in fact, the unchained beast of prey. Nietzsche considers this teaching the most clever point of attack by resentment morality, and a successful one. For since by his Dionysian faith the whole of man must be affirmed and by sublimation the drives of the beast in man must be recreated into cultural power without loss of their original vigor, the blond beast cannot be denied. Among equals, that is among those who together fight the battle of culture, these "evil enemies" are severely restrained in their relations with each other by "manners, reverence, custom, gratitude, and even more by mutual watchfulness and envy of related attainment." They are very resourceful in showing regard for each other in "mutual consideration, self-control, loyalty, pride, and friendship." [1] But toward those alien to their way of life and those who obstruct their battle, they are indeed unchained beasts of prey and delight in destroying. Before strangers, Nietzsche explains, they allow themselves relief from the tension of their battle and for the moment become unchained. Moreover, even in their highest culture there is a trait of defiance and pride; so that it is not strange that they leave the concept of a "barbarian" with those unable to understand them. When their battle is less than finished—as he considers it to be the case with the Germans—distrust of them is quite natural as the result of all the horror with which Europe had to watch the blond beast's madness for centuries. But Nietzsche prefers even that to the disgust that he professes at sight of the destruction of man's dignity by the resentment morality.

Thus Nietzsche attempts to draw the picture of what he considers to be the aristocrat who, out of a complete faith in the autonomy of man, this life and its moral values, battles progressively and without compromise to recreate his inherent powers to their highest human forms. The goal is still vague to him and exceedingly distant. But he is certain that there can be no approach to it other than through the complete affirmation of life. Consequently, every evaluation out of a negation of the powers of this life, or the distortion of them out of hatred of life's fullness in the manner of the resentment morality, is to him false, deceitful, and a will to mediocrity—and therefore nihilism, rather than a will to power. This he attacks relentlessly and seeks to destroy it. Because he discovers this nihilism in the Christian democratic culture of the Europe of his day, and yet asserts that the European in his best examples is still the fine blond beast capable of regenerating his powers to the highest culture, he plumbs for the reason of this degeneration and believes to have found it in the revolt out of resentment of the Jewish priests and its success in Christianity. Such procedure may properly be called a psychological investigation, or more properly experiment, but not history. To Nietzsche, however, it is true because it inescapably results from his basic faith. That is to say, in theory.

When, at the end of the essay, he engages in psychological analyses of the element of resentment in modern institutional behavior, particularly in the administration of justice and the culmination of it in the dogma of the Last Judgment, he is sharp and telling. But when he ventures to find in history examples of the distinguished warrior of culture, he is far from convincing and even awkward. For example, he calls the aristocrat of Rome the ideal classical man and Rome's writings best, "provided one can divine *what* is written there."

At the end he takes a glimpse into the future in the teasing manner that delights him and suggests that at some time a more terrible but far more carefully prepared example will appear who will flourish "beyond good and evil" but *not* "beyond good and no-good."

C. *"Guilt, Bad Conscience, and the Like," The Morality of Nihilism*

In the second essay Nietzsche pursues the origin and functioning of nihilism from a point of view that must have seemed a truer genealogy to him than that of the resentment of the priests and the "revolt of the slaves." The new presentation finally results in very much the same picture, but the origins of the disease of nihilism are traced further back into man's history, into what he sees as the violent emergence of the organization of the first state. Again, however, it is a psychological study of his peculiar brand and not properly historical. It is another experiment, on the basis of his persistent hypothesis of the development of man's will to power through sublimation, in an effort to diagnose the root and reason of the disease which obstructed it, and to examine the possibility of a cure.

The idea of the will to power through sublimation within the steady maintenance of the Dionysian faith is here formulated in moral terms as "nature's task in respect to man to breed an animal who *has the right to promise*." [1] By this is meant the development of the fully responsible and autonomous conscience as the full integrity of the will to power. Though to promise means to remember, Nietzsche points out that memory cannot be indiscriminate, because that would lead to a serious congestion of experiences. Therefore, nature in man makes use of an active forgetfulness which acts as a restraint to memory to allow the assimilation and incorporation of experiences, which he calls spiritual assimilation *(Einverseelung)*. This provides some repose to consciousness so that there may be room for more distinguished functions. It is the "guardian of spiritual order, serenity, and etiquette."

As a counterforce to this selective forgetfulness, man is endowed with an active memory (as distinct from the purely passive one) which stops forgetfulness for the sake of promises. It is the will not to let go, a will to will, a "memory of the will." This is to Nietzsche the origin of responsibility: the result, however, of long training to distinguish the necessary from the fortuitous action, to be able to calculate. During an extended period of his pre-history, man, in the course of such training, first made himself calculable, regular, and necessary. This is his basic moral history. In its final stage it took on the form of what Nietzsche calls *Sittlichkeit der Sitte*, habitual moral behavior, common decency, or mores. This is described as the fixed moral behavior that had developed over a long period as unconsciously as the assimilation of food. It is accompanied by a disturbance similar to all digestion, but, once formed, it represents man's responsibility and controls his actions within his society like a straitjacket. Though the average man is content to stop at this stage of his development, there yet arises as the final meaning of the long process, the sovereign individual who has freed himself from the merely habitual moral behavior to become an autonomous, more-than-moral *(übersittlich)* individual with a personal, independent will that gives him the right to promise and the consciousness of power and freedom. He supplies the real meaning of the process that had hardened into the *Sittlichkeit der Sitte*. He is now the master of a freed and sublimated will and as such awakens much confidence, respect, and also fear. He honors his equals and has no regard for the weaker. His long, unbreakable, autonomous will acts as his dominant instinct and conscience in "the highest, almost surprising form." [1] He makes himself the measure of things by the genuineness of his sublimated power.

This master, as the final phase of man's moral development, is, like Zarathustra, a picture of Nietzsche's hope for the future. It is still strangely vague, considering that it is not very different from Goethe's autonomous conscience *(selbstständiges Gewissen)* which Nietzsche, however, in all probability interpreted as a gift and, therefore, not similar to the actively acquired sublimation and freedom forged into the instinct of his "master." It seems as though he was impelled to project his master far into the future so that he could devote himself to describing the obstacles to his coming and then attempt to clear them away.

To elaborate on the origins of moral behavior and custom, he seeks to pursue by his "historical" psychological method the origin and purpose of responsibility, obligation, and conscience. He finds that the idea originated first from the contractual relation of the stronger creditor to the weaker debtor, as between individuals, rather than under the usually accepted idea of a social contract. Relying on the German word for guilt *(Schuld)*, which still signifies both debt and transgression, he identifies the two ideas in their origin. In return for the debt owed to the creditor, the latter demanded an equivalent which, if it could not be paid materially, was exacted by the infliction of bodily and later spiritual harm that was subsequently called punishment. By means of such equivalents there was produced in the debtor a memory or conscience, which was necessary to uphold the contract and which included all manner of cruelty meant to establish the superiority of the creditor.

Nietzsche goes to considerable length to describe the element of cruelty and the festive delight in cruelty employed to stimulate memory and conscience within the debtor. He finds it not only in the old German criminal law, the later festive witnessing of executions, and the like, but he observes that the punishment of the wicked even today gives an unholy satisfaction to the righteous. In most of the moral concepts that originate in the rights arising from obligations—such as guilt, conscience, duty, sanctity of duty, and the like—he discovers some element of cruelty.

Nietzsche finds nothing pessimistic in this festivity of suffering, and no element as yet of "bad conscience" in the memory it produces. It is still a healthy process by which nature develops the animal in man into one who can promise, as well as a will to healthy power. From this point of view he studies "historically" the nature of punishment as the equivalent for a breach of contract, in order to discover at what point "bad conscience" is introduced and under what conditions. In the oldest form of social activity—the contract between individuals—he finds the first manifestation of the measuring of human wit against wit, and perhaps even thinking itself. The word for man, *manas*, he suggests by an etymology peculiar to himself, is meant to convey man's pride as the "evaluating animal *per se*." The initial ideas of exchange, contract, debt, rights, and responsibility constitute the rudimentary forms of the personal law of the powerful individual who can force others to an agreement. These later transferred themselves upon early social complexes. "Everything has its price, everything can be paid for," he calls the oldest canon of justice.[1]

He finds the attitude of the early communities to their members to be a similar one, and in part still to persist. The German word for the criminal *(Verbrecher)*, for example, connotes generally a "breaker," a man who violates a contract and promise against the whole, a debtor. His punishment is meant to remind him of the value of the social good, and it is meted out to him on the same principle as indemnities are imposed upon the conquered in a war. As society increases in power, it can afford to be more lenient in its punishments, and it demonstrates its strength by the degree to which it can tolerate infractions. At its peak, what is ordinarily called justice is set aside for mercy, thereby demonstrating, so Nietzsche argues, that mercy is the privilege of the most powerful who can afford to act beyond the law.

He finds that the procedure of punishment has an essentially persistent character, as evidenced by its related customs throughout the changes of history. The purpose of punishment, however, as that expected from the execution of the procedure, is a constantly changing interpretation put upon the procedure. This is Nietzsche's real point of interest, because in the changing purpose he sees the manifestation of the creative will to power. "But all purposes, all usefulness are merely *indications* that a will to power has become master of something less powerful and has attributed to itself the meaning of a function."[2] In the function the will to power is always creative in its expression and therefore, by constant reinterpretation and reforming, each time expresses the mastery of the stronger over the weaker.

The history of punishment is to him the history of the purposes. But in modern punishment he discovers not a particular purpose, but a synthesis of the whole of this history which is quite impossible to analyze or define. A series of purposes can, however, be isolated. In doing so, he discovers what he has originally set out to find: an assumed, and consequently false, usefulness to be distinguished especially in modern punishment. This assumption is the belief that the value of punishment lies in the feeling of guilt which it awakens and in its use as an instrument for the spiritual reaction, called "bad conscience" or "pangs of conscience." This Nietzsche calls historically and psychologically false. Punishment, he maintains, rarely produces a bad conscience, but rather a feeling of being a hopeless and helpless victim of fate, who sees the wrongdoing not in himself, but in the procedure of the judge and in the execution of the judgment. At best, its effect is the historical one of fear and the sharpening of memory. Punishment may well make use of what he calls the disease of bad conscience and the feeling of guilt. But the origin of this he sees in quite a different direction from punishment, namely, in man's denial of his nature; in becoming ashamed of himself; in turning his will to power toward a negative, rather than a positive, creative sublimation.

His hypothesis for the origin of bad conscience is, in a sense, a modification of the "revolt of the slaves" described in the first essay of this book, or better, an attempt to find in the "disease" of the static behavior a deeper psychological origin than in the "historical" revolt. When man, the "half animal who had successfully adapted himself to the wilderness, war, roaming, and adventure," finally and irrevocably found himself under the restrictions of society and peace; when he had attained the stage of the fixed *Sittlichkeit der Sitte* under the organization of the state, he became as awkward as a fish out of water. The instincts which had unconsciously, but surely, regulated his behavior were made taboo and had to be repressed in favor of conscious thinking, calculating, and combining cause and effect. As a result of this, a deep distress came over man since the old instincts continued to make demands on him. But the restrictions of society prevented their expression and forced a repression.

The ordered behavior which the State organizations forced as a habit upon man were like the bars of a cage against which he wounded himself out of a "longing for the wilderness." So he created an insecure and dangerous wilderness out of himself. "This fool, this longing and despairing prisoner got to be the inventor of the 'bad conscience.' By him there was introduced the most severe and uncanny disease from which man has not yet recovered: the suffering of man from man, from himself."

In upholding this hypothesis Nietzsche makes the assumption, first, that this change was neither voluntary nor organic but so sudden an imposition that there was no opportunity to oppose it or even resent it; secondly, that it was a violent action, a "terrible tyranny" by the few untamed, unspoiled, and consequently still creative masters who forced the "hitherto uninhibited and unformed mass" into the definite form that Nietzsche calls the first State. It is a familiar idea of his that, when the will to power and the instinct of freedom becomes retarded in a condition of peace and static behavior, and even more when it becomes repressed, some few stronger individuals will arise to exert their will in violent creative activity. To see the beginnings of the State in these uninhibited and creative tyrants is consistent with his theory, but probably has no other basis.

Christian religion, he contends, has attempted finally to cancel the debt in a pessimistic manner by fostering the bad conscience to the point where the discharge of the guilt became hopeless. The debtor invented to his self-abuse the concept of eternal punishment; made his progenitor the Old Adam and the source of original sin; considered nature and life inimical; and landed in nihilism. Finally he sought his redemption by having God Himself assume the punishment for his guilt, letting the creditor pay for the debtor—"out of love of the debtor!"

Thus the "crude logic" of Nietzsche goes, and must go by the dictation of his Dionysian faith and of the will to power by sublimation to which any attitude of escape or a pessimistic negative approach is contradictory and destructive. He sees man employing his feeling of debt toward God as an instrument of self-torture.

Nietzsche's faith dictates to him a wishful solution. It must lie in continuing boldly, with strictest integrity, with what he calls "the great health," to expose the prevailing Christian ideals as escapes; to regain the full faith in life and full knowledge of it; to work progressively at the will to sublimate its power through the joyous recreation of it. He would call it to redeem the actuality of life. It is an emotional solution, and he consoles himself about the strange oddity of it by saying that the comprehension of it is almost impossible in modern times and, at best, depends on some new philosopher of the distant future.

D. *What Do the Ascetic Ideals Signify?*

Having established modern man's disease as the nihilism arising from the frustration and exhaustion of life, and having shown to his satisfaction that this disease prevailed throughout European history, Nietzsche examines in a third essay the ascetic ideals that express this nihilism. To these ideals he applies his psychological method of depth penetration to discover, first, whether they are truly nihilistic—that is, wholly deny life as the will to power and consequently deny the will itself. To him that would mean to be able to see life wholly devoid of a goal, or the attempt to live in a vacuum as though life did not exist. He then establishes that, since non-willing is an absurdity and man must have a goal, the diseased man by the ascetic ideal attempts to will the nothingness rather than not to will at all, or persuades himself that he is doing so, and thus does not rid himself of the will in spite of his nihilism. Besides, he discovers that to certain men the ascetic ideal is not a symptom of the disease of nihilism, but merely a mask they assume to establish a distance between their search for power and the lack of understanding accorded them. But he finds this a dangerous game and a threat to the robust health necessary to the philosopher. In the ascetic ideals of those whom he takes to be definitely diseased, however, he discovers no mask, but a great lack of intellectual integrity which may be self-deception or a disguised will to power by a false show of sublimation.

So this essay is primarily an exhibition of Nietzsche'

psychological penetration of the behavior of the ascetic ideal. Thereby he makes discoveries of the behavior of exhaustion and repression that are startling for his time and of significant suggestions to later investigators. But they all result from his premise and throw light upon his difficult theme of autonomous sublimation in a negative way only. The theme upon which the psychological analyses are built he recapitulates in a final paragraph in so clear and characteristic a manner that it is well to quote it in its entirety in the selections to this chapter (p. 241).

With his interpretation of the ascetic ideal and the claim that it saved the will in spite of itself, Nietzsche examines the particular meaning of the ideal as employed by various artists, philosophers, or groups. Characteristically, he treats mostly of those with whom his experiences had been most intimate and with whom he had to battle most for his own integrity. It is in such cases that he is harshest and kindest.

He speaks of Wagner first, but as though he were analyzing a case scientifically, and makes no direct mention of the personal elements of their friendship or of the story of their break. He uses him as an example of what the ascetic ideal means, or, in the case of an artist, may mean.

Wagner's attitude toward the ascetic ideal in his early days is described as quite healthy and cheerful. He mentions that before writing the *Meistersinger*, in "his strongest, most exuberant and courageous period," Wagner had planned a comedy on the subject of Luther's marriage that would have been equally in praise of chastity as of a frank sensuality of the kind that Luther was not loath to admit. True to his principle of sublimation, Nietzsche saw no contrast between chastity and joy in the senses. The labile balance of the two in well-conditioned men, particularly good artists, might well be taken as one of the charms of life. Nietzsche himself repeatedly battled, or claimed to battle, with the uncertainty of this balance. The problem interested him all the more because he himself was not too well conditioned—at least physically. So he tried to solve it to his encouragement, if possible, in those once closely related to him, the poet Wagner and the philosopher Schopenhauer. He suggests that perhaps even the *Parzival* is not the pessimistic tragedy that it has been taken for, but a kind of farewell satire.

But if this attempted "rescue" of Wagner should be too fantastic, and if the *Parzival* must be taken seriously, then Nietzsche suggests that in his dotage Wagner had occupied himself with medieval Christianity to his own undoing; that he had fallen prey to the "typical velleity" of a senile artist; that he had succumbed to a misunderstanding of Schopenhauer's theory of music and turned into a metaphysician and "ventriloquist of God." Either interpretation presents Nietzsche with the point which he desires to make: that the use of the ascetic ideal by an artist such as Wagner proves nothing as to the worth of the ideal itself, in that it is either mere material for him or an aberration.

The case of Schopenhauer and the ascetic ideal concerned him even more, for he had never turned away from Schopenhauer's influence with equal distress as from Wagner. However much he found himself in disagreement with the metaphysics, Schopenhauer still remained the example of the real philosopher. Consequently he had to find an explanation for Schopenhauer's homage to the ascetic ideal which would not deny his own thesis. He does so by turning this homage into the kind of discipline, training, and pathos of distance that he considers generally characteristic of the life and sublimation of a philosopher under present adverse conditions.

He maintains boldly that in the case of Schopenhauer, or any real philosopher, the ascetic ideal does not mean a denial of life, but rather the affirmation of his own particular manner of life; that Schopenhauer cannot even properly be called a pessimist. In asserting that beauty lies in the freedom from the will—that is, the vulgar will to live—Schopenhauer merely desired to free himself from the obstruction to his contemplative life and from the spiritual torture caused by the vulgar will. His denial of the senses was very different from the disinterestedness of Kant. Like every real philosopher he was intent only on the most essential and most natural conditions of his best living and productivity. With his ascetic ideal he flirted with the optimum of those conditions which would enable the highest and boldest spirituality. His attack upon women and sex, as expressions of the vulgar will, was essentially his delight in a fight, as was his pessimism, to rid himself of the torture of that element of the will.

By implication Nietzsche even identifies his own fate with that of Schopenhauer and asserts that all philosophers have a hatred of sensuality and a strong inclination toward the ascetic ideals not, however, for any moral reasons, but for the sake of the expression of their power. They have a dislike of marriage and the sensuality leading to it because of the fetters which this puts upon the philosophical life. Consequently, poverty, humility, and chastity in a true philosopher are not moral ideals at all, but the best conditions for the best life and highest fruitfulness. His dominant instinct is his will to power through sublimation. In almost autobiographical terms Nietzsche insists that poverty gives the philosopher an opportunity to be by himself, even in society. He may make a show of humility in order to avoid enemies and friends that are uselessly disturbing. Chastity is merely his training to remain in fittest condition. Such ascetic behavior is simply good sense and quite without "virtue." As severe and cheerful restraint a certain asceticism belongs to the favorable conditions of highest spirituality and to the best will to power through sublimation.

The ascetic ideals may also serve the philosopher as an effective weapon by which to gain recognition and the power over lesser men which is necessary for his mission. Contemplative men have always had to live under the weight of the hatred which they awakened. By this they "built their own hell" for themselves, but also created the conditions by which they could be themselves. Thus they were forced, by the conditions about them, to live in a sort of cocoon. Perhaps, Nietzsche says, now that the world has become saner, warmer, and more enlightened, there may be a chance that the philosopher can leave the cocoon and at last emancipate himself.

Having found some excuses and even some advantage for

the use of the ascetic ideals by the poet and philosopher, because they are both related to himself and because the torture of their struggle with the ideal was an intimate experience of his own, he now turns to his favorite attack upon the ascetic priests as the example of the wholly pessimistic use of the ideal and of the resultant danger to culture.

To Nietzsche the ascetic priests are completely false philosophers devoid of intellectual and spiritual integrity, motivated, like all living, by a will to power which, however, is exerted to deceive themselves and others, rather than for sublimation. They attempt the impossible: to express the will to power of life by the complete denial of life and by the enjoyment of that denial. Their ascetic ideal, like all observations to Nietzsche, is indeed a perspective, but a complete reversal of the healthy person's perspective. Actuality with them becomes appearance; they deal with mystic absolutes: "a realm of truth and essence is decreed but reason is above all excluded from it." [1] They become the victims of Nietzsche's persistent and consistent hatred of absolutes and of idealism as the fatal contradiction to his perspective procedure. He grants, however, that their perversion is still a mere interpretation and that the sickness which it represents to him is, therefore, not necessarily real, but perhaps a kind of indigestion of life. Their ascetic ideal, he thinks, may arise from "the instincts of a degenerating life to find protection and cure." For them life has been suppressed and exhausted and they find themselves in a state of severe discomfort. They represent man, the great experimenter, as completely exhausted and nursing his wounds by means of the ascetic ideal—a sort of trick by which to save life. Though the ideal in its denial of this life fosters in them a great longing for another life, the very intensity of that wish still binds them to life. Thus they complete the paradox which they represent. [2]

Since they completely contradict his point of view, these ascetic priests are to Nietzsche the great enemies and danger for all those who are luckily strong and healthy. Moreover he sees them as the prevailing influence in Christian Europe and he therefore goes to extremes to unveil them and warn against them. Out of their weakness and lust for power he finds that there arises a sick resentment against all that is healthy, and that they employ every distortion in the effort to claim for themselves all virtues, "even to their insistence on designating their revenge and hatred as justice." The greatest threat to the health of man lies in the disgust with man and in the debilitating sense of sympathy the sight of such degeneration may produce. If these two should ever come together, they might well produce "the last will," man's will to nothingness, his nihilism, the gravest danger to the free spirit. So concerned is Nietzsche with this danger that he invokes the protective "pathos of distance" and cautions the healthy to stay away from the ascetic priests and their teachings in order to guard themselves against the *"great disgust with man"* and *"the great sympathy."* [1]

The ascetic priests are described as the physicians of those who suffer from the depression of life and its resultant pessimism. But they themselves suffer from the same disease and therefore know its symptoms thoroughly, though they are unable to comprehend its cause. By virtue of their cleverness, however, they are strong enough to prescribe in the ascetic ideal a narcotic and depressive by which they make the patient dependent upon themselves and thus gain power over him. They succeed in this primarily by being what Nietzsche calls *"the changers of the direction"* of the sick resentment. [2] The emotion of resentment, which is itself a kind of narcotic, the priests turn upon the sick themselves. They attribute the depression to the guilt of the patient himself, thus creating in him bad conscience and the sense of sin, and then develop in him a longing for the redemption from his guilt. They do so not by treating the cause, which they do not understand, but by increasing the narcotic. They whip up all kinds of ascetic emotions and excesses, even to the extent of an insane frenzy which, in the nature of a narcotic, first decreases the discomfort, but then revenges itself. Thus man learns to castigate himself, to long for suffering, and to cherish pessimism. [3]

In bitter and satirical terms Nietzsche then analyzes the various forms of the ascetic ideal prescribed by the priests and by which they hypnotize and rule over the masses of the weak. These prescriptions represent a complete lack of integrity to him. And yet, since he considers the priests themselves sick, he finds a degree of innocence in them, and even a kind of positive act in the intensity of their hypnotic negations. As a psychologist, however, he undertakes what he calls the disagreeable task of uncovering this "innocence" as moral sweetening and an inner feminism which likes to call itself idealism. He brands every form of the ascetic ideal some kind of an escape and, as such, the direct contradiction of the courageous confrontation of life demanded by his Dionysian faith. He also finds a total absence of the creating of values in sublimation. Instead, this idealism calls for abstention of willing and emotions, and creates the "great sleep," about which he becomes highly satirical and which he finds powerfully represented in the teaching of vicarious redemption in the great religions.

The greatest bitterness, however, he directs against religious ecstasy as the debauchery of emotions which clothes deceit in attractive, innocent forms and acts as a criminally false hypnosis. He finds every kind of neurosis resulting from such deceit, as well as a serious loss of spiritual health and of good taste in the arts.

These psychological analyses of the ascetic ideal are extremely bitter and sharp because they represented his meeting with the most immediate enemy of his struggle for his own faith and because he personally had experienced their power thoroughly. But if he found the power deceitful and the means to it devoid of integrity, he was obligated to define genuine power and to describe the honest means towards sublimation in an idea other than the ascetic. In this attempt he examines science, which he had once followed as the safest road to integrity. He now finds that science and the modern atheist produced by it is not genuine enough nor sufficiently free from idealism. He now suspects that modern exact science, with its worship of facts, may be only another narcotic, like all mere hard work which mistakes the mass of quantity for quality. Perhaps it is only propaganda and has no faith in itself and no ideal over itself, and so cannot create values as sublimation must. At best, he suggests, it is only the newest and most distinguished form of the ascetic ideal. "It is the restlessness over the loss of idealism itself, over the loss of a great devotion," and so also an escape and devoid of "a goal, a will, an ideal, a passion of great faith." [1]

By "faith," Nietzsche here, as always, refers to his Dionysian faith and the will to power through sublimation which he considers wholly different from any metaphysical belief in whatever garb. He sees in it the basic assumption of any cognition: "There must always first be a philosophy, a faith, from which scientific investigation receives its direction, meaning, limits, method, and a *right* to existence." [2] Its goal is the never-ending experimentation toward clearer and more honest cognition and the eternal effort of the will to power through clearer sublimation, however great the torment may may be as the path leads through new and unforeseeable difficulties and has no end in time. The way of procedure must be by an intellectual and spiritual integrity which is ever suspicious of itself and constantly seeks a possible contradiction of itself, lest it come to rest in some metaphysical truth. It is always brutally exacting.

However, he finds that modern scientists, philosophers and scholars are far from being bold, unceasing experimenters with their worship of facts as the truth, "their fatalism" of the addition of minute facts, and their refusal of creative interpretation. The belief in "truth" in their sense he calls their madness and very much an ascetic ideal, though more spiritualized than the denial of the senses. Believing in the value of truth *per se,* they give truth a metaphysical value and thereby divorce themselves from his method. A courageous experimenter like himself would break free from the ascetic ideal to the extent of adopting for his search the motto of the Ismailian assassins: Nothing is true, all is permitted. He would reject the dogma of the divinity of truth and assume the risk of making the value of truth his new problem. "The will to truth needs a critique—let that be our particular problem—as a matter of experiment the worth of truth must be *questioned.*" By this kind of attack Nietzsche severely divorced himself from those "free spirits" who would claim relationship with him, as though he feared they would adversely influence his integrity or somehow disturb the isolation of which he was as jealous as of his uniqueness, however much he complained of it. Nevertheless, the saying, "Nothing is true, all is permitted," is consistent with his theory of the persistent intellectual and creative activity of the will to power through sublimation. To it the final truth would mean an end of activity and of the meaning of life itself. To the experimenter and perspective thinker and artist, all is indeed permitted that does not violate his integrity. The intellectual and spiritual conscience must everywhere be the touchstone of the genuineness of the will to power and sublimation. It is the morality, he believes, on which the "weaker" morality of the ascetic ideal must founder, when moral courage rises to the venture of posing the problem of the value and meaning of truth.

It is with the "torture" which he claims to experience as the necessity to contradict each result attained with painful "rectitude," even to the extent of questioning the value of truth—that he seems to justify his claim as lawgiver and enlightened teacher of the autonomous culture by which all that is best in man can and will aim at ever truer sublimation. Like the end itself, even the method can have no final definition. Even the final answer as to what constitutes intellectual and spiritual integrity must be scrutinized and attacked as far as possible by questioning the very worth of truth.

Thus, at the end of this book, also, little progress has been made in dispelling the element of vagueness as to the nature of the proper sublimation of the will to power, except to question the disadvantage of the vagueness itself. However, in the process of searching for genuine integrity and in testing past accomplishments, behavior, and institutions of religion, scholarship, and art in order to discover what degree of integrity they contain, he succeeds in many sharp psychological analyses that are highly enlightening, even though the resultant judgments are merely consequences of Nietzsche's initial hypothesis of the will to power by autonomous sublimation and of his dominant Dionysian faith.

from:

A Genealogy of Morals

We need a *critique* of all moral values; the *worth of these values themselves must first be questioned.*

[FOREWORD: 6]

Thus far no one has in the least doubted or hesitated to claim a higher value for the "good" than for the "evil." What, if the opposite were true? What, if in the "good" there were a symptom of regression, also a danger, a temptation, a poison, a narcotic by which the present were perhaps living *at the expense of the future?* More comfortably perhaps, less dangerously, but also in a meaner state, lower? . . . Can it possibly be the fault of morality if the highest potential power and glory of man never has been reached? That the supreme danger should be morality?

[FOREWORD: 6]

It is perfectly obvious to me at the start that in this [utilitarian] theory the real source of the concept "good" is looked for and posited at the wrong place. The judgment "good" does *not* arise from those to whom "goodness" is shown. Rather it was the "good" themselves, that is the distinguished, powerful, outstanding, and high-minded who considered and posited themselves and their acts as good, as of first rank in contrast to all that is low, low-minded, mean, and plebeian. This *"pathos of distance"* gave them the right to create values and coin the names for values. What concern of theirs was utility?

[ESSAY 1:2]

The welfare of the many and that of the few are opposite perspectives of value. To consider the former *per se* of higher value we will leave to the naïveté of English biologists.—*All* sciences must henceforth prepare the future task of the philosopher, the task being, that the philosopher must solve the *problem of worth,* must determine the *order of rank* of the kinds of worth.

[ESSAY 1:2]

Is it not part of the hidden sorcery of a truly great policy of revenge; a far-sighted, slowly expanding and calculating revenge, that Israel had to deny and crucify the real instrument of its revenge before all the world as though it were a mortal enemy, so that "all the world," that is all the enemies of Israel, would readily take this bait. And yet, could a *more dangerous* bait be conceived by any subtlety of intellect? Anything that in enticing, intoxicating, stultifying, destructive power would equal that symbol of the "sacred cross"; that mystery of an inconceivable, extreme, final cruelty and self-sacrifice of God for the *salvation of man?* . . . One thing at least is certain: *sub hoc signo* Israel with its revenge and transvaluation of all values has thus far triumphed over all other ideals, over all *more distinguished* ideals.

[ESSAY 1:8]

It may be wholly right that the fear of the blond beast at the heart of every distinguished race cannot be avoided and must be guarded against. But who would not a hundred times rather fear, if at the same time he can admire, than not fear, but never be able to rid himself of the disgusting sight of the crippled, debased, absurd, and poisoned. And is not that very thing *our* fate? [The blond beast at least affirms this life against the denial of it by the tame and hopelessly mediocre man of the resentment morality. Here Nietzsche is like Dionysus calling upon man to be] stronger, more evil, deeper, and more beautiful.

[ESSAY 1:11]

Rome found the Jew guilty of hatred of all mankind; rightly, in so far as one has the right to tie the welfare and the future of mankind to the unconditional rule of the aristocrat, the Roman values. [In the same paragraph he eulogizes Napoleon as] the most unique and latest-born person there ever was who incorporated in himself the problem of the *aristocratic ideal per se*—one must consider well what this problem is: Napoleon, this synthesis of *beast (Unmensch)* and *superman*.

[ESSAY 1:16]

To see suffering pleases, to inflict it even more; that is a hard saying but an old, mighty, human, all-too-human principle. "Without cruelty no feast." Thus the oldest, longest history of man teaches—and in and about punishment there is so much that is *festive*.

[ESSAY 2:6]

The terrible bulwarks by which the State organizations protected against the instincts of freedom caused all the instincts of the wild, free, roaming man to turn within *against man himself*. The enmity, cruelty, joy in persecution—all this turning against the possessor of such instincts—that is the origin of "bad conscience."

[ESSAY 2:16]

This fool, this longing and despairing prisoner got to be the inventor of the "bad conscience." By him there was introduced the most severe and uncanny disease from which man has not yet recovered: the suffering of man from man, from himself.

[ESSAY 2:16]

[He describes the organizers of the first State as] a pack of blond beasts of prey, a race of conquerors and masters who, with a warlike organization and the power to organize others, blandly set their terrible paws upon a group which may very greatly outnumber them but is still unformed and roaming . . .

Their work is an instinctive creation and imposing of forms; they are the most involuntary, unconscious artists imaginable. Where they appear there is suddenly something new, a form of government [*Herrschaftsgebilde*] that *lives*, the parts and functions of which are defined and interrelated, in which there is nothing to which meaning has not first been given in respect to the whole.

[ESSAY 2:17]

This *instinct for freedom*, forcibly made latent, suppressed, retrograded, locked up within, and finally expending itself and letting itself out only upon itself—that and that alone is *bad conscience* in its beginnings.

[ESSAY 2:17]

[But, Nietzsche continues, this repressed and inverted instinct for freedom is still a will to power, though a negative form of it. It finds its activity in negative creations, in concepts and ideals contradictory to power—such as selflessness, self-denial, and self-sacrifice—that, however, suggest a fund of strange new beauty and affirmation. It may even be the source of what we call beauty.] What would be beautiful if its opposite had not first become conscious of itself; if the ugly had not said to itself: I am ugly.

[ESSAY 2:18]

[He then undertakes to state under what conditions this "disease" of man reached its most terrible and most sublime height, in order to discuss modern nihilism as its necessary result. He explains that at one point of history, which he calls remarkable and odd and sets back into pre-historic times, the civil contractural relation of debtor to creditor was interpreted into the debt owed by descendants to their ancestors from whom they had received the gifts that enabled their existence. They expressed their obligation to them in reverence and sacrifice to the point of ancestor worship. Moreover, the greater and more distinguished the descendants, the greater the consciousness of obligation, so that] If this crude logic is carried to its conclusion, then the ancestors of the *mightiest* races must have gained immense stature in the imagination of an increasing fear until they receded into the obscurity of a divine mystery and ineffability;—finally the ancestor necessarily is transfigured into a *god.*

[ESSAY 2:19]

[According to this reasoning, when blood relationship is lost in the more complex societies the consciousness of debt is not lost with it, but changes from a particular to a universal ancestor god; and in the Christian God, as the maximal god, it has produced the maximum consciousness of debt. In the interest of his faith Nietzsche allows himself the following wishful fantasy.] Assuming that at last we have entered upon the *opposite* course, we might then with some probability deduce from the irresistible decline of the faith in the Christian God that there is already a significant lessening of the consciousness of guilt. Yes, the prospect cannot be denied that the complete and final victory of atheism may free mankind from the whole feeling that it is indebted to its origin, its *causa prima.* Atheism and a kind of *second innocence* belong together.

[ESSAY 2:20]

In God he [man] seizes upon the extreme opposite to his real and inescapable animal instincts; he translates these instincts into a transgression against God (as enmity, insurrection, revolt against the "Lord," the "Father," the progenitor and the origin of the world); he ties himself to the opposites of "God" and "the devil"; every No that he pronounces to nature and the naturalness of his being he projects into a Yes as a living actuality, as God, as the holiness of God, as God the judge and executioner, as life beyond, eternity, as torture without end, as hell, as the immensity of punishment and guilt. This is a madness of the will of a spiritual cruelty that has no equal anywhere. [To Nietzsche this is the most terrible

disease imaginable. It is making this earth into a madhouse
out of a pessimism of which the bad conscience is the symptom and symbol, and nihilism the end.]

[ESSAY 2:22]

This man of the future who will free us not only from the
prevalent ideal but equally from that which had to proceed
from it: from the great disgust, the will to nothingness, the
nihilism; this signal of noon and of the great decision who will
again free the will, restore to the earth its goal and to man
his hope; this anti-Christian and anti-nihilist; this conqueror
of God and nothingness—at some time he must appear. . . .

[ESSAY 2:24]

Man, man the beast, has hitherto had no meaning except
for the ascetic ideal. There was no goal to his life on earth.
Why man at all? was a question without an answer; the will
to man and earth was missing; every great human fate contained the greater refrain: In vain! The very meaning of the
ascetic ideal is this: that there was something missing, that
an immense void surrounded man;—he did not know how to
justify, explain, affirm himself; he *suffered* from the problem
of his being. He suffered in other ways, too. Mainly he was a
diseased beast. However, suffering was not his problem, but
the fact that he had no answer to the distress of the question:
suffer for what? Man, the bravest and most long-suffering
beast, does *not* deny suffering in itself; he wants it, he even
searches it out, provided a meaning for it be shown him, a
"what for" of his suffering. The senselessness of suffering,
not suffering, was the curse that had hitherto been lying upon
man;—*and the ascetic ideal provided a meaning*. Thus far it
has been the only sense, and any sense is better than no
sense at all; it was in every respect the *faute de mieux par
excellence* that ever was. In it suffering was *explained;* the
terrible void seemed filled; the door was closed against all
suicidal nihilism. This interpretation—no doubt about it—
brought on new suffering, deeper, more inward, more nox-

ious, and gnawing more at life: it put all suffering under the perspective of *guilt*. But in spite of all that—it *saved* man, it gave him a meaning. From now on he was no longer a leaf in the wind, a playball of nonsense; he could henceforth *will* something—initially quite indifferent as to whither, what for, or with what he willed; *the will itself was saved*. It is simply impossible to disregard *what* all the willing that received its direction from the ascetic ideal really expresses: this hatred for all that is human; still more for what is beast; more still for the material; this disgust with the senses, with reason itself; the fear of happiness and beauty; this longing to be rid of all illusion, change, becoming, death, wishing, even longing itself—all this signifies—let us risk an understanding of it —a *will to nothingness*, a repugnance to life, a revolt against the most fundamental premises of life; but it is and remains a *will!* . . . And—to repeat at the end what I said at the beginning—man still prefers to will the *nothing* to *not* willing.

[ESSAY 3:28]

[In *Parzival*] Wagner the composer of tragedies meant to take his leave of us, of himself, and especially of the tragedy in the manner most becoming and worthy of him, that is, by an excessively high and most audacious parody *on the tragic view of life;* on the whole of the former gruesome seriousness of life; on the finally discarded monstrosity of the ascetic ideal.

[ESSAY 3:3]

That which is inactive, brooding, unwarlike in the instincts of contemplative men causes a deep distrust to be spread about them, which could be met by no other means than to awaken *fear* of themselves.

[ESSAY 3:10]

Is there enough pride, daring, bravery, self-assurance, will of the spirit to responsibility today to at least make the philosopher possible?

[ESSAY 3:10]

The ascetic ideal never and nowhere has been a school of good taste and less of good manners.

[ESSAY 3:22]

It [science] is the restlessness over the loss of idealism itself, over the loss of a great devotion, [and so also an escape and devoid of] a goal, a will, an ideal, a passion of great faith.

[ESSAY 3:23]

There must always first be a philosophy, a faith, from which scientific investigation receives its direction, meaning, limits, method, and a *right* to existence.

[ESSAY 3:24]

[Nietzsche here examines the modern scientists, the philosophers and scholars who believe themselves free of the ascetic ideal.] These deniers and aloof men of today, unyielding in one thing: their claim to intellectual cleanliness. These hard, severe, abstaining, heroic spirits who are the honor of our times; all these pale atheists, anti-Christians, immoralists, nihilists; these skeptics, aphetics, hectics of the spirit (in some way or other they are all hectics); these last idealists of cognition in whom alone today the intellectual conscience dwells and has its being;—they do indeed believe that they have freed themselves from the ascetic ideal, these free, *very* free spirits.

[ESSAY 3:24]

The will to truth needs a critique—let that be our particular problem—as a matter of experiment the worth of truth must be *questioned*. What is the meaning of all will to truth? . . . What sense would all our existence have if not this: that it should have become conscious of the will to truth itself *as a problem?* From this light of consciousness thrown upon the will to truth, morality will from now on founder—there is no doubt about it—: . . . that great drama in a hundred acts, which is awaiting the next two thousand years of Europe; the most terrible, most questionable, and perhaps also the most promising of all dramas.

[ESSAY 3:27]

9.

Works:

The Wagner Case, a Letter from Turin of May, 1888

The Twilight of the Idols, or How to Philosophize with the Hammer

The Wagner Case

After finishing the *Genealogy of Morals*, Nietzsche set himself the task of preparing a comprehensive presentation of his philosophy, the preparation of which he had mentioned toward the end of his last book. It was to bear the title *The Will to Power: An Essay on the Transvaluation of All Values*. Quite naturally, the urge for the systematic elaboration of his teaching pursued him as an obligation proper to his claim as a philosopher and as an answer to the many challenges to that claim from the world of scholars. But he had neither the health nor the temperament for persistent scholarly and systematic procedure, nor the genius for the necessary orderly and calm presentation. Indeed, in the first pages of *The Twilight of the Idols*, the second of the shorter writings which he finished during this last busy year, he states as a maxim: "I distrust all systematists and avoid them. The will to system is a lack of integrity." This certainly would have been true in his case, since it would have meant a mere compromise.

In the winter of 1885-86, he spent more time than was to his liking in Naumburg and at the university library in Leipzig to do the research necessary for the proposed project, but there is no evidence that he was able to subject himself to such discipline. He notes various plans for the work and makes careful divisions and subdivisions under which to treat his philosophy, which, however, prove to be only titles and subtitles under which the aphorisms are to be ordered. When, after having completed the manuscript for the *Genealogy* in the spring of 1887 and seen it published in November, he claimed to have finished the first version of *The Will to Power,* he still had only a large collection of aphorisms ready to arrange under the selected titles and no thought whatever of deviating from his established style. Also, his health was sadly deteriorating at this time. With intervals of high euphoria and great activity he devoted himself in part to the writing and rewriting of the aphorisms of the proposed work, but more to several short publications, primarily *The Twilight of the Idols,* which he called his "philosophy in a nutshell," [1] and *The Antichrist,* a kind of advance warning of what the larger work was to elaborate. The printing of the first of these two concise books was completed but had not yet appeared on the market, and the manuscript of the second was ready for the printer when Nietzsche had his complete breakdown at the very end of this year.

Preceding the writing of *The Twilight of the Idols,* he had prepared and completed a short essay which he called *The Wagner Case, a Problem for Musicians.* The manuscript was sent to the publisher in June to be printed as a short pamphlet or, as designated on the title page, a "Letter from Turin of May, 1888," but he added two appendices and an epilogue before its appearance in September.

Wagner's influence, by virtue of the interpretation which he had received or might still receive, represented to Nietzsche a vital illustration of the "degeneration" against which he was carrying on his war. Because of this, he could feel that the pamphlet might prepare for the reception of his great work when it appeared, or even help to present his main theme if it never should see completion. Also, it was to serve as a case history, so to speak, of the method by which such a "degeneration" can be thoroughly known by experience and finally avoided. Nietzsche had lived through a period of complete subjection to Wagner which gave him the right, he thought, to claim full knowledge of him but, according to the principles of his integrity, also imposed upon him the duty to analyze his influence sharply and battle against it, should it prove contradictory and therefore harmful to the ascending life of the will to power. Having found this to be so, he attacked it as a disease from which he had now recovered and which he must disclose as a danger to life. Moreover, the influence of Wagner appeared to him as one of the greatest obstacles in modern Europe to the understanding and acceptance of his own mission.

The attack is vehement beyond measure. It shows none of the respect he maintained for the person of Wagner and none of the courtesy he insisted upon as a mark of distinction, even in the most bitter wars. He calls it a "jolly piece with an almost too serious basis," [1] but humor can be interpreted into it only by seeing his picture of Wagner as a caricature with the serious purpose, however, to unsettle the Wagnerians and to shock them into attention upon himself. That would make the pamphlet propaganda and thereby, by Nietzsche's own standard, lacking in integrity, though that lack is his principal accusation against Wagner. The fact seems to be that the writings of this last year of Nietzsche's sanity, as the products of intermittent periods of high euphoria, are all extremely intense and impatiently centered upon a last chance, as it were, to force attention upon his mission. However, it is best to take *The Wagner Case* as a separate chapter of *The Twilight of the Idols* in which it serves as a conspicuous, even shocking illustration to the less readily understood idols.

The pamphlet begins with a high praise for Bizet's *Carmen* at the expense of Wagner's operas. Immediately before his breakdown, he calls this a jest and insists that Bizet could not possibly be of significance to him. He had made the comparison, he says, solely because of its "strong effects as an ironic *antithesis* to Wagner. It would have been in the poorest possible taste to have begun with praise of Beethoven, for example." [1] His interpretation, indeed, builds up a forced antithesis by making *Carmen* a Dionysian drama, and Wagner into a decadent champion and the redeemer of the "poor in spirit." He interprets the early revolutionary Wagner and some of "The Ring" into an illustration of attitudes like those of Zarathustra. But then he lets Wagner founder on the rock of Schopenhauer's philosophy and be "redeemed" to his nihilistic self. Wagner the diseased, or better the disease, becomes like Nietzsche's other enemy, the priest, the tricky deceiver of the weak and exhausted. Everything within him and of him now denies the Dionysian life and the will to power by sublimation, and is therefore false. He is made to be a diseased physician, clever at administering narcotics and stimulants to exhausted nerves in order to make them more diseased, knowing that the modern decadent world desires just that.

Nietzsche allows Wagner no integrity anywhere and describes his idealism as a crafty sentimental bait. His music is without beauty or melody; his writings devoid of style. As a dramatist he is at best an excellent miniaturist or merely a decadent trickster in love with the drama, but incapable of creating any development in the action beyond clever turns, or any other than decadent and sterile characters. He sees in Wagner the play-actor *par excellence*, and as such the arch-deceiver and dangerous hypnotist of the audiences—all the more alluring because he is without the instinct for music as a musician, and so abuses it for clever rhetorical effects.

All this is presented in an extremely cavalier fashion and with the exaggeration and exuberance that Nietzsche liked to assume when he fancied himself—at his desk—the great warrior against a redoubtable enemy. But beyond that there is the very serious anger, and almost fear, at the realization of the wide and strong influence Wagner was exerting, and thereby building a most formidable obstacle to the hopes that Nietzsche entertained for an understanding of his teaching or even an attention to it. The prevalence of Wagner, together with the new spirit of Bismarck's Reich, meant to him the modern spirit of decadence. Therefore the cudgeling blows. Of Wagner as a person he would never have allowed himself such tactics.

While the pamphlet was still in the hands of the printer, Nietzsche added two postscripts and an epilogue. He declares the first postscript to be a condensation of an essay on the theme: What Wagner costs us.

In the Postscripts he expresses some hope for the Germans in that some healthy instinct had made them slowest to succumb to the enticements of Wagner, and so they may be the first to free themselves of them. These enticements are ascribed to the cynical duplicity of Wagner, as though by means of his music he consciously were intent upon corrupting whatever intellectual integrity or health the audience may still possess into a sensuous sentimentality.

Nietzsche considered the epilogue very significant and claims to have rewritten it several times to find the most effective formulation. It serves to make the pamphlet less an attack upon Wagner and to raise the case of Wagner more to a significant illustration of the danger confronting the modern times, the understanding of which will clear the way for the recovery of the free spirits.

The Twilight of the Idols

Nietzsche had finished the manuscript of *The Twilight of the Idols* within a very few weeks, while *The Wagner Case* was still in press, and had sent it to his publishers on September 7. During the course of the printing he added several supplements: the entire section, "What the Germans Lack," and twelve aphorisms to be included with the "Excursions of a Non-timely." Though the proofs were complete by the end of October, the book did not appear until January 1889, a few weeks after his collapse.

While Nietzsche wished to have this book also considered

a witty relaxation during the arduous task of preparing his great work, he described his real intent as a "very bold and very precisely sketched condensation of my essential philosophical heterodoxies in the hope that the book may serve to initiate and excite some appetite for my 'Transvaluation of All Values.' " [1]

It is quite evident that Nietzsche feared that the definitive work might be forbidden in Germany and that he wished to have this "condensation" act as a challenge to that threat. But the claim of relaxation was perhaps merely a defense, if not an apology, for the loose arrangement of the book. It is another item of evidence that, because of his delight in aphorisms and his pride in the daring of each of them, the severe final composition was causing him great unrest and would continue to do so. The claim of "precisely sketched condensation of my heterodoxies" does not apply strictly even to this short book. Indeed, the title first chosen was "Idle Hours of a Psychologist." Not until the printing of the manuscript was almost completed did he change to the present more challenging title: *Twilight of The Idols or How to Philosophize With the Hammer.* Thereby he translated the idea of relaxation into his delight in battle, and, moreover, directed attention particularly to his method of investigation as that of the thoroughly informed and keenly discerning psychologist of stern integrity, to whom the hammer is the well-tempered tool by which, as with a tuning fork, he will test the rocks or "truths" or idols of moral values and institutions to determine whether or not they are hollow. These idols are his familiar enemies and their hollowness will be attributed to the exhaustion, escape, and intellectual falsity of nihilism, as before. But the justification for the attack and his qualifications as an investigator, clear observer, and analyst of high integrity, as an experienced psychologist and "ratcatcher," are defended in this book with new directness and passion. As always, however, he can see no intellectual integrity and no solid approach outside of the Dionysian view of life; also he finds no spiritual integrity in interpretations outside of the evaluation of life through the will to power by sublimation. Obedience to that view constitutes freedom.

The first section of the book, a collection of forty-four "Proverbs and Darts," is undoubtedly meant as an appetizer for the more serious offering.

With the second section, called "The Problem of Socrates," Nietzsche enters upon his more serious task and selects Socrates and his influence as his first "idol." It is a pithy parallel to the case of Wagner in that Socrates, however much Nietzsche found to admire him in other respects, here becomes the sick physician of the sick and an equally clever detraction from an understanding of the sublimation of power as the way to health and genuine culture. He enters upon his war with Socrates with gusto, confident of his analysis because he is certain of Socrates' contradiction to his own assurance. Nietzsche believed he had disposed as poor sense of the idol, "reason, virtue, happiness," of Socrates. "Socrates was a misunderstanding; the whole improvement morality, including the Christian—was a misunderstanding."

In the two sections on "Reason in Philosophy" and "How the 'true' World finally got to be a Fable," Nietzsche disposes in a few self-assured paragraphs of all philosophy up to his own. All, he contends, are based upon deceptive falsehoods due to their inability, because of moral prejudices, to understand the Dionysian view of life. Instead of beginning with the ability to see and accept life as it is, together with the battle of the instincts, the contradictions of the senses, and the bold experimentation towards sublimation, he decrees that all have, in one way or another, taken an unreal escape into some kind of metaphysics and unreal abstractions, and have worshipped the idols constructed from them. He makes the early assumption of "divine reason" *(Vernunft)* in man the culprit of this prevailing error, by which the philosopher created unreal abstracts which he labeled as the true worlds, the being and essence. Then, because this "true world" could not be seen, he consigned the world of the senses to a world of appearances only. Nietzsche attributes this "aberration" to a clever terminology constructed by philosophers to present "divine reason."

First they conceived the "I" and from it built "being" or essence, and finally the things; thus they confused, as the error must, according to his view, the first and the later and the last, misled by their belief that the highest concepts, such as being, absolute, the good, the true, the perfect, must be *causa sui*. The source of all these highest concepts they then stipulated to be in God so that there should be no contradictions between them. All this means to Nietzsche the betrayal of life, since in his view the "true" world must equal nothingness, and the "phenomenal" the only real world. Therefore he ends the first of these two sections with the statement of his own four theses:

The proofs advanced by the philosophers of the phenomenal world are proofs only of its reality. Since the phenomenal character given to the actual world is an illusion only from the conventional moral point of view, the "true world" can mean only nothingness. To speak of "another" world, a world beyond, proves an instinct to deny this world and a resentment against it. To divide the world into "true" and "phenomenal" is merely a symptom of decadence, of descending life, and a fatal error.

In the succeeding section Nietzsche succinctly outlines what he calls the history of the error. He sees its beginning in Plato's "I, Plato, *am* the truth," by which the "true world" is taken as attainable for the wise, pious, and virtuous by simply identifying themselves with it. Then, in the subtler, more enticing, and less tangible Christian form of the idea, the "true world" becomes unattainable for the now, but promised to the wise, pious, and virtuous, meaning the sinner who repents. Later, in the "pale, northern Koenigsberg mist," the "true world" eludes attainment, proof, or promise but turns into an obligation and a necessary postulate. Nietzsche then sees the first evidence of awakening reason in the beginnings of positivism by which the "true world" is unknown because unattained, and because unknown can be neither comforting nor obligating. Then the "free spirits" see that the idea of the "true world" is empty, useless, and superfluous, and it is consequently refuted and dispensed with. The day then brightens with the light of good sense and joyousness towards the hour of Zarathustra and the noon that puts an end to the error with the realization: *"with the true world we have dispensed also with the phenomenal world."* With such strained confidence, Nietzsche, in his loneliness at Sils-Maria, would turn his euphoria into a joyous vision of a Dionysian victory.

But adherence to the Dionysian view of nature means to accept life exactly as it is and as it passes through its eternally recurring transformations. The activity of the man who accepts it must be to humanize it to the extent of his courage and intelligence. He must realize the power which he truly represents with his passions, instincts, and drive by sublimating life through the higher discipline of merging it with his spirit and making it "intelligent, beautiful, and divine." Thus the Dionysian believer also has his morality, but one that affirms nature in contrast to the institutional morality of the denial of life and the escape from nature. It is the morality of the discipline and battle towards sublimation, for which Nietzsche here also uses the term *Vergeistigen*—spiritualizing or intellectualizing in a broad sense. His free spirit is slow to act upon the stimuli of his passions. In a constant contest with them he imposes the restraint of intelligence and his sense of quality upon them. Indeed, he calls the sublimation of the passion of enmity the attainment of respect for the enemy and the realization of the need of him in order to avoid complacency. The Dionysian warrior towards sublimation will refuse nothing and rather use everything to affirm life. His morality is considered healthy, in that it is natural and ruled by some instinct of life and in that every step of sublimation renounces some repression.

In contrast, the conventional Christian morality is called unnatural, in that it turns against life's instincts and suppresses the passions instead of seeking to sublimate them. To be sure, he expounds, all passions have a period when they are crude and drag down their victim with the weight of their stupidity. But, he argues, "to destroy the passions because of their stupidity, merely to avert the evil results of their stupidity, seems an acute form of stupidity to us today." He calls this the "castrating" of life which is resorted to by men of weak will, whose repression of passions is not the discipline of the true ascetic, but merely a timid escape of the exhausted who have abandoned the struggle with life and, therefore, can know nothing of life.

In the next chapter, called "The Four Great Errors," he exposes what is to him the false thinking that produced this "metaphysics of the hangman," as he calls the unnatural morality. Instead of courageously facing Dionysian nature and taking life as it is; instead of realizing that each person is part of the whole and represents that whole, each in his fashion, both backwards and forwards, that there can be no responsibility for being what one is but only the intellectual courage to accept it wholeheartedly with an "*amor fati*" and the will to sublimate its power—to accept, in a word, the "innocence of becoming" and pursue it with *amor fati*; the unnatural morality resorts to clever tricks of false thinking and assumptions to make life evil and man responsible for it.

The chapter on the "Improvers of Mankind" is an interesting example of his method of composition. Up to this point his book may be said to be a severe concentration of his teaching. Now, however, he engages in an enthusiastic discussion of Indian law, occasioned by a chance discovery of a French translation of *The Code of Manu*. It is difficult to determine how well he studied it, though his enthusiasm about it would tend to the assumption that the reading was selective and exciting rather than thorough. He takes it to be the prototype of all later moral laws, which are either imitations or caricatures of it. The Manu is to him a thoroughly Arian production and, therefore, aristocratic, bolder, and more honest. Even though formulated by priests and raised to a religion, it is less pessimistic than later codes because it frankly serves the purpose to establish the superiority of a single caste as masters and, with brutal but openly stated discipline, establishes and restricts the order of rank and rights of each descending caste down to the lowest mass of the *Chandala* who, being of undefined mixture, have no rights and privileges whatever.

In a letter to Peter Gast of May 31, 1888, he lets his enthusiasm decide that all other moral codes—including those of Egypt, the ethics of Confucius and Plato, and finally the Jewish-Christian code—are imitations of the Manu. He interprets the Jews as a *Chandala* race which had learned from its masters the principle by which it could establish its rule, but in its instance with the pessimistic values of decadence, which it then transmitted to the Christian institutions. Consequently, merely because he believed to have the basic principle of this in the Manu, he considered himself scientifically justified in his theory of the illusionary and decadent character of the conventional moral laws with his pet statement that "All reasons by which mankind was to be made moral—were thoroughly immoral." By this theory, the so-called "improvers of mankind" first tame mankind by means of a pessimism that robs it of its power and then let the moral law train and breed it to impotent obedience.

The book ends as though he had established that a new era or culture will arise on the basis of it. With tragic fanaticism he persuades himself the world will now have to comprehend that, beginning with Plato and culminating in Christianity, the courage for the Greek faith has increasingly lessened. Man had become weakened and exhausted, had built ideas and institutions on the resultant pessimism, and in them erected idols whose hollowness was now at last being exposed by the unrelenting, "hard" prophet of Dionysus with his hammer of keen perception and the integrity of his intellectual freedom.

from:

The Wagner Case

In Wagner modernity speaks its most intimate language; it hides neither its good nor its evil and has lost all sense of shame. Vice versa: the worth has about been settled when one has cleared his mind about the good and evil in Wagner.

[FOREWORD]

[Speaking of "The Ring," Nietzsche says:]
Siegfried and Brünnhilde; the sacrament of free love; the rise of the Golden Age; the twilight of the old morality—evil is done with.

[4]

It was the philosopher of *decadence* who first restored the musician of *decadence* to himself. [The philosopher is Schopenhauer; the musician, Wagner.]

[4]

His [Wagner's] art is the most tempting mixture of the three stimulants that the world needs most: the *brutal*, the *artistic*, and the *innocent* (idiotic).

[5]

What makes an actor is that he has developed one insight further than have others, namely, what is to have the effect of truth must be lacking in truth. This proposition, developed by Talma, contains the whole psychology of the actor; it also contains his morals—no doubt about it. Wagner's music is never truthful.

[9]

[Nietzsche's Three Demands:]
That the theater should not become the master of the arts.
That the actor should not become the deceiver of genuine people.
That music should not turn into an art of lying.

[CONCLUSION]

In the art of seduction *Parzival* will forever maintain its rank as the stroke of genius. . . . [Young men become] moon calves —idealists; [and women in Wagner are in complete surrender] to the most attractive ambiguity to be found these days.

[FIRST POSTSCRIPT]

No God can save music from the general *rule* that degeneracy is in the saddle, that degeneracy is fatal.

[SECOND POSTSCRIPT]

The case of Wagner is a lucky chance for the philosopher . . . to cast glances at the master morality, the *distinguished* morality (the Islandic saga is almost its most important source) and at the same time use the contrasting teaching, that of the "gospel of the lowly," of the *need* for redemption!

[EPILOGUE]

from:

How to Philosophize with the Hammer

Proverbs and Darts

Do we immoralists do *harm* to virtue? As little as anarchists harm princes. Only since they are being shot at are they again firmly established. Moral: one must take a shot at morals.

[36]

Posthumous people—I for example—are understood less than the timely but *heard* better. To be more exact: we are never understood—*hence* our authority.

[15]

Problems of Socrates

Perhaps wisdom [in Socrates] appeared on earth as a raven excited by a slight odor of carcass.

Socrates was the buffoon who made people take him seriously.

[Socrates] became the first fencing master of this art for the distinguished.

As long as life is on the upgrade happiness equals instinct.

Socrates was a misunderstanding; the whole improvement morality, including the Christian—was a misunderstanding.

Morality as Opposed to Nature

Fruitfulness is possible only at the price of being rich in contrasts; and we remain young only provided that the soul tries to expand rather than to long for peace.

To destroy the passions because of their stupidity, merely to avert the evil results of their stupidity, seems an acute form of stupidity to us today.

The Four Great Errors

The whole realm of morality and religion belongs to the concept of imaginary causes.

Forays of a Non-timely

[Nietzsche satirizes the idea of the Prussian *Kulturstaat* under Bismarck.]

What was great in a cultural sense was always nonpolitical, even antipolitical.

Art is to *have to* transform into completeness.

It is impossible for the Dionysian man not to understand a suggestion; he misses no indication of an effect; he possesses the highest degree of the comprehending and divining instinct, as well as the highest degree of the art of expression.

[10]

The mere discipline of emotions and thought is worthless— the *body* must be won over first.—It is decisive for the fortune of a people and for humanity that culture begin at the *proper place*—not with the "soul" (as was the fatal superstition of priests and semi-priests); the proper place is the body, the posture, the diet, the physiology; the *rest* will follow of itself. That is why the Greeks will remain the *leading cultural event* in history—they knew, they *did* what was necessary; Christianity that despised the body was the greatest misfortune of mankind thus far.

[47]

Wherever man is at all depressed he suspects the presence of something "ugly." His feeling of power, his will to power, his pride—lessens with the ugly and increases with the beautiful. The ugly, whether physical or spiritual, expresses man's hatred of the degeneracy of his species. It is the deepest hatred there is.

[20]

Goethe was the last German whom I revere.

[51]

Such a spirit *who has won his freedom* lives by a joyous and confident fatalism within the All, in the *faith* that nothing is to be rejected but the unrelated; that in the whole everything is to be redeemed and affirmed—*he no longer denies.* . . . But this faith is the highest of all possible faiths. I have baptized it in the name of *Dionysus.*

[49]

What is the task of all higher education?
　　To make a machine of man.
What are the means to this end?
　　The student must learn to be bored.
How is that accomplished?
　　Through the concept of duty.

Who serves as the example of this?
　　The philologian: he teaches to *grind.*

Who is the perfect man?
The civil servant
What philosophy provides the highest formula for the civil
    servant?
>   That of Kant: the civil servant as the thing per se
>   placed as judge over the civil servant as phenome-
>   non.

[29]

What I Owe the Ancients

Only in the Dionysian mysteries is there expressed the
basic fact of the Greek instinct—its will to life. In the mysteries
and the orgies, the Greeks found the guarantee for *eternal* life,
the eternal return of life, the future promised and dedicated
in the past; the triumphant Yes to life beyond death and
change.

[4]

10.

Works:
The Antichrist: An
Attempt at a Critique of
Christianity

After completion of *The Twilight of the Idols*, Nietzsche apparently changed his plan about his *magnum opus* and decided to reduce it to a much more concise presentation in four "books," to which he gave the title, *Transvaluation of All Values*. According to what is called the final plan of the autumn of 1888, the first book carries the title, *The Antichrist: An Attempt at a Critique of Christianity;* to be followed by *The Free Spirit: The Critique of Philosophy as a Nihilistic Movement;* then, *The Immoralist: The Critique of Morality, the Most Fatal Kind of Ignorance;* and finally, *Dionysus: The Philosophy of the Eternal Return.*

This change of plan is thoroughly characteristic of Nietzsche's distrust of system, and even of his inability to build his philosophy—or better, his teaching—into a system, rather than into an impassioned polemic. On September 12, 1888, he writes to Peter Gast that the first book is about finished, and there is every evidence that it was completed before the end of the month in the form in which it was published in 1895. He found no opportunity to work at the other three books, though there are some notes on the third.

As published, *The Antichrist* carries a foreword presumably intended for the whole of the *Transvaluation of All Values*. It is held to an extremely defiant note against all contemporary society, whether it be conservative or advanced, because the conditions necessary for the comprehension of his own point of view have nowhere been sufficiently won: "the integrity in spiritual and intellectual things to the point of relentlessness." He is insisting, of course, on the Dionysian view as the only truthful approach and as the sole way to win "freedom within oneself." He despairs of being heard until a "new conscience for truths that have not yet been voiced" be developed, and, thereby, an audience come into being destined for his message. It alone interests him. The others, he exclaims in this excessive moment of strangely mingled euphoria and despair, are "merely human. One must be superior to the human kind by virtue of strength, height of soul,—of contempt." Thus Nietzsche introduces this final formulation with a challenge that is almost desperate and which permits the suggestion that this new conscience for unvoiced truths is more a strained show of courage than a clear freedom, though in the body of the book itself the strain is not so apparent.

The Antichrist is concerned with the critical examination of Christianity as against the Dionysian view of life. As expected, he will prove it to be false where it denies and betrays life as he sees it, or lacks the courage and strength to embrace it. The critique is, therefore, not at all objective, but a condemnation on the basis of the assumption, not only of his definition of reality, but even more of the possession of a highly developed instinct for that reality and its sublimation. Among other terms, he likes to speak of his method as philological and explains philology as the "ability to read facts *without* falsifying them by interpretation or *without* the loss of care, patience, and subtlety in the desire to understand." [1]

True virtue is what the instinct of life compels one to be: genuineness of power in the Renaissance sense. The loss of this instinct is identical to him with disease and degeneracy which resorts to metaphysical concepts like "pure spirit." The instinct for life concentrates on the sublimation of the will to power: how man is to be trained and bred into one of higher value, more worthy of life and more certain of the future through the elevation, enhancement, and strengthening of his genuine power.[1] By this sublimation a higher type of man can be aimed at as distinct from the fortuitous examples that life has produced in the chance course of history—also decidedly different from the superficial modern belief in the evolutionary process. Sublimation is the endless experiment to express the will to power of nature in terms of human culture. Its primary condition is the intellectual integrity to see life in his Dionysian manner until this condition becomes an instinct beyond mere conscious observation and search. Since this instinct is wholly a matter of quality, there must proceed from it a culture of rank. It is topped by the few, highly select, free spirits who are austere and clear in understanding, of reverence for themselves and their equals, with an instinctive pathos of distance toward those of lesser understanding or small creative power. By virtue of the same instinct, however, they will comprehend and appreciate the worth and the function of the rank immediately below, which comprises those of sufficient intelligence to understand, but who lack the power to create, and consequently have the secondary function of disciples and executives of the leaders. Beyond that, they will also appreciate the worth of the great masses who are incapable of understanding, but who can and must be encouraged and employed for all the groundwork, intellectual and physical, which must exist as the broad basis of culture. To Nietzsche, as we know, this is the order of nature which the experiments of sublimation must obey. To him, this is a fact rather than a faith, though it remains as dogmatic as the most fundamentalist faith.

Sublimation is the "great passion" of the free spirit of full and overflowing power. He remains a skeptic and experimenter at every attained conviction, in order to use it in further battle for higher sublimation. Thus he will keep himself free and strong, since he considers every final conviction or faith as evidence of slavery or weakness, or as a deliberate lie to distort nature for the purpose of gaining mastery over the strong.[2] This last is Nietzsche's accusation against Christianity, as also against every "priestly or philosophical priestly power organization."

To give a sharper perspective of this, he again presents in the Laws of Manu a case which, though he considers its order truer to nature, is still a product of weakness, in that it is based on final authoritative conviction and, therefore, deprived of genuine Dionysian creative power. But in spite of this "holy lie," it is much preferred by Nietzsche to other holy books, because, by clever interpretation, he is able to make of it a convenient illustration of an approach upon his own point of view. Such cleverness seems permissible to this man of integrity. He takes pains, however, to explain from it the nature of any national code of laws, anticipating some of the characteristics which a future Zarathustra or his equals might sometime conceive for the culture of mankind. At some point of the national development, a group of the keenest and most farsighted men decrees that there must be an end to the pains and dangers of the infinite experiments with values, and builds a "double wall" against it: first, that of revelation, which erases the idea of experiment in favor of the non-historical, non-human divine origin of the law; second, that of tradition, to create a pious acceptance of the laws out of reverence for the founders of the nation. The aim is to stop conscious examination and to produce, instead, a "completely automatic instinct" in observance of the laws as the precondition of their authority as the order of nature.[1]

In the organization of the castes, as proscribed and protected in the Laws of Manu, Nietzsche finds the order of nature least violated. He was clearly fascinated by his discovery of this book as a support for his idea of the "order of rank" and the disciplinary measure to uphold it. He reads it solely for that support, forcing upon it the interpretation of most help to himself. He would probably defend such arbitrary procedure by the claim that it was merely for illustrative purpose, very much as he, in this very connection, defends the lie if useful to the enhancement of life.[2] He quite ignores the fact that the masters of the Laws of Manu were the priests and attributes to them the virtues of his own higher men. To him their rights are the realistic expression of their genuine superiority in power and complete instinct for integrity. They represent happiness, beauty, and kindness on earth; they are the hardest men because of their wisdom and integrity, but also the kindest and most cheerful. They know how to evaluate the importance of the lower ranks and how to train them to their best contributions, so that they know their place and remain content. To the lowest, the slave class, the purely physical *Chandala* they apply the most rigid prohibitions.

All this he probably hoped to present in detail in the last planned book, *Dionysus*. Here it is used as background for his attack on Christianity. But the attack is essentially a confession of his own faith, everything contrary to which is taken to be in error. The telling disclosures of certain weaknesses in Christianity are of the kind that generally result when an established institution is examined from a point of view diametrically opposed to it. They are very useful as correctives, but do not constitute the proofs that Nietzsche sought.

The principal accusation is that in Christianity neither morality nor religion at any point touches reality, but that everything about it is imaginary: its *causes* in God, soul, ego, spirit; its *effects* in sin, redemption, grace, and punishment; its anthropocentric natural science; its psychological fallacies of repentance, pangs of conscience and the like; its teleology with its eschatology. All these are fictions of distress and decadence to Nietzsche, invented by the priests and their philosophers in their battle to win acceptance for their views in their vengeful revolt against their natural masters.

Nietzsche is not only highly prejudiced and dogmatic in this attack, but also cynical, as, for example, in the exhibition of bad taste with which he parodies the story of Genesis, turning it into an unbroken series of mistakes.[1] God is bored and creates man. Man becomes bored and God gives him beasts to entertain him. Failing in that, God gives him woman and all the evil which woman represents. The woman introduces man to knowledge to make him like God and a rival of God. Out of fear of the rival, God teaches him morality by making knowledge the original sin, and then drives him from paradise in order to rob him of the leisure to think. Work brings on distress and disease, but knowledge grows in spite

of it. So God invents wars from which only the priests profit.
Man, however, in spite of all, succeeds in emancipating himself from the priests, and so no other means are left to God
to rectify his mistakes than to bring on the deluge.[1] There
are qualities exhibited in this that Nietzsche would not permit
his higher men to possess, but which he nevertheless showed
—and not only in this last year of threatening disease.

The greater part of *The Antichrist* is concerned with the
history of Christianity, as his point of view forces him to see
it: as the history of the betrayal of nature by degenerate
priests and their philosophers who skillfully conduct the
revolution of the *Chandala* in order to establish their own
mastery, and who usurp the method of the genuine masters.
He makes of it the most crude and deceptive of all decadent,
nihilistic religions. Since he saw in Christianity not only the
immediate, but also the most powerful enemy of his teaching,
he attacks it viciously and with an "objectivity" in historical
interpretation which has its definition only in his own conception of the phenomena of history.

To begin with, he compares Christianity to Buddhism
which, though also nihilistic, is still infinitely more realistic to
him. He calls it the "only positivistic religion in history," in
that in its exhausted surrender of the will to power, it strives
for the only thing it can realistically produce, namely, the
lessening of suffering. In a negative way it is honestly egotistic
in that purpose, for it recognizes the supreme sensitivity of its
nerves and its tenuous spirituality after too long an exercise
with conceptual and logical thinking as physical exhaustion
and loss of power. The result was a serious depression which
Buddha tried to cure by means of a realistic system of hygiene,
through which perfection can be reached as the normal condition of the highest classes, without the false strain even of
prayer not to mention that of Christian asceticism or categorical imperatives; also with complete exclusion of the idea of
resentment. By contrast Nietzsche finds Christian asceticism
directed against the higher classes because of its hatred, not
only of the body and the senses, but also of intellect, pride,
and courage; it is also the very opposite of hygiene in that

it irritates the nerves still more, rather than soothes them. Buddhism he calls the religion of late men and gentle, over-intellectual races, which suffer too easily and need to be directed back to cheerfulness and peace. Christianity, on the other hand, desires to rule over the strong by making them diseased by means of a taming it calls civilization.[1]

To develop this point he resorts to what he calls the historical origin of Christianity, which, however, means his psychological interpretation of the roots of Christian theology and morals. He maintains that these must be found in Jewish history, for Christianity must be seen not as a movement in opposition to the Jewish instinct, but as the final, "terrifying conclusion" of that instinct at the point where it had become completely degenerate. He pictures the Jews as the toughest race in history who, in their struggle to persist, succeeded "with most uncanny consciousness" to falsify all nature and to turn religion, morality, history, and psychology, one after the other, into the very opposites of their natural values; all this with such thorough cunning that it denatured mankind. The Christian of today is but the final Jewish product, even when he feels strongly anti-Semitic. Nietzsche thus makes a very special case of the Jews, who deliberately assumed values of decadence as an instrument of power and with it constructed a system of religion and morality to rule over others.

The Jewish priests translated the realistic history into a religious one, making of it a "stupid salvation mechanism of guilt towards Jehovah and punishment; of piety towards Jehovah and reward."[2] On this they based their "moral" world order by which the society, as determined by the priests, is called the "Kingdom of God," and the means to establish it as the "will of God"; and the authority for it cleverly established by a "holy revelation." So the power of the priests was made secure and able to dominate all thinking and living. Nietzsche turns passionately against this moral world order, because it is a complete denial of his Dionysian nature.

In Christianity, Nietzsche develops further, this denial was carried to its logical extreme. The new Jewish reality itself was denied and the revolt turned against the priests and their organization. In the earliest Christianity, especially in Christ Himself, Nietzsche does not see a revolt against the corruption of the Jewish priest, but against the hierarchy itself as a privileged caste and formula for superiority, and consequently against the support of Jewish existence. Nietzsche doubts, however, that Christ was conscious of all this, and he therefore attempts to give his own psychology of the person of Christ as redeemer. He calls His deepest instinct and morality that of complete non-resistance, *"not being able* to be an enemy." His "glad tidings" he interprets as meaning that the true, eternal life has been found. He insists that there is no eschatology in the teachings of Christ, but that the "Kingdom of God is *within you"* and everybody a child of God. Because of an extreme sensitiveness, which cannot bear to be touched, he finds in Christ an "instinctive hatred of all reality." Because this sensitiveness made of all enmity a mortal danger, His instinct was to exclude every dislike, opposition, and every feeling of distance; to find bliss only in non-resistance and love the only possible way of life.

Nietzsche sees in Christ a prolonged childishness, similar to a retarded adolescence, but living wholly in the spirit. He had no realization of realities nor did He care for them excepting as they had their use as symbols or in parables. He naïvely lived the life of His faith. He did not deny the world because He had no idea of it or of its institutions. In his interpretation of the Gospels Nietzsche finds in Christ's teachings no trace of guilt, of punishment and reward, or even of sin, because there is in them no sense of distance to God. Like the Kingdom of God, eternal bliss is at hand in the instinct of the brotherhood of man with God. The inner realities are the sole realities and the truth.

Nietzsche finds in Christ's teaching a new way of life, a new conduct of life, rather than a new faith. With it the whole of the Jewish church theory was abandoned, together with its concept of sin, forgiveness, and redemption through faith. Christ's death was a demonstration of this new way of life.

It is this over-sensitive, wholly unworldly without being

other-worldly, almost purely symbolic figure of Christ, that
Nietzsche extracts from his reading of the Gospels, more by
instinct than by research (which he calls idle in this question).
But he finds the figure too delicate to be understood by His
disciples, or capable of later tradition. He decides also that
the early Church could not use such a figure in its struggle
with the priests and theologians. The Church was in need of
a "judging, avenging, maliciously clever theologian and
created its God according to its needs," primarily by attributing to Him "wholly unevangelical," but useful concepts, such
as "second coming and day of judgment," wholly contradictory
temporal expectations and promises.[1] Thereby it cynically
made of Christ's figure and His conduct, particularly His
death, the very opposite of what He represented. Nietzsche
sees in the early interpretation of the crucifixion the point
most fatal to Christianity. It was incomprehensible to the
disciples, and appeared to them a disgrace, and even a possible refutation of their cause. So they sought to fix the blame
for it and settled it upon the ruling class of Jews, the priests,
who had executed the leader of their revolution. "The most
unevangelical sentiment, *revenge*, then again gained the upper
hand," [2] and out of Christ was made a judge, avenger, a
Pharisee and a theologian, especially by the teachings of Paul,
whom Nietzsche calls the "embodiment of the type contradictory to the 'bearer of glad tidings,' the genius of hatred, the
vision of hatred, of the inexorable logic of hatred." [3] He finds
that Paul invented for himself a history of the earliest
Christianity and even changed Jewish history in order to pre-
dict his kind of redeemer.

Paul is the very special target of Nietzsche's attack, since
he saw in him the originator and organizer of those concepts
of Christianity and of the theology and morality of the prevailing Christian Church which most directly contradict his
Dionysian view and are the formidable impediment to an
understanding and acceptance of it. Since he is convinced
that his view can be contradicted only by a denial of facts,
and the hatred of the method of his brand of intellectual
integrity in the interpretation of the facts, he must depict

Paul as the archdeceiver of early Christianity. Thus he shows
Paul as falsifying the personal history of Christ and corrupting
His teachings, in order to fashion out of them a tool for his
own purposes. Because of Paul's influence he condemns the
whole of the New Testament. Nietzsche sees the democratic
idea in Christianity as not only a contradiction of nature, but
also its corruption arising from the lowest motives for selfish
power by clever, designing demagogues who are able to
invert the values of nature, hallow impotence, and succeed in
stamping health, "integrity, manliness, and pride, beauty and
freedom of the heart as simply 'world,' evil per se." [1] All this
he calls the greatest crime against mankind instituted by Paul,
the diseased priest and organizer of the diseased priesthood,
which administers to the masses the degenerating poisons of
the concept of guilt and punishment, together with the teachings of grace, redemption, and forgiveness, so as to keep the
masses dependent and deprive them of the help intelligence
might give.

With the growth of Christianity, Nietzsche goes on to explain, the Church spread among still cruder people who
vulgarized and barbarized the original symbol still more,
until a sick barbarism seemed to assume full power. He
insists, however, that at last the consciousness of the contrast
between the Christian and the distinguished values is dawning
—because of himself, of course.

Clearly, the arguments of the *Antichrist* are not in any
accepted sense scholarly, in spite of all the claims of intellectual integrity or of a sound and healthy instinct of interpretation. They are only Nietzsche's full realization that the
Christian teachings of the Church or of the dominant philosophies, however much they may seem to liberalize the former,
are in direct contradiction to his Dionysian affirmation of life,
and that this authority must, therefore, be eliminated if
human culture, as he sees it, is to be saved. Being, therefore,
an attack on his principal and most powerful enemy, it becomes more virulent as it progresses. Nietzsche's anger becomes more dogmatic and direct, until he expends his greatest
scorn upon the "barbaric" instincts of his own Germans for

having helped most towards vulgarizing Christianity, betraying nature, and bringing disaster to culture.

He ends the essay with an angry review of the development of this "disaster." It includes characteristically exaggerated eulogies for the periods in which he finds that his view of nature prevailed, or was at least honored, especially, but not exclusively, in Greece and Rome; but also equally characteristic violence against its defamers, primarily the Germans.

In his indictment of the Germans for further corrupting culture at every historical moment when it might have gained a distinguished quality, he then turns to the crusades. He calls them "superior piracy" and wars merely for booty against a distinguished culture before which the crusaders might better have bent their knees. But the Church knew well what it was doing in calling upon the German Knights in order to wage its wars of hatred of all that was distinguished with German swords and courage. For to Nietzsche, at least in the heat of this attack, Islam and the "marvellous Moorish culture of Spain" is of more significance and present help than even Greece and Rome.

Nietzsche then tells his story of what is to him the even more disastrous failure in the battle for culture: the German defeat and corruption of the Italian Renaissance. The cause of the Renaissance he identifies with his own as the great attempt at a transvaluation of all values undertaken "with all means, all instincts, all genius to bring victory to the *counter* values, the *distinguished* values" at the very center of the power of the Church.

But the German monk came to Rome and defeated the Renaissance with "the vengeful instincts of a shipwrecked priest." Instead of seeing that the papacy was on the point of embracing a sound affirmation of life, he saw only what he called corruption, revolted against the Renaissance without understanding it, and thereby restored the Church and defeated the restoration of life. This interpretation of Luther is wholly one-sided and possible only from Nietzsche's definition of the Renaissance and from his wishful demand that intellectual enlightenment must establish his Dionysian view of life as the only reality. Since it failed to do so, the fault must lie with the founder of the Reformation and the resultant Protestantism as the false and compromising enlightenment which has since ruled over all German religion and thinking and has barred the way to the enlightenment of the complete intellectual integrity which his view claims to represent. Thus the Germans are villains.

This note of melancholy is very strong in the *Dionysian Dithyrambs* which he prepared to accompany the *Transvaluation*. They read as though they were to function as a final enticement to disciples at some distant, more favorable future to follow his teaching in spite of its harshness and even though it precludes the comfort of rest or final attainment. He describes the dithyrambs as "Songs of Zarathustra which he sang to himself that he might bear his last loneliness." He speaks of it also as his "seventh loneliness," as though it took the place of a seventh heaven, but not a happy one. It seems to signify the attainment of a wisdom that none is prepared to share with him, but which will yet expend itself ceaselessly. He warns that the wisdom has no definable content, but for that very reason should guarantee the joy of eternal adventure with enigmas. It cannot be pursued in person beyond the span of mortal life, and life itself must therefore seek no pleasant repose from the pursuit, yet it still can act for those willing to be errant adventurers, it can act as beacon on the rock in the vast sea of living. Thus the wisdom seems to signify the attainment of the method of pursuit out of loyalty to life and a bold acceptance of the eternity of the enigma. That should be enough to guarantee dignity and promise joy. But in all these poems it is a joy with a heartbreak. It may be the melancholy of one who is asking the impossible of himself by demanding happiness from uncertainty, but perhaps it is more the fear that his best followers may tire and translate the enigma into cheap and ready answers.

from:

The Antichrist

Pure spirit is pure nonsense. . . . If we reckon without the nervous system, the senses, the "mortal veil," then our calculations are wrong.

[14]

For this one must realize: every natural institution (state, legal procedures, marriage, care of the sick and poor), every demand arising out of the instinct of life; in short, everything that has worth *within itself* is made fundamentally worthless, inimical to worth by the parasitism (or the moral world order) of the priest.

[26]

An attack [by Christ and Christianity] upon it [the Jewish hierarchy] was an attack upon the deepest national instinct, the most stubborn instinct to live that ever existed. This holy anarchist who called upon the lowly, the outcasts, the "sinners," the *Chandala* within Judaism to oppose the ruling world order—in a language, if the Gospels are to be trusted, which even today would lead to Siberia, was a political criminal, in so far as political criminals were possible in an *absurdly nonpolitical society*. This is what brought him to the cross; the proof is in the inscription on the cross. He died for *his* guilt—every reason is lacking, however much it has been maintained, that he died for the guilt of others.

[27]

The concept of the "Son of Man" is not a concrete historical person but an "eternal" fact, a psychological symbol free of the time element.—The same is true of the God of this typical symbolist—. [The concept of a personal God, of the kingdom to come, and of the second person of the Trinity, Nietzsche calls a] *world-historical cynicism* of mockery of the symbol.

[34]

This bearer of glad tidings [Christ] died as he lived, as he taught—not to "redeem men" but to show how one must live. It is the *practice* which he bequeathed to mankind: his behavior before his judges, his captors, the accusers and every kind of false witness and mockery,—his conduct on the *cross*. He does not resist, does not defend his right; he makes no move to avert the extreme; even more, *he provokes it*—And he begs, suffers, loves *with* those who do him wrong. . . . *Not* to resist, *not* to fix responsibility. . . . Above all, not to resist him who is evil, . . . to *love*. . . .

[35]

[St. Paul is the] embodiment of the type contradictory to the "bearer of glad tidings," the genius of hatred, the vision of hatred, of the inexorable logic of hatred.

[42]

His [St. Paul's] need was *power;* in Paul the priest wanted to return to power—he had use only for those ideas, teachings and symbols by which masses are tyrannized, herds formed.

[42]

[Of the New Testament:]
Humanity has not made even a beginning here; the instinct of *cleanliness* is lacking. There are only bad instincts in the New Testament and there is not even the courage of these bad instincts. . . .
[The doctrine of personal immortality is] the most despicable of impossible promises [and] the most malicious attempt upon the life of *distinguished* humanity.

[43]

Christianity waged a war to the death against every feeling of reverence and distance between man and man, this *primary condition* for every heightening and growth of culture. Out of the darkest depths of low instincts;—out of the resentment of the masses it forged its *principal weapon* against *us*, against everything distinguished, joyous, magnanimous on earth, against our happiness on earth. . . .

[43]

All the ideas of the Church are now recognized as the most vicious counterfeits for the purpose of devaluating nature and natural values.

[38]

[Nietzsche's eulogy of the spirit of antiquity and the disaster that befell it from Christianity:]

The whole work of the ancient world *in vain:* I have no other word to express my feeling about a thing so monstrous. . . . The clear eye in presence of reality, the careful hand, patience and seriousness in the smallest detail, the whole intellectual integrity. . . . Added to this good, fine tact and taste. *Not* a drilling of the brains! *Not* German culture with boorish manners! But as body, native gesture, as instinct— in a word as reality. . . .

[Antiquity was] put to shame by sly, secretive, invisible, anemic vampires [Paul and the first Church fathers, whom nature] had neglected—had forgotten to supply with a modest dowry of respectable, decent, *clean* instincts.

[59]

[Of the German nobility, the staunchest supporters of the Christian church:]

Always the Swiss Guard of the Church, always at the service of the low instincts of the Church—but well paid, but without the sentiments of Christians.

[60]

[Of the Renaissance, which Nietzsche identifies with his own attempt at a transvaluation of all values and portrays as a battle against the power of the Church:]

[The Renaissance might have produced] an art, divine, devilishly divine [by an act] so rich in meaning and yet so marvellously paradoxical that all the gods of Olympus would have had reason for undying laughter. —*Caesar Borgia as pope*. Do you understand what I mean? . . . Very well, that would have been a victory that *I* long for today—;with that Christianity had been *done for*.

[61]

[But the battle was lost, and Nietzsche returns to his vilification of the Germans and the Reformation:]

Ah, these Germans. What have they not cost us! All "in vain" has always been the work of the Germans.—The Reformation; Leibniz; Kant and the so-called German philosophy; the wars of "liberation"; the *Reich*—each time an "in vain" for something that was already there, for something *irretrievable*. . . . They are *my* enemies, I acknowledge it, these Germans. I hate in them every variety of uncleanliness of concept and value, of cowardice in presence of every honest Yes and No. For almost a millennium they have snarled and confused everything that they touched; they are responsible for all half —three-eighths truths from which Europe is suffering;—also they are responsible for Protestantism, the most unholy kind of Christianity that there is. . . . The Germans must be blamed if Christianity cannot be dealt with.

[61]

from:

Dionysus Dithyrambs
Between Birds of Prey

> Knower of self!
> Hangman of self!

A short time ago proud and strutting about on all the stilts of your pride; living alone without God, living by two with the devil as the scarlet-robed prince of every audacity; now bent by the weight of two noughts, a question mark, a tired enigma, a problem for birds of prey to watch him fall.

from:

Fame and Eternity

> Shield of necessity!
> Highest star of life!
> —which no wish attains,
> —which no No defiles,
> eternal Yes of life
> ever am I your Yes:
> for I love you, oh eternity!—

11.

Works:
Ecce Homo
Will to Power

Nietzsche claims to Peter Gast that he began writing the *Ecce Homo* on his birthday, October 15, 1888, and to have finished the manuscript very early in November. He sent it to his publisher, Fritzsch, with whom, however, difficulties arose over the purchase of the rights. As a result, he recalled the manuscript and then, after some revision, entrusted it to his new publisher, Naumann. On December 22nd he writes to Overbeck that he had received two galleys of the print, but shortly after this the project had to be dropped because of Nietzsche's collapse, and the book did not appear until 1908 and in a private printing.

It carries the subtitle, "How one gets to be what one is," and so suggests an autobiography, but only as the psychology of his development as a philosopher and writer. It thus supports the appeal of the main title for that interpretation of himself he wished to impress upon those seriously interested in him, in contrast to what the professional critics or the official censors of the State would certainly present. "It will perhaps prevent," he says in a letter of October 30 to Gast, "that I be mistaken for the opposite of what I am."

The appeal is presented as a sharp polemic and with occasional high euphoria, even resulting at times in almost senseless exaggerations. In spite of this it still contains accurate statements of what he had aimed at in his writings, whereas the excesses are either desperate wishful pictures of final accomplishments, or they are deliberately used to shock his readers into attention. In a letter to Gast, shortly after he had sent the manuscript to Fritzsch, he describes the work as "a fire-belching prologue of the *Transvaluation*." Again on December 9, after having sent it to his new publisher, he says of it: "It by so much transcends the concept of 'literature' that even in nature the simile for it is lacking; it literally blasts the *history* of mankind into two parts—it is the highest superlative of dynamite."

In the foreword he again sharply contrasts his Dionysian faith to everything that is held to be true. This sharp formulation of his persistent issue dominates the interpretation of his method and his writings that constitute his "biography." He begins with a chapter called "Why I am so wise." Wishful even in retrospect, he lays claim to fundamental, robust health, together with a wide experience in disease and exhaustion. He insists that no suffering which he had ever undergone had been able to get the better of him. He had always been able not only to view it objectively but, moreover, to employ the greater sensitiveness which it had brought with it to become an expert in the nature of degeneracy and its evaluations of life, and because of such understanding also to know the nature of true health the better. This had helped to make him the keener psychologist and had developed in him the power of perspective observation.

It is true that Nietzsche had to battle with serious physical and nervous disorders all his mature life; that he had to resign his professorship at Basel because of them, and that the remainder of his life was a restless search for a climate in which he could produce. It is equally true that he fought consistently to get the better of his disease and to translate the experience of it into a richer understanding of life, and that this developed his psychological acumen. Nevertheless, the claims in this section are more the hoped-for, ideal qualities of the free, triumphant spirit who consistently affirms, or else shuns, what cannot be turned into an affirmation of himself. He claims a rich and varied heritage which sharpens his sense for the prejudices of the modern day and, with it, an instinct for health that enables him to test all stimulants for what they contain of health for himself. In his relation with others he is always able to elicit some positive quality, if he concerns himself at all with them, and he never expresses sympathy because it is always directed upon negative qualities and so does harm and generally insults. His assurance of his own riches forbids him ever to justify himself and even less to feel resentment in the presence of enmity. As a healthy man he rather repays enmity with friendship, as an indication of his greater resources. "That is not morality, that is psychology." Aggression, he explains, is quite another thing and a necessary attitude of strength, provided, however, that it be directed against a cause worthy of attack and thus coupled with respect rather than resentment. He insists that he is instinctively free of resentment, which he considers an evidence of weakness, and that he can free himself of it as a dietary precaution if a weak moment threatens. At other times he finds it beneath him.

Thus he attributes his wisdom to an extreme sensitiveness, due to his wide experience in both health and decadence, but directed by a robust instinct for health and cleanliness and resulting in "psychological feelers" to understand life and men. Out of this there may arise a disgust with men. Not only did his instinct for affirmation teach him to tolerate them, but it also supplied him with the *"great good sense"* to accept himself as fate and not to want to be "different." It can be said of this that he was, in fact, a psychological analyst of what he called decadence and escape, and he also sought to develop more and more his instinct for a courageous affirmation of life as he found it, but the triumphant and serene success remained a longing.

The following two sections, on "Why I am so clever" and "Why I write such good books," are exaggerated almost to the point of being merely amusing. Perhaps they had better be interpreted as a conscious tantalizing of his prospective hearers, rather than as an autobiographical sketch.

The first is a lengthy discussion of his intellectual growth, as though it had been either a fortunate or a carefully directed dietary process for the development of subtlety and healthy instincts. He describes, inaccurately, that he had been fortunate in his youth in having been able to avoid "harmful" intellectual food; that he had never experienced religious difficulties or had ever paid any attention to God, immortality of the soul, redemption or sin; and that the only fateful experience with which he had to battle was the climate of German idealism, which he makes responsible for whatever errors he had made in the choice of his occupations. In the same dietary sense he speaks of the reading of books as his principal relaxation, but as relaxation only and to be avoided as obstructive influences in productive times. He let his instinct for self-preservation, the avoidance of all things that demanded a negative attitude, constitute his taste. So he shunned German writers generally, he claims, in favor of the French, especially Stendhal, as the only "witty culture and keen psychology" extant. He makes an exception of Heine as having "that divine malice without which I cannot imagine perfection." He proudly identifies himself with him and predicts that some day it will be said that Heine and he are "by far the best artists in the German language." He says of Wagner in this optimistic retrospect: "I do not know what the experience of others with Wagner has been. Over our skies never a cloud has passed." [1] That is far from accurate, but he selects his early acquaintance with Wagner when he thinks of him as full of Paris and daring, even though already decadent. His music, however, he calls the "opium for my youth," but still a necessary relief.

Of particular interest is the ninth paragraph of the second of these two sections in which he gives the formula of how he got to be what he is. It is again little more than half accurate, and for the rest a wishful interpretation of the facts. It describes the camel phase of the growth of the free spirit who willingly assumes all chance burdens as he enters the desert, and then takes the part of the lion. Thus he accepted all the chance experiences of his early life, such as the fortuitous assignment as philologist during his days as student at Leip-

zig, or the unexpected appointment to a professorship at
Basel, without any consciousness of a goal or any grand attitude of importance, but merely as phases of life with which
to experiment in order to detect their error or health for his
self. This self is not at once a consciously directing guide, but
at first a hidden "idea," which, though destined to rule,
gradually by way of the various chance experimental tests
takes command over the self as its instinct by which all genuine potentialities are perfectly coordinated. Nietzsche even
makes the surprising, perhaps wishful, claim that struggle
plays no part in this emergence: "there is not a trace of the
heroic in my nature. To 'will,' to 'strive' for something, to
have a 'purpose,' a 'wish' in view—of all this I knew nothing
from experience." This is certainly not factual, however much
he would have it so in order to demonstrate the genuineness
of himself.

In the few remarks on "Why I write such good books,"
this desired genuineness turns into an absolute uniqueness.
Consequently, he upholds his claim to the excellence of his
writings by denying to anyone the intellectual experience, or
the courage and subtlety that would enable a judgment, or
even an understanding, of them. On this basis he can boldly
assert to be the first of all Germans to have created the "grand
style" out of his extreme riches, or to be the psychologist
without equal anywhere.

After all, however, all this is a teasing, somewhat humorous
preparation for the more important remarks that follow, con-
stituting not merely an interpretation, but a translation of his
books into the evolution of his basic ideas and of the instinct
that guided them.

In *The Birth of Tragedy* he finds his ideas first emerging.
He considers the book not as a philological study, and even
less as a discussion of the works of Wagner, but a discovery of
himself; the first clarification of himself to himself; his own
awakening instinct through the exposition of the contrast between Dionysus and Socrates. In the Dionysian, as "the only
example and parallel in history to my own inmost experience,"
he had found the formula for the highest affirmation of life

born of an overabundance of life, "a yes-saying without reserve, even to suffering, guilt, and all that is questionable and strange in life." This discovery he calls not only the highest insight into life, but the deepest as well, "confirmed and upheld in the strictest sense by truth and science." He explains that the complete understanding of the Dionysian as true nature had given him an instinct for reality by which he was able to detect with assurance the health or degeneracy of all expressions and evaluations of life. Thus he was the first to understand Socrates as the typical decadent in whom dialectics stifled and degenerated the instinct and led to the fear of life, and because of it to a revenge on life by substituting for the Dionysian formula that of idealism and morality.

So it is instinct for "reality" as his native endowment, plus the instinctive courage of the full acceptance of it, and, as part of it, the clear psychological sense for its fullness or poverty, as against the degenerate instinct that must falsify life because it denies it, that he claims to have discovered in writing this his first book. This Dionysian instinct and the courage to apply it to the full, including the sacrifice of its highest representatives, is seen as the philosophy and psychology of the tragic; as the training of man to his height in the bold battles of the will to power through sublimation.

It is apparent, as he now reviews the book, that he is no longer interested in the philological or historical problems of it, but exclusively in presenting the startling anticipation of what he considers his most genuinely native instinct. Even a discussion of the Apollonian principle is missing. He admits that his study of Heraclitus and the Stoics helped him uncover his instinct. But he insists that they had no clear grasp of it themselves; that his discovery is wholly original with him and the product of his search for clarity and complete honesty about himself. Because of this instinct he saw himself as a turning point in history, when, after two thousand years of exhaustion in which reality was denied and man thereby became degenerate, man would now again accept nature in its entirety and joyously regain his dignity in the tragic battles of the will to power through sublimation. The highest expression of this battle he makes the paradoxically optimistic tragedy in which the highest types of men sacrifice themselves for their own potentialities in assuming the unrestricted responsibility for mankind with the courage of their complete intellectual integrity. In this, God has no place, unless He be the picture which man makes of his own potentialities out of gratitude for them. Degeneracy, on the other hand, is the false will to power out of a conscious abuse of intellectual integrity, which counterfeits weakness as strength and quantity as quality. In contrast to the autonomy of man, it relies upon the love of God for man in his insufficiency and hopes for salvation and grace.

In thus interpreting his later development into his first book, as though he were intent upon creating a legend of complete consistency, it is not to be wondered at that he also insists that all descriptions of Wagner here and in the somewhat later *Richard Wagner in Bayreuth* are of himself alone, and that even Zarathustra is foreshadowed.

Having thus established to his satisfaction this anticipation of his "true self" in his first book, he then reviews *Reflections Out of Season* with its collection of the four essays from the following four years on education, the study of history, Schopenhauer, and Richard Wagner in Bayreuth to show that his instinct thoroughly dominated the interpretation of each subject in turn. It enabled him to be the first to demonstrate how German school and university training was obstructing the fostering of real culture by neglecting the rigorous search and training of self. Again he insists that Schopenhauer and Wagner in these essays are shadow figures of himself and speak only of himself. He believes that with these essays his instinct had entered upon a very bold and hard fight with the prevailing German standards, when he insisted upon his severe definition of culture and his conception of a philosophy as "a terrible, explosive affair in the presence of which everything is in danger." He claims that with the exception of a near friend, Karl Hillebrand, "the last *humane* German," none was able to understand him and that he was feared by most. The popular European and American freethinkers who hailed him as related to themselves in spirit he discards with disgust as superficial and without comprehension of the depth and severity of his instinct.

His next book, *Human, All-Too-Human,* he describes as the "war" by which he freed his nature of all in his past that was not germane to it: idealism, beautiful sentiments, and other "effeminate" things; Wagner, Schopenhauer, "German art, German music, German beer." "The meaning of the title is this: where *you* see ideal things *I* see human—alas, all-too-human." He makes the writing of this book the crisis in which his instinct was finally cleared and set free from the all-too-human prejudices and "opiates" against which he had long been struggling and which he would now attack with an easy sense of superiority. He calls it a war, but a "war without powder or smoke; without warlike attitudes, pathos, or grimaces—for all that would still be idealism." He tells dramatically how he had disciplined himself to use his illness and his enforced retirement to free himself of his professional and sentimental attachments in order to win himself and his insights for himself alone, so that he might now go his way without compromises. "At that time my instinct led me to the irrevocable refusal ever to yield again, or to follow, or to mistake myself for another." From now on, with a sure instinct for reality, he would enjoy uncovering what is idealistic as unreal and of a degenerate nature. All this meant that he would now more than ever delight in psychological diagnoses on the one basis of a robust Dionysian nature, as against the escape from it into some kind of idealism. The discussion of the more serious, more positive part of his labor, the sublimation of the will to power, does not enter here.

Dawn of Day he reviews calmly, though his pride is more exaggerated still. Certain now of being the first to have seen that morality, with its denial of this life in favor of soul, spirit, free will, and God, is a disease fatal to the Dionysian man and his culture, he feels compelled as a good physician to excise it. Now that he is confident within himself of his Dionysian faith, he is equally certain that the moralist priests and philosophers are dangerous healers, in that, out of sympathy for the distress of life, they prescribe no cure except the denial of life and the reliance upon a savior and a better life beyond. The honest procedure, he dictates, must be the courageous and joyous acceptance of each individual actuality and a rigorous therapy and training. He is very proud and delighted with the book, and even more with *Gay Science*, the tone of which seems perfect to him, as though his insight were now crystal clear and ready for the revelation of Zarathustra.

Thus Spoke Zarathustra receives the longest and most exultant discussion, almost as something sacrosanct. Now everything is complete: affirmation, training, and sublimation. As though he were establishing the saga of a sacred book, he relates how, in August 1881, "six thousand feet beyond man and time," the idea of the Eternal Return came to him as the greatest of all affirmations; how it needed a period of gestation twice that of man; the final words written in the "holy hour when Richard Wagner died in Venice." How with the figure of Zarathustra everything suddenly became clear and a long-sustained rhythm took hold of him by which each thing fell into its proper place, and the metaphors, particularly, suggested themselves. In recollection of his exultation at the conception of the figure of Zarathustra, he even ventures the naïve claim that it was an inspiration such as nobody had experienced for a thousand years, and supports it by telling of the swift composition of the first three books.

However exaggerated, this is still not the mere euphoria of the increasing illness of this last year. It is reminiscent of the excitement actually experienced when, in his struggle to maintain strict intellectual integrity with its demands of close observation, penetrating analysis, and careful scientific procedure, he was able also to turn artist and find a plastic form to clarify his conflicts into a unity. It was the time in which he wrote some of the poems and composed the music of which he was most fond. But the figure of Zarathustra appeared to him to be his greatest success and his most powerful metaphor, in that, like the best of its kind, it not only gave body to his thoughts and insights, but has a life that can expand infinitely. In the fourth book, which is more distant from the original

inception, he believes he succumbed to the danger of having
added too many details to the figure and thereby hardened it.
In the plans for still further development with the saga of
Zarathustra's death, there was even the risk of overloading it
and thus stopping the metaphor. But these attempts are not
mentioned in this review, as though, in spite of euphoria, his
instinct were still reliable.

The interpretation of Zarathustra is still naïvely excited,
but is nevertheless a fairly accurate statement of what he
conceived to have accomplished with it. First, he quotes the
passage from the fifth book of *Gay Science* in which he describes how he had lived through the experiences of the best
of the past warriors and discoverers of the ideal. But his great
health and courage had given him the power to see the degeneracy and escape in these ideals as the danger to life, and then
to strike out for the new discovery of the Dionysian "ideal"
which, with its joyous affirmation, demanded, in addition to
the great health, the great seriousness of acceptance and sublimation. "The fate of the soul takes a turn, the hand of the
clock moves on, the tragedy *begins*." [1]

These two ideas: that his discovery of the Dionysian interpretation of life has initiated an entirely new era, and that its
full acceptance in the Eternal Return and the will to power
through sublimation signifies the bold and optimistic acceptance of tragedy, occupy him most and bring him extreme
pride in their utter greatness. He is confident that they must
prevail because they alone are true and real, though at
present he alone is conscious of the change, and everything
and everyone else is strange and distant. He even imagines
that the new ideas themselves in their uniqueness resent his
intrusion and rejoice in his discomfort. But this merely feeds
his pride, and he flatters it by calling it the sad joy of the
sculptor who sees the image of man in the crude block in
which it has slept thus far, and who has now been able to free
it. To him Zarathustra is that image, new and necessary as the
true disciple of Dionysus and created in language as new and
true as the image itself. His fondness for Zarathustra, or perhaps the fear of his reception, leads him to say that in him

he has completed the picture of the superman, and that in being "Yes to all things," unrelenting but kind, he is himself Dionysus.

Nietzsche was not, above all else, a poet, and the figure of Zarathustra is not as compelling and clear as he would have us accept. But he has made him a sharp analyst and an impassioned, stimulating missionary for a view of life that he believed to be the only true reality. When he discovered the metaphor of Zarathustra, it was perhaps natural that his excitement was extreme, as it is apt to be in a thinker who distrusts mere rational formulation for fear that it be neither deep nor comprehensive enough, and who then succeeds in creating a figure as the living incarnation of his searchings and insights, and by whose completeness he can test, so he thinks, the genuineness of his intellectual depth.

In this review Nietzsche plainly means to have *Thus Spoke Zarathustra* taken as his principal contribution, as the "yes-saying part" of his work, after which his efforts can be directed to clear away all values and institutions that he finds to be a denial of the new. He would now proceed to the "transvaluation of the hitherto prevailing values." After having enjoyed with Zarathustra the wide and far view upon life and participated in his clear and bold instinct for reality and truth, he says that in the following books he had forced himself to examine nearest things to see the nature and effect of the escape from reality and the degeneration of the instinct caused by it. He speaks of this as unpleasant but necessary work— psychology manipulated "with deliberate harshness and cruelty," but which gave him a kind of relaxation after the extravagant gentleness of the divinely aristocratic Zarathustra. Even God, he jests tactlessly, on his seventh day after his creative labors, sought relaxation in the form of the serpent under the tree of knowledge. "The devil is merely the relaxation of God on every seventh day."

He presents himself as enjoying the devilish sport of psychology in all these later writings; of uncovering unreality, and lack of integrity, cleanliness, and health in all prevailing living, in the expectation that it will be compellingly clear that the Dionysian approach alone can restore life to its reality and man to his health and dignity. It is interesting to insert, however, that, as a result, he has in fact produced many a sharp diagnosis of prevailing escapes and weaknesses, but still did not sufficiently clarify the Dionysian basis or the resulting affirmations. Paradoxically, the intended most complete affirmer became one of the most clever deniers.

Thus when, in reviewing the *Genealogy of Morals*, he claims to have given in its first book the psychology of Christianity as born out of resentment against aristocratic values, he fails to see that it presents important studies of resentment in itself, but little more. While the second book makes significant contributions to the psychology of guilt, as he claims, it falls far short of offering a convincing proof that guilt is consistently used as an instrument of torture to secure the power of the Church. So also the psychology of the priest in the third book adds greatly to an understanding of the nature of a dictatorship, but fails in its extravagant historical claims. He is not far wrong in calling this work "the most uncanny thing ever written," but in doing so he also senses the mystic cloud from which he never was able to free his Dionysus.

The review of *Twilight of the Idols* expresses a particularly exuberant delight in the ease and assurance with which he believes he has destroyed beyond repair all the old "truths" and idols of the day, because he alone had possession, in his Dionysian reality, of the standard by which to arrive at the soundness of an ideal, or to determine the path toward genuine culture. But again, there is more flaming enthusiasm than clear intellect. "In all seriousness, none before me knew of the right way, the way *upwards;* beginning with me there again are hopes, tasks, ways to be prescribed to culture—*I am the bearer of the glad tidings of them.*" He suggests that all his preparatory work was complete and he could now, as he did, go to work at once at his definitive "transvaluation of all values"; and he ends with a saga-like description of bright, productive September days in Sils-Maria, followed by the dangers of flood which he miraculously escaped to reach

his favorite haven in Turin. Little did he suspect that he was
to escape into utter darkness.

He says of the Germans that they have no conception of
"how vulgar they are, but that is the superlative of vulgarity."
As before, he makes them responsible for every crime against
culture of the last four centuries, culminating in the most
recent crime which will probably be fatal to his mission also.
This is what the Germans called the Wars of Liberation, which
brought about the fall of Napoleon, who might have been
strong enough to unite Europe and perhaps the world.

In a last section to this "autobiography," "Why I Am a
Fate," he sums up the basic elements of his teaching and
reiterates his claim that it must inevitably disestablish all the
old values and institute his new ones. While this section is
also passionate, it is nevertheless an accurate recital of his
teachings, first in detail and ending in a pithy, grand resumé
as a final challenge to all that is established, but a warning
also as to the great difficulties for those who would accept the
new.

Again he presents himself as a crisis and a terrible one.
"I am not a man, I am dynamite." In being the first to have
discovered that there can be no other reality than the Dionysian reality, because it alone is life affirmed without reservation with all its changes and chances, its eternity and its
return, he has placed the terrible responsibility of life's will
to power by sublimation upon the man of culture. It is
terrible because of the severity of the discipline in the endless
battle for every still undiscovered greatness. Terrible also, because the discovery of the "truth" must necessarily mean that
all that has hitherto been held as true now discloses itself to
be a lie. Therefore the institutions built upon it, foremost the
Christian and idealistic morality, must be destroyed to enable
the building of the new culture and man.

Because of his insight into reality and his courage to affirm
it, he calls himself the first to have developed an instinct for
complete intellectual integrity, as well as a keen psychological
sense for its presence or absence. He is proud to have made
what he calls his classical discovery of the falsity of Chris-

tian morality. Not to have discovered this before is to him the supreme crime, "the crime against life." He explains that he took the name of Zarathustra for his hero because the historical Zarathustra (Zoroaster), while the first moralist, had still been a man of integrity and had finally succeeded in overcoming the moralist within himself. Thus, out of this curious sense of integrity, which in the end means the unflinching adherence to his dogma of reality, he makes a Dionysian even out of the historical Zarathustra so that he could function as the prototype of his hero, and of himself. As a result, all three become mythical and endowed with mysteriously divine instinct for reality. This instinct has made him the new philosopher and the first dependable psychologist to diagnose the presence or absence of truth in institutions and men. All philosophers before himself he considers to have been "higher swindlers" because of their devotion or surrender to some kind of unreal idealism.

His instinct, he firmly, all-too-firmly, asserts, must spell the end of Christian morality and the Christian man, the "good and righteous man." As though it were his most significant accomplishment, he repeats that he has once and for all disclosed the "good man" as false, in that he refuses to see reality; and as degenerate, in that he suffers from the disease of the fear and hatred of life. He calls him the "last man," the beginning of the end, the most harmful kind of man. He sees his Christian virtues, with their instinct for benevolence, small happiness, so-called goodness, serving the weakening of life, rather than "the great economy of the whole" for which "the terrible elements of reality (in the emotions, desires, and the will to power) are necessary to an incalculable degree."

The good man and the Dionysian man are contrasts: each can persist only at the expense of the other. Since each lays claims to the truth, the good from his point of view calls the Dionysian evil, and the Dionysian sees the good as false and degenerate. The good man is treated as human, all-too-human; the Dionysian in relation to him as the superman who has his greatness in that he is the sublimation of reality, together with what is terrible and dubious in it.

Thus Nietzsche considers that the battle must be joined, which he predicts will be a "monstrous war," but of a nature different from all past wars in that the whole idea of politics will have changed into a war of intellect. This is surely not a prediction of anything resembling modern ideological conflicts. He imagines something far more radical, though even here in this final appeal it is none too clear on its affirmative side.

Early in January, on a street of Turin, Nietzsche suffered a paralytic stroke which plunged him into a mental and spiritual darkness from which he did not recover. The frequent moments of euphoria, especially during the last year, foreshadowed the collapse. It cannot be said, however, that he had lost control of himself, in spite of the mounting tension, until the final disaster overcame him. Nor has it been clearly established to what extent physical causes aggravated the hypertension under which he had long been laboring. To be sure, it must be accepted that an early, insufficiently treated syphilitic infection contributed further to weaken his constitution, which had never been robust even from childhood. But it has never been proved how this infection was contracted, whether in personal intercourse or from the patients whom he had in charge during his service as medical officer. Whatever its nature, little was made of it in the clinical reports after his collapse, and less in known previous medical findings. Some of the later interpreters, even Thomas Mann, have made a great deal of it to account for the extremes in Nietzsche's teachings. But that has served only to obfuscate the picture of Nietzsche. Without regard to whatever infection there was, the mental and spiritual hypertension which his militant mission progressively caused in him as he found himself more alone and misunderstood during the final years of wandering, would have been enough to destroy a stronger constitution. Besides, in spite of occasional outbursts of euphoria, the writings immediately preceding the attack show no dementia and his power of language and the metaphor remained characteristic.

For a few days Nietzsche lay in his room in Turin in

delirium and lethargy. On January 6, Professor Burckhardt, who had not kept in close touch with Nietzsche, received a letter from him with clear indications of derangement and took it to Nietzsche's closest friend in Basel, Professor Overbeck. The latter went to Turin at once, brought the patient back with him, had him entered at the local asylum, and sent for his mother. She succeeded in having him transferred to an institution in Jena not far from her home, in order to be nearer in the hope that he would recover. She was permitted to visit with him freely, and after a month even to spend most of the day with him at a lodging which she took to prepare to move him to Naumburg and assume full charge of him there. At the end of March she received permission to take him home, since the danger of violence seemed lessened by her care, even though there was no promise of recovery.

Nietzsche remained at Naumburg during the next seven years, for the last four of which his sister, Elisabeth Foerster-Nietzsche, assisted the mother and also made herself the sole authoritative intermediary between her brother's affairs and the outside world. At the death of the mother in the spring of 1897, she established her brother in a pleasant villa on the outskirts of Weimar, the city of Goethe, hoping that the greater freedom and the view upon the center of classic German culture would aid his recovery. In her biography of her brother she gives optimistic reports of returning lucidity during this period that are probably excusable, fond myths. We know that the paralytic strokes soon became more progressive, and after a very severe recurrence, on August 25, 1900, Friedrich Nietzsche died.

The villa at Weimar became the Nietzsche Archive, directed by the intelligent, affectionate, nonetheless dictatorial authority of the sister as the sole literary executor. She has rendered valuable service in collecting and preserving the Nietzsche material; has herself contributed biographical, critical, and editorial studies, and encouraged research by others. But her stern concern for what she considered a favorable interpretation has also been a hindrance. Upon her death in November 1935, the Nazi influence, which she herself had favored, took a stronger hold upon the memorabilia; and the Russian occupation of Weimar was first said to have done great harm to it, but it has now been established that all Nietzsche material is housed in the Goethe-and-Schiller Archives and is accessible to scholars there.

But, in spite of the paradoxical nature of his life and teaching, Nietzsche is too brilliant a master of language and the metaphor not to persist. He attempted the impossible with his mission of the completely autonomous genius of a human culture which he must endlessly strive to perfect as he perfects himself, but which he must also forever refuse to accept as final, so that the cycle of return may always continue to prove the eternity of life. He must believe in a reality which is fixed in space and energy and which reveals itself in an endless cycle of identical configurations in endless time, but which is yet ever awaiting the creative genius who will transfigure the most sublime revelations of reality in terms of culture, as he eternally struggles to transfigure himself into its lawgiver. His integrity must constantly be on the alert to see and seek nothing but reality and not let his eyes rest upon transcendental and metaphysical promises and comforts. And yet that reality, though fixed, must still be taken as of a quality whose sublimation must be ever sought, but never completed. He must find his joy in his love for that reality and be kind to all things; but he must be unrelenting in his efforts to destroy all social institutions and intellectual or spiritual values which express and direct life as configurations of a reality other than his. He is the enemy of that which is held most sacred in our evaluation of life; and yet he waged this war for the sake of what he considered to be an honest devotion to life.

Why, then, should his brilliance be enough to make him persist? We have seen that his mission ended in the strange heroics that the genius sacrifice himself joyously for an eternally future sublimation. His personal life ended in a final pitiful tragedy. Much of his influence, through misunderstanding and arbitrary interpretations, has been used to depreciate and even brutalize life, instead of sublimating it, and so tended to deprive the tragedy of what dignity it possessed. Nevertheless, the severity of the intellectual discipline that he exercised upon himself and upon his particular Dionysian perspective makes him a stimulating and valuable educator. The constant striving to clear his own perspective with watchful intellectual integrity made of him a master of the perspectives underlying other evaluations and gained for him a psychological acumen that produced valuable insights and analyses of behavior. The fact that he depreciated, even passionately, all perspectives but his own is his real and personal tragedy. But that very limitation, when clearly seen, makes it possible to read him sanely and with pleasure and to profit from the keenness and breadth of his mind.

After Nietzsche's death, his sister, with the help of Peter Gast, gathered a great bulk of stray notes which they assumed he would have arranged and edited to form his definitive philosophy. For the arrangement they used a plan which Nietzsche himself had outlined in the spring of 1887 under the title, *Will to Power*. It is futile to speculate how he would have used these notes, if at all. Very few further clarify the ideas which he had already presented, or have the poetic quality of his published writings. The fourth book, however, in which the posthumous notes on the discipline and breeding of the new philosopher are collected, is significant for the continued discussion of the qualities of the good teacher as necessary for the task. A note of kindness and even humility enters into the otherwise severely aristocratic exclusiveness of the figure, as though much of the harshness had merely been meant to shock a Germany which had become materialistic, complacent, and crude, back to a realization of its potential qualities, even if he had to overextend his demands upon himself to do so. Of the teacher himself he would ask the utmost: "Man is the transfigurer of life if he knows how to transfigure himself." He is not so severe, however, on those whom he hopes to influence. His only concern here is to administer to that which they need most to make life more significant.

from:

Ecce Homo

[Nietzsche contrasts his Dionysian faith with everything that is held to be true:]
Up to now the *lie* of the ideal has been the curse resting
upon reality; by means of it mankind itself has become cor-
rupted and falsified to the very lowest of its instincts—
until it worshipped the values which are the *reverse* of those
which might promote health, future, and the lofty right to
the future.

[FOREWORD]

[He discusses the keenness of his own insight:]
From the optics of disease to get a view of the *more robust*
ideas and values; and conversely out of the full self-assurance
of a *rich* life to look down into the hidden workings of the
instinct of decadence.

[WHY I AM SO WISE, 1]

[His intellectual growth:]
The tempo of metabolism bears an exact relationship to the
sprightliness or haltingness of the *feet* of the intellect; the
'spirit' itself is merely a kind of metabolism.

[WHY I AM SO CLEVER, 2]

[Nietzsche then discusses all his works in chronological
order:]

The Dionysian View of Life

. . . a yes-saying without reserve, even to suffering, guilt, and all that is questionable and strange in life. [Moreover, it is an insight that is] confirmed and upheld in the strictest sense by truth and science. . . .

He who not merely understands the term "Dionysian" but has a comprehension of himself in the term needs no refutation of Plato and Christianity—he *smells the decay*.

I promise a *tragic* age. The highest art in the affirmation of life, the tragedy, will be born again when man knows that he has passed through the severest but necessary wars, *without suffering from them*. [By these wars Nietzsche is not prophesying the cataclysms of our century, but is merely alluding to the hard spiritual battles of sublimation.] The proximity of the clearest and most fateful energies, the will to power such as no man has yet possessed, the relentless bravery in intellectual things; the unlimited strength to learn without the danger that the will to act be stifled by it.

Human, All-Too-Human

[He has freed himself from] German art, German music, German beer. . . . The meaning of the title is this: where *you* see idle things, *I* see human—alas, all-too-human. . . .

[The book is] a war without powder or smoke; without warlike attitudes, pathos, or grimaces—for all that would still be idealism. . . . At that time my instinct led me to the irrevocable refusal ever to yield again, or to follow, or to mistake myself for another.

[1, 2, 4]

Thus Spoke Zarathustra

[The idea of the Eternal Return came to me] six thousand feet beyond man and time.

[1]

The greatest ability in the use of the metaphor that was ever known is poor and child's play in comparison to this return of the language to the nature of imagery.

[3]

With every word he [Zarathustra] contradicts, this most affirmative of all spirits. In him all opposites are bound into a new unity. The highest and lowest powers of human nature, the sweetest, the most frivolous, and the terrible flow from a single spring with immortal certainty.

[6]

Twilight of the Idols

In all seriousness, none before me knew of the right way, the way *upwards;* beginning with me there are again hopes, tasks, ways to be prescribed to culture—*I am the bearer of the glad tidings of them.*

[2]

The Wagner Case

[The Germans do not even know] how vulgar they are, but that is the superlative of vulgarity.

[2]

[The Germans have released on Europe] disease and stupidity that is as opposed to culture as anything can be: nationalism, this national neurosis of which Europe suffers; the permanence of Europe's particularism, of *small politics.* They robbed Europe of its meaning, of its reason—they brought it into a blind alley. Does anyone besides myself know the way out of this blind alley?—Know a task great enough again to bind the peoples? [But he expects that his country-men will spoil this chance as well and try their best to have his "mountainous labor" produce a mouse. Therefore he will turn away from them.] They shall never have the honor to connect as allied to them the first *integrious* spirit in intellectual history, an intellect by which truth sits in judgment on the counterfeiting of four thousand years.

[2, 3]

Why I Am a Fate

I am not a man, I am a dynamite.

I was the first to discover the truth in that I was the first to conceive the lie as a lie—to smell it.

[Christianity] is the idiosyncrasy of decadents with the hidden intention *to take revenge upon life*—and with success. . . . Is not history a refutation by experiments of the principle of the so-called moral world order? [Not to understand this is] the crime against life . . . [and all philosophers before me are] higher swindlers.

The flash of truth has just struck down what has hitherto stood highest; whoever can comprehend what was destroyed by it, let him examine carefully whether he still has anything in hand at all.

The Will to Power

To conceive of a philosopher as a great educator who, down from his lonely heights, is powerful enough to attract long series of generations, it is necessary to grant him also the uncanny privileges of a great teacher. A teacher never says what he himself thinks about a subject but only what he believes to be of benefit in relation to the student. But this dissembling must not be detected; it is part of his mastership that his honesty is not questioned. He must be skilled in all ways of discipline and rearing. Some natures he will be able to promote only by the whiplash of scorn; others, the indolent, indecisive, timid, and vain, perhaps by exaggerating praise.

Such an educator is beyond good and evil; but no one must be aware of it.

[APHORISM 980]

[In the following remark he even relinquishes much of his exclusiveness in order to encourage the reader to learn from the way in which he pursued his perspective—to examine his own for the honesty with which it is held:]

The assumption for all living and its life is that there must be a body of *truth;* that *judgments* be made; that there is an *absence* of doubt in respect to all essential values. Consequently, it is necessary that something *must* be held to be true—*not* that it is true.

[APHORISM 507]

Notes and Sources

Chapter 1

Most quotations in this chapter are taken from the projected, but still incomplete, definitive edition under the auspices of the Nietzsche Archives in Weimar:

Friedrich Nietzsches Werke, Historisch-Kritische Gesamtaugabe (Hist. Krit. Aus.), C. H. Beck, München, 1933ff.

p. 16	1. Hist. Krit. Aus. III, 69ff.	
p. 19	1. ibid.	III, 217.
p. 20	1. ibid.	III, 289.
	2. ibid.	III, 352ff.
p. 21	1. ibid.	III, 353.

Chapter 2

Writings discussed:

Homer and Classical Philology (Introductory lecture at the University of Basel on May 28, 1869).

Published by the Nietzsche Archives as preliminary studies to *The Birth of Tragedy: The Greek Musicdrama (Das Griechische Musikdrama),* Leipzig, 1926; *Socrates and the Tragedy (Sokrates und die Tragödie),* Leipzig, 1927; *The Dionysian View of Life (Die Dionysische Weltanschauung),* Leipzig, 1928; *Socrates and the Greek Tragedy (Socrates und die Griechische Tragödie),* München, 1933.

From *The Greek Musicdrama*.

p. 25   1. p. 30.
         2. p. 3.

From *Socrates and the Tragedy*.

p. 26   1. p. 16.
         2. p. 26ff.

From *The Dionysian View of Life*.

p. 26   3. p. 3.

         4. p. 3.
         5. p. 6.
         6. p. 11.

p. 27   1. p. 22.

From *The Birth of Tragedy*.

p. 29   1. section 7.
         2. section 25.

p. 30   1. section 18.

Chapter 3

Writings discussed:

On the Future of Our Academic Institutions, 1871/72.
Philosophy in the Tragic Age of the Greeks, 1873.
Truth and Lie in an Extra-moral Sense, 1873.

Chapter 4

Writings discussed:

Human, All-Too-Human I, 1878 (in 638 aphorisms).

    1. "On First and Last Things."
    2. "Toward a History of Moral Sentiments."
    3. "The Religious Life."
    4. "On the Soul of Artists and Writers."
    5. "Symptoms of Higher and Lower Culture."
    6. "Man Communicating."
    7. "Woman and Child."
    8. "A Look at the State."
    9. "Man Alone with Himself."

Epilogue, "Among Strangers."

Human, All-Too-Human II.

   1. "Various Opinions and Sayings" (408 aphorisms).
   2. "The Wanderer and His Shadow" (350 aphorisms).

p. 46	1.	89.		p. 63	1.	170.
p. 47	1.	109.		p. 65	1.	41.
p. 48	1.	113.				

Chapter 5

Writings discussed:

The Dawn of Day: Thoughts on Moral Prejudices, 1881 (a collection of 575 aphorisms in five books).

The Eternal Return, 1881 (from posthumous writings in 43 aphorisms).

The Gay Science (a collection of 382 aphorisms in five books), First four books 1882; Book five 1886.

From *The Dawn of Day.*

p. 71	1.	439.
	2.	456.
p. 72	1.	423.
p. 73	1.	453.
	2.	547.
p. 74	1.	503.
	2.	199.
	3.	201.
	4.	262.
p. 75	1.	271.
	2.	449.
	3.	506.

From *The Eternal Return.*

| p. 77 | 1. | 20. |
| p. 78 | 1. | 25. |

From *The Gay Science.*

p. 78	2.	46.
p. 79	1.	324.
	2.	33.
	3.	310.
p. 80	1.	346.
p. 81	1.	276.
p. 82	1.	371.
p. 83	1.	382.

Chapter 6

Writings discussed:

Thus Spoke Zarathustra: A Book for All and None (Zarathustra's preface and his aphoristic addresses to his disciples in four parts), Part 1, 1882/83; Part 2, 1883; Part 3, 1884; Part 4, 1885.

p. 102 1. "Die Sprachkunst Friedrich Nietzsches in Also Sprach Zarathustra," Bremen, 1951, p. 68.
p. 104 1. "On Love of Neighbor."
p. 107 1. "On Famous Sages."

Chapter 7

Writings discussed:

Beyond Good and Evil: A Prelude to a Philosophy of the Future, 1886 (Nine chapters of 296 aphorisms and an epode).
  Chapter 1. "On the Prejudices of Philosophers."
         2. "The Free Spirit."
         3. "The Religious Person."
         4. "Sayings and Interludes."
         5. "Toward a Natural History of Morality."
         6. "We Scholars."
         7. "Our Virtues."
         8. "Peoples and Fatherland."
         9. "What Is Distinguished."
         Epode "On High Hills."

p. 205	1.	32.		p. 207	1.	46.
	2.	36.		p. 209	1.	188.
p. 206	1.	42.		p. 212	1.	262.

Chapter 8

Writings discussed:

Toward a Genealogy of Morals: A Polemic, 1887 (Foreword —8 paragraphs; Essay 1—"Good and Evil," "Good and Mean," of 17 paragraphs; Essay 2—"Guilt," "Bad Conscience, and the Like," of 26 paragraphs; Essay 3—"What Do Ascetic Ideals Signify?" of 28 paragraphs).

From Foreword.			p. 229	1.	8.	
p. 219	1.	6.		2.	12.	
From Essay 1.			From Essay 3.			
p. 222	1.	14.	p. 236	1.	12.	
	2.	15.		2.	13.	
p. 223	1.	9.	p. 237	1.	14.	
p. 224	1.	11.		2.	15.	
From Essay 2.				3.	20.	
p. 226	1.	1.	p. 239	1.	23.	
p. 227	1.	3.		2.	24.	

Chapter 9

Writings discussed:

The Wagner Case: a Letter from Turin of May, 1888 (12 paragraphs with two postscripts and an epilogue).

Twilight of the Idols, or How to Philosophize with the Hammer, 1889. Sections:

"Proverbs and Darts," 44 aphorisms.

"The Problem of Socrates," 12 paragraphs.

" 'Reason' in Philosophy," 6 aphorisms.

"How the 'True World' Finally Got To Be a Fable," 6 aphorisms.

"Morality as Opposed to Nature," 6 paragraphs.

"The Four Great Errors," 8 aphorisms.

"The 'Improvers' of Mankind," 5 paragraphs.

"What the Germans Lack," 7 aphorisms.

"Forays of a Non-timely," 51 aphorisms.

"What I Owe to the Ancients," 5 paragraphs.

"The Hammer Speaks," from *Thus Spoke Zarathustra*.

p. 250   1. Letter to George Brandes, Oct. 20, 1888.
p. 251   1. Letter to Peter Gast, July 17, 1888.
p. 252   1. Letter to Carl Fuchs, Dec. 27, 1888.
p. 254   1. Letter to Peter Gast, Sept. 12, 1888.

Chapter 10

Writings discussed:

   The Antichrist: An Attempt at a Critique of Christianity, 1888, published 1895 (62 paragraphs).

   Dionysus Dithyrambs, 1888/1895 (6 appended poems).

p. 266	1.	52.	p. 271	1.	22.
p. 267	1.	4.		2.	26.
	2.	54.	p. 273	1.	31.
p. 268	1.	57.		2.	40.
	2.	58.		3.	42.
p. 269	1.	48.	p. 274	1.	46.
p. 270	1.	48.			

Chapter 11

Writings discussed:

   Ecce Homo: How One Gets To Be What One Is, 1888, published 1908.

   The Will to Power, planned c. 1887, published 1904.

Foreword.

"Why I Am So Wise."

"Why I Am So Clever."

"Why I Write Such Good Books."

Reviews:
The Birth of Tragedy.
Reflections Out of Season.
Human, All-Too-Human.
The Dawn of Day.
The Gay Science.
Thus Spoke Zarathustra.
Beyond Good and Evil.
A Genealogy of Morals.
Twilight of the Idols.
The Wagner Case.

"Why I Am a Fate."

From "Why I Am So Clever."
p. 285   l.   5.
From review of *Thus Spoke Zarathustra.*
p. 293   l.   2.

Index